THE *American* PEOPLE

THE
American
PEOPLE

A Timely Exploration of a Changing America
and the Important New Demographic
Trends Around Us

BRYANT
ROBEY

T·T

TRUMAN TALLEY BOOKS
E. P. DUTTON
NEW YORK

Published in the United States by Truman Talley Books · E. P. Dutton, 2 Park Avenue, New York, N.Y. 10016

Library of Congress Cataloging in Publication Data

Robey, Bryant.
  The American people.

  "A Truman Talley book."
  Includes index.
  1. United States—Population. I. Title.
HB3505.R63 1985   304.6'0973   85-1481
ISBN 0-525-24296-1

Published simultaneously in Canada by Fitzhenry & Whiteside Limited, Toronto

Designed by Nancy P. Danahy
W

10 9 8 7 6 5 4 3 2 1

First Edition

Contents

Contents

Note to the reader:
The statistics in this book
come from public sources,
except where noted,
and they are up to date
as of summer 1984.

THE
American
PEOPLE

Introduction: The Demographic Revolution

"Despite their increasingly frequent mention in newspaper articles, corporate reports, and government documents, demographic trends are not yet widely known or appreciated. That makes them all the more valuable to those who do understand them."

Americans in the 1980s are different in almost every way from Americans just a generation ago, and these differences have profoundly affected the American way of life. Consider some of the trends: In the past, husbands went to work while most wives stayed home to raise families. Today, a majority of wives work. Among today's married couples, more have two earners than have just one earner.

More than two thirds of the women born since 1950 are working or looking for work, and women now play increasingly important roles as politicians and business executives. Two thirds of women with school-age children are working and, incredibly, fully half of all mothers with preschool children.

Divorce used to be rare. In 1950, for every 1,000 Americans, only 2.6 got divorced. Now, divorce is common. For every 1,000 Americans in 1980, 5.2 got divorced, twice the 1950 rate.

Fewer than 3 percent of Americans lived alone in 1950. Today, more than 8 percent live alone. Households containing only one or two persons made up 40 percent of all households in 1950. Today, they have risen to a majority—54 percent. The days when the typical household contained mom, dad, and two kids have ended. The average number of people living in a household has dropped to well under three.

Why has the family changed so much? What accounts for this revolution in American life-styles? In 1950, the country had just begun the baby-boom years. During the next fourteen years, over 60 million babies were born. The average woman had three children, or even four. Americans did not talk about "life-style" then because there was only one style—families. The 1950 census counted 44 million households, and nine tenths of them contained families.

Today, members of the 1947 to 1964 baby-boom generation comprise nearly one third of the American people. They are a dominant feature on the social landscape. As baby-boomers pass through life's stages, America's customs and concerns travel with them. In the late 1960s and the 1970s, when most baby-boomers were teen-agers, alternative life-styles and the challenge of authority were in vogue.

In the 1980s, as the baby-boom generation grows up, the young-professional life-style is at center stage. Families are returning to style, but today's families are different from those of the previous generation. Large families are still not in style; fertility, the birthrate of the population, is only about half of what it was in the 1950s.

Americans live in different places than they used to. With Bing Crosby, a majority of Americans in 1950 could dream of a white Christmas and have a meteorological chance of seeing their dream come true. The Northeast and Midwest contained 55 percent of the national population. The South was thought to be a backwater and the West still a frontier.

The cities were once the seat of progress, and their suburbs were growing as families sought space in which to raise children. Americans continued to leave the rural areas. Then, during the 1970s, Americans left the cities in record numbers to live in small towns and rural areas. For the first time since the industrial revolution, the population growth rate outside the nation's metropolitan areas was higher than within them. The service economy of the 1980s no longer requires ever-growing industrial centers.

Americans are more dispersed across the country than ever before. A majority of people now live in the South and the West. All but one of the top-ten growth states of the 1970s were west of the Mississippi. The nation's population center has crossed the Mississippi River and is unlikely ever to move back.

Suburbs are no longer the same. Those suburbs closest to the central cities are becoming more like the cities themselves. As the young adults who settled there in the 1950s and 1960s grow older, the inner suburbs are graying just like the cities. New suburbs are spreading farther from the center, attracting today's young families. American workers are now more likely to commute from one suburb to another than from the suburbs to the city. The city center is no longer the magnet that it once was. The periphery has a greater attraction, pulling people outward.

In 1950, farming still occupied one worker in eight. A majority of workers wore blue collars. Only about 33 percent of all adults had finished high school, and a mere 6 percent were college graduates. Now, more than seven of every ten adults have a high school degree, and 18 percent are college graduates. Less than one worker in thirty-five is a farmer, and over half the labor force wears white collars.

The racial balance has changed. The 1950 census counted 15 million Negroes—but no blacks. That term did not appear on the census questionnaire. Nor did the 1950 census inquire directly about Hispanic origin. Now, the country has over 28 million blacks and 15 million Hispanics. The 1980 census questionnaire inquired about fourteen different races, versus only six in 1950, and the latest census found members of each race in every state.

America has always been a nation of immigrants, but in the 1950s, only a handful of immigrants came from Asia; the melting pot was still simmering full of Germans, Irish, Italians, and Scandinavians. Today, the melting pot is serving up a new kind of American. The immigrant flows are not from Europe, but rather from Asia and Latin America, where growing populations far outstrip the number of new jobs. Europe accounted for only 18 percent of immigrants in the 1970s. Mexico has overtaken Germany as the number one country of ancestry for America's foreign born.

The 1950 census detected a historic first: The number of women surpassed the number of men, by about 1 million. Today, however, the gap has widened to 6 million. In 1950, the average sixty-five-year-old American man could expect to live another thirteen years, a woman fifteen years. A woman aged sixty-five in 1980 could expect to live another eighteen and a half years, three and a half years longer than in 1950, whereas a man's odds were for another fourteen years of life, only a little over one year more than in 1950.

TOGETHER, APART

Americans in the 1980s are better linked than ever before—by interstate highways, jet airplanes, chain stores, satellites, and computer banks. Sharp regional differences are giving way to a homogeneous national economy, shaped by a new technology, new kinds of jobs, and new population shifts.

The differences between the cities and the countryside used to be profound. Now, they are disappearing. Americans used to migrate from farm to city to improve their living standards. One reason people and jobs have been moving back to rural areas is that these areas now offer a better standard of living than the congested large cities.

Sex roles that were once clearly defined are fading fast, as women enter men's occupations and men assume more household roles. In the 1950s, the terms *A man's world* and *Woman's work* defined opposites. That is no longer the case. Educational differences between young men and women are not as wide as they are between older men and women. Today, more women than men are enrolled in college.

However, in other ways America today is more fragmented than it was a generation ago. Most women used to play only the role of home-maker; now they play many new roles as well. The changing role of women may have made women and men more equal, but it also has created new differences among women, according to their age, their level of education, and their status in the work force.

Black America is becoming fragmented, too. Although blacks still lag behind whites of similar background, younger blacks who have attained a higher education and whose families are intact have approached whites in income, occupation, and residential status. But blacks who live in single-parent families, those with less education, and those who hold lower-status jobs are farther behind whites than blacks were a generation ago.

American coins still carry the motto *E Pluribus Unum,* Latin for "Out of Many, One," but the income gap among Americans has widened. The middle class is reversing a historic growth trend and has been shrinking for the past several years. Some families have broken away from the pack and become affluent, whereas poverty has become, increasingly, a black and a female problem.

The mass market has splintered. Companies now face a tangle of targets at which to aim their products. To hit one target is to miss the others, so instead of firing a fusillade of products and advertising at the masses, firms must take more careful aim.

In today's labor force, it is specialties that separate people instead of hierarchies. The division of workers into labor and management has blurred, as service and professional jobs supplant manufacturing and farming in the economy.

Americans have always been separated by a generation gap. Now the size of the baby-boom generation in relation to the age groups that come before and after it is so great that age differences affect everything from presidential politics to fast food franchises. Nor are Americans of the baby-boom generation all alike. They too are separated by family status, education, occupation, and income. Muppies and yuppies grab headlines, but they are not the full story.

TODAY, TOMORROW

Americans change faster than their institutions. As a consequence, most organizations suffer from a generation gap. The succession of generations brings new life-styles, but most of the nation's leaders belong to the older generation, with its different values. Their background makes it hard for them to understand why things are changing.

Most Americans alive today were born after 1950. But most of the country's leaders were born before 1950. And in 1950, when today's senior statesmen and business executives were growing up and forming their own attitudes, the majority of Americans had been born before 1920—the year women won the right to vote. The country always has one foot in the past, yet the challenge is to move into the future.

The national census, taken once every ten years, is one of the most important signposts on the road from past to future. In its charting of the characteristics of the American people, each census is a mirror of society at a single point in history. Over the decades, the succession of censuses reveals the changing face of the American people.

The government takes the census to obtain an accurate count of the number of Americans so that members of the U.S. House of Representatives can be fairly apportioned among the states. But the census has never been a simple head count. From its start in 1790, the census has also asked Americans to provide additional information about themselves. Today its questions cover age, income, education, occupation, living arrangements, and many other important facts.

The census does not reveal information about individuals, which would violate the law, but it combines individual responses and reports these summarized statistics. It is these numbers that tell us so much about ourselves. The 1980 census was taken April 1, 1980, but its results will be analyzed, digested, and acted upon up to and after 1990, when the results of a new census become available.

Government programs at the federal, state, and local levels; corporate marketing strategies; political campaigns; new product development; advertising and promotion; television and radio network ratings; and magazine circulation all make use of demographic statistics. Investors should understand demographic trends if they wish to avoid declining markets and anticipate emerging trends. School systems and universities need demographic data to forecast enrollment. Young people can assess career opportunities better if they understand how the population is changing. Politicians are almost as interested in the census head count as they are in the count of ballots each November. They recognize the power of the numbers.

The census and the annual surveys that update it provide a guide to how the American people are changing. No longer a matter of interest only to statisticians and academic researchers, demographic information is also a key to performance in a wide variety of fields. Demographics are in demand, and the Bureau of the Census is the source of many statistics.

Using the most recent information available, this book explores the demographic trends revealed by the 1980 census and other recent national demographic surveys. It examines how the size of the different generations fluctuates; how Americans' living arrangements are changing; how the country's population map is being redrawn; and how the status of women, blacks, Hispanics, and ethnic groups is changing. The book reports key findings about occupation, education, and income. A final chapter brings these themes together to report ten powerful demographic trends that are shaping America.

Despite their increasingly frequent mention in newspaper articles, corporate reports, and government documents, demographic trends are not yet widely known or appreciated. That makes them all the more valuable to those who do understand them. The subject is not dull, or even complicated. On the contrary, few subjects are more fascinating. After all, demographic facts and figures tell us about ourselves. What could be more exciting than that?

The Power of Positive Demographics

"Why are today's Americans more interested in staying in shape than were previous generations? Why is everybody running?"

A magazine advertisement for the American Express Card portrays a thirty-year-old mother skiing cross-country with her baby strapped to her chest. The caption: "The American Express Card; it's part of a lot of interesting lives."

Better than most, this advertisement illustrates some top trends of the 1980s. Americans are getting into shape. Small families are in fashion. The pursuit of happiness is the pursuit of wealth. Women are a dynamic new force in business and government.

Why are today's Americans more interested in staying in shape than were previous generations? Why is everybody running? Why do so many men and women attempt to rescue their bodies at fitness centers by "pumping iron" and fervently pedaling away the hours and the fat?

The most important reason is that America's baby-boom generation, the more than 70 million people born between 1947 and 1964, are entering their thirties. Interests change with age, income, education, and other demographics. College classrooms filled when the members of this generation were of school age, now health centers are filling as they approach middle age.

Today's Americans are more educated than those of previous generations. Educated people are more likely to be joggers, health-club members, and nonsmokers. With the surgeon general, they understand that smoking can be hazardous to their health. As the baby-boomers age, the lighter alcoholic beverages, which cause less damage to the physique and the psyche, are more popular than the strong stuff.

Singles express more interest in fitness than do marrieds. When half of a generation is likely at some point to be on the prowl for a new mate following a divorce, appearing trim and attractive takes on new importance. Spouses have a new incentive to stay fit, too, surrounded as they are by so many trim unattached men and women.

As America's dominant age group moves into its forties, toward the end of this decade, the fitness craze probably will take a different form, becoming less strenuous and better suited to physical limitations. A government study, for example, has shown that interest in Alpine skiing peaks at age twenty-nine. Because, physically, it's all downhill after that, ski manufacturers are wise, along with American Express, to emphasize the less breakneck sport of Nordic skiing if they hope to retain the interest of the baby-boomers.

Families are returning to favor not because of a reversal of attitudes about marriage and childbearing after a decade of divorce but because a larger proportion of Americans are in the age groups when people marry and have children. As members of the less populous generation born in the 1970s and the latter half of the 1960s reach their childbearing years, the number of children will decline again—in fact, the number has already started to drop.

More than 40 million Americans will be turning thirty this decade (Is this why the phrase "don't trust anybody over thirty" has vanished?), and as these millions move into their forties, it will mean a profound change for business. Interest in financial matters will grow in coming years because a larger share of people will be of an age that values saving and investing. The number of affluent middle-aged Americans will rise dramatically for the rest of this century.

American companies have become avid consumers of information about demographic trends, and a growing number are acting on this information in plotting strategy, producing new products, and updating their marketing and advertising. *People* magazine believes its success has come from avid readership by baby-boomers, so as the baby-boomers age, the people featured in *People* will age with them. *The Wall Street Journal* sees prosperous years ahead because its prime readers are people in their forties and fifties who have investments, and more Americans will be fitting this description.

Merrill Lynch started a new mutual fund, the Fund for Tomorrow, in which investments are geared to products and services likely to be of interest to America's largest population group. The investments of a "Sunbelt Growth Fund" in Houston are designed to benefit from population and business growth in the booming areas of the South.

The Ford Motor Company has an advisory committee on older consumers. Chrysler's director of merchandising a few years back was quoted as saying that the company was not attracting "the younger upscale college-educated buyers we need." Since then the company has taken steps to retool, faced with the fact that imports have captured half the market among buyers under thirty years old, whereas less than one third of all car buyers prefer imports.

Gannett's *USA Today* relies on the fact that America has become a different kind of economy, in which the hometown may be where a person lives but in which his or her interests are national. The nation's economic and social life no longer revolves around the activities of a few major urban centers, but encompasses virtually the whole land, as the population and the jobs have become more widely dispersed.

McDonald's and its competitors now serve breakfast. The number of people eating breakfast in restaurants has been growing faster than the number eating other meals out, while expenditures on eating out have been growing faster than the food dollar spent at home. As family size has fallen, the traditional hamburger has made room for chicken and other meals designed to appeal to the on-the-run adult crowd instead of the kiddie market that accounted for McDonald's rapid growth.

United Airlines, a generation ago, had a television advertisement aimed at traveling businessmen in which wives were singing "take me along if you love me," to which a chorus of men responded "I love you little cutie but the office is my duty." Now that nearly two thirds of women below retirement age are working, and a growing share of business travelers are women, airline commercials have become unisex. Men have joined the ranks of airborne attendants, women are airline pilots, and the word *stewardess* has become *flight attendant*.

Today's demographic trends may benefit the airlines not only because the national economy depends on frequent business travel, but even because of an age difference between the East Coast and the West Coast. Young adults are more likely to uproot and move than older Americans, and the number of births is higher in the West than in the Northeast because adults in their childbearing years have been moving West, while their parents have remained back East. These trends suggest more coast-to-coast travel to unite grandchildren and grandparents.

The dispersion of population also bodes well for the direct-mail business. As the population has become less concentrated geographically, it has become more efficient to reach customers by mail. Mail can be targeted to only those potential consumers likely to be interested in a product, whereas stores are rooted in neighborhoods, whose characteristics can change.

Demographic trends affect virtually every facet of business. *The Wall Street Journal* has reported that the Campbell Soup Company was concerned that "many of its products had failed to entice a new generation of shoppers with more sophisticated tastes and life-styles," so the company is adding new products, "apple juice, low-sodium soups, low-calorie pickles, and ham and cheese encased in a pastry that can be eaten on the run—tailored for shoppers who are dieting, health conscious, and usually in a hurry."

Club Med, which used to cater to the singles crowd, featuring army tents and the opportunity to wash one's own dishes, is now going after what *Business Week* has termed "sun-seeking, sybaritic high-income couples," as well as its traditional market.

America's best-known companies are responding to demographic trends, realizing that rapid changes in consumer groups mean that they can no longer have a business-as-usual attitude. *The New York Times* reported, "Retailers plan to divide and conquer the buying public. They talk of dividing consumers into categories by age, income, sex, life-style, taste, and preferences, and then targeting products at each group with great precision."

The Newspaper Advertising Bureau's Alfred Eisenpreis has said, "Retailers will have to recognize in their marketing and store planning that there are various levels of working women—the young career woman, the pregnant career woman, the working mother, and the older woman are just a few examples." J. Walter Thompson's Rena Bartos makes the distinction between women to whom work is a career and those to whom it is "just a job."

Businesses increasingly engage in *segmentation*—an ever finer slicing of the consumer marketplace. Targeted marketing requires that companies understand who their best customers are, as defined by such demographic characteristics as age, income, education, or family status. Then, they may reach more people who share these characteristics but who are not yet customers.

In earlier years, and simpler days, every mom-and-pop store knew its customers. Today, it is impossible for a national firm to know its customers personally, but it can still know them and their tastes by studying demographic characteristics. Some people object to the idea of faceless and distant companies using the data the government has obtained in the census and other surveys to sell them products. Others believe that better targeting of products assures that marketers approach only those people who probably would be interested in the product, leaving everyone else in peace. But businesses have little choice, if they wish to stay competitive, but to follow demographic trends, analyze their customers' characteristics, and target their products. In this, businesses are not alone.

DEMOGRAPHIC DIFFERENCES

Not only markets but virtually every activity—from who watches football to who wears contact lenses—varies according to demographic characteristics. People who wear glasses, for instance, tend to be better educated and have higher incomes than people who don't wear glasses, in addition to their obvious difference in eyesight. More than two thirds of football spectators are white-collar workers who earn at least $25,000 per year.

The average marriage that ends in divorce lasts seven years, but the residents of some states get the itch much sooner than others. In Massachusetts, according to the National Center for Health Statistics, marriages that end in divorce last an average nine years. But in Wyoming and Utah, the average length is only five years.

Twenty-seven percent of persons aged thirty-five to forty-four who head a household have a college degree—7 percent higher than American household heads in general, according to Fabian Linden of the Conference Board, reported in *American Demographics* magazine. The magazine has also reported the following demographic differences among Americans, some profound, some trivial—but all remarkable:

– Blacks are less than 12 percent of the American population, but they account for 34 percent of hair care expenditures, according to Business Trends Analysts, a research firm.

– Nearly two thirds of the people who own shares of stock in small banks are at least fifty years old, according to Shearson/American Express. These statistics suggest that many shareholders may not be able to sell their investments as they approach retirement; small banks are notoriously illiquid.

– The biggest tippers are people who eat alone; the smallest those who eat in large parties (where the safety of numbers deflects the waiter's disapproval). Big tippers are younger, live in smaller households, have higher incomes, and live in the large metropolitan areas of the Northeast, researchers at the University of Illinois found.

– People between ages twelve and twenty-four are just over one quarter of the population aged twelve and over, but they account for over half of all movie admissions, a Motion Picture Association study has shown. In contrast, people aged forty or older are 44 percent of the population aged twelve and over, but account for just 13 percent of moviegoers.

– Of the female readers of *Newsweek*, according to the magazine's reader surveys, more than 50 percent are college graduates, nearly 75 percent are employed full time, and 42 percent are the sole earner in their households.

– More than 25 percent of disabled Americans live in poverty; only 22 percent of disabled men worked full time for the entire year of 1981, versus 61 percent of healthy men, the Census Bureau has reported.

– Whereas 22 percent of men reported to the Wheat Council that they are concerned with staying away from snacks, 31 percent of women gave this response. Less than one third of men worry about maintaining their proper weight, but about half of women.

– Households likely to burn large amounts of firewood are those headed by a person aged 35 to 44, those in rural areas, and, surprisingly, those with high incomes.

Americans can be divided and subdivided demographically as they pursue life, liberty, and happiness. Demographic characteristics can be compared from one geographic area to the next, guiding government agencies in their quest to serve (or tax) the public, or businesses in their desire to locate branches in convenient spots or near suitable sources of labor. Demographic differences can be compared from one time period to the next, revealing trends that show how America is changing.

THE SURPRISING 1970s

Every decade turns up its share of surprises, and the past decade turned up more than its share. One of the country's leading demographic analysts, Calvin Beale of the U.S. Department of Agriculture, discovered five key trends of the past decade that even the experts failed to forecast.

First, wrote Beale in a bulletin from the Washington-based Population Reference Bureau, the Census Bureau's lowest projection of births for the 1970s overshot the mark by some 17 percent, and its most widely accepted projections were off by 23 percent. In 1971, the bureau issued four projections of births, ranging from 40 million to 49 million. But American couples produced only 33 million babies. The Census Bureau had no way of predicting the changes in patterns of marriage and childbearing that resulted in fewer births.

Second, the same Census Bureau projections anticipated 21 million deaths during the decade, but only 19 million Americans obliged by dying during the 1970s. The nation's vital statisticians projected that life expectancy would rise by only 6 months, Beale wrote, but it rose by 3.4 years instead, as advances in medical science and healthier life-styles reduced mortality from heart diseases.

Third, the number of people living in an average household dropped much faster than had been predicted. By 1980, average household size was only 2.76 people, far below a generally accepted projection for 1980 made by the Census Bureau in 1968 of between 3.08 and 3.19 people.

Fourth, migration to the South and West was much greater than the experts predicted, according to Beale. In 1972, the Bureau of Economic Analysis, part of the U.S. Department of Commerce, projected that the West would gain 4.0 million new residents during the 1970s. Instead, it gained 8.3 million—more than twice as many. The bureau projected that the South would gain by 7.8 million people, but the actual gain was 12.5 million, or three fifths more.

Fifth, and most surprising of all, nobody thought that the population growth rate outside the metropolitan areas—large cities plus their suburbs—would be greater than inside these areas. This reversal of Americans' historic patterns of migration was stunning because it went against so many familiar assumptions about how cities expand. The Bureau of Economic Analysis projected that metropolitan areas would grow 11.4 percent and nonmetropolitan areas only 5.3 percent. But instead, metropolitan areas grew only 10.2 percent, while nonmetropolitan areas zoomed 15.1 percent—triple the forecast.

The past two decades have brought dramatic demographic changes. And though the future never turns out just as we expect, or hope, understanding today's demographic forces will help businesses, government planners, and individuals alike foresee the attitudes and values that Americans will hold in the future. Demographic trends provide powerful clues to the future. Because they reflect the actions of millions of people, these trends have a momentum that can last for decades before there is a turn in a new direction, often in reaction to the trends of the past.

2 | *Generation Gaps*

"Positioned between the small generation born between World War II, when births were depressed along with the economy, and the small generation born after 1964, when small was beautiful, the baby-boom generation towers above its neighboring generations."

If thirty is the age that sets the young apart from the not-so-young, America has ended its affair with youth. More than half of all Americans have reached the age of thirty. A country that only yesterday was teeming with teen-agers, is fast becoming full of the middle-aged.

The median age, the age at which as many people are older as are younger, rose more between 1970 and 1980 than it had risen in any other decade but one. Its two-year rise from twenty-eight to thirty years has been matched only by the 1930s, when the median age rose from twenty-six and a half years to twenty-nine years.

In 1950, at the beginning of the baby boom, the median age was also thirty years, but then it fell under the weight of so many babies. Now it is rising again. By 1990, the median age should be thirty-three years. By the turn of the century, it will be thirty-six years—signaling a dramatic change in how Americans live. Never again are there likely to be as many people under age thirty as there are today. Ours will become a middle-aged society.

The median age is rising for three reasons. The average woman is having fewer children, so there are relatively fewer youngsters in the population to pull down the average. People are living longer, so there are relatively more older Americans, which pulls the average up. Most important, the baby-boom generation—that enormous group of more than 70 million Americans born in the 1950s and early 1960s—is moving from youth to adulthood.

This is America's dominant generation. Its attitudes become America's attitudes, its needs and interests appeal to legislators and attract manufacturers. As the baby-boom generation ages, the youth culture that so shaped the 1960s and 1970s may someday appear simply as an interruption—albeit a resounding one—in a long-term trend toward an older society.

Our era is unique for the sharp differences in the size of its generations. Throughout history, the size of each generation declined as its members grew older and death thinned the ranks. A chart of the population by age, with the youngest at the bottom and the oldest on top, resembled a pyramid. As long as each generation had children at the same rate during the childbearing years, nothing could change this pattern except the periodic plagues, wars, and exoduses that depleted only certain age groups.

But Americans have changed the shape of their pyramid. In the United States and a few other countries, primarily in Western Europe, the pyramid's base is narrowing and its top expanding as children become scarcer and older people more numerous. The U.S. age chart no longer resembles a pyramid as much as it does a python swallowing a pig. With apologies to over 70 million people, the pig is the baby-boom generation being swallowed by middle age.

A better analogy might be that of a rock thrown into a quiet pond. The rock splashes, and ripples spread outward from the center, creating a series of diminishing troughs and crests behind it. Eventually, the ripples spread so far from the center that they hit shore and the pond becomes still again.

If the average number of births per woman of childbearing age does not fluctuate widely again, the splash of the baby-boom generation in the 1950s will create a series of large generations followed by smaller generations. These crests and troughs will ripple through America for years to come—until time reduces their successive size, the generations reach the end of their life span, and the surface of the pond becomes still.

During the 1920s and continuing through the Depression to World

War II, American birthrates dropped so rapidly that many forecasters were predicting an elderly society by the 1950s because so few children were being born. But then came the rapid unexpected rise in birthrates that created the baby boom. Instead of becoming elderly, America was reborn. Just as abruptly, another fall in fertility followed in the mid-1960s and 1970s to produce the baby-bust generation.

HARD TIMES, GOOD TIMES

Positioned between the small generation born before World War II, when births were depressed along with the economy, and the small generation born after 1964, when small was beautiful, the baby-boom generation towers above its neighboring generations. The eighteen-year binge of births that began after World War II and lasted until 1964 surprised all the forecasters.

The postwar baby boom was a reaction to hard times. American family life had been interrupted first by world depression, then by world war. Not only had the plans of young adults been disrupted, but the turmoil had affected a generation of children as well. They grew up knowing hardship, hunger, rationing, and family separation. The seeds of the baby boom were sown in the turmoil that came before it.

Americans born in 1929, the year the stock market crashed, turned twenty-one in 1950. The baby boom resulted not from enormous families, but rather from the decision of a whole generation of families to have a third child, as a whole generation sought the safe harbor of home after two stormy decades. Families sprouted out of the rubble of the 1930s and 1940s. The 1950s would be different.

And they were different. Between 1947 and 1964, American mothers gave birth to more than 72 million babies. Between 1954 and 1964, the years of record births, more than 4 million babies were born each year. The 42 million children born between 1955 and 1964 were the most recorded in the United States in any single ten-year period. The peak year for births was 1957, with a record 4.3 million births. Fertility —the number of births per 1,000 women aged fifteen to forty-four— also peaked that year at 122.9.

The baby boom ended just as abruptly as it began. When it became their turn to marry and have children, Americans born in the 1950s found families unfashionable. Memories of the Depression and World War II had long since faded, women's opportunities were expanding, and young people had more exciting plans than to raise large families. Fertility rates and the number of births both declined abruptly in 1965, after having fallen gradually for the previous three years. The 3.8 million births in 1965 were fewer than in any year since 1950.

In 1965, the fertility fell below 97 births per 1,000 women of child-bearing age, a rate below that in any of the previous nineteen years. And to everyone's astonishment, fertility rates kept on declining—until they bottomed out in 1976, at 65. Since then, births and the birthrate have been rising again, but not because large families are now in favor. Instead, the number of people in their childbearing years is higher than it has ever been before. The baby-boom generation is now squarely in the middle of the traditional childbearing years, fifteen to forty-four.

The baby-boom generation is now making its waves in the age group when people settle down and start families. The 1980 census counted an astonishing 793,000 more Americans aged thirty-three than aged thirty-four. Thirty-three-year-olds were the nation's fastest growing single age group in 1980: the people born in 1946 and 1947, when births began to boom. (At the other extreme, the age group that fell the most was age six, down 843,000, according to the 1980 census. These youngsters were born during 1973 and 1974, at the bottom of the baby bust.)

Births have risen again, almost to their baby-boom highs of the 1950s. But in the 1950s it took only 35 million women of childbearing age to give birth to more than 4 million babies each year. Now it takes 56 million women to produce fewer than 4 million babies. Fertility remains near the record lows of the 1970s, only about half what it was in the family-happy 1950s.

Because fertility has fallen, the share of children today who are firstborn or only children is much higher than in the 1950s. Because young women today expect to have only one or two children, on average, the share of all births represented by first births should continue to rise.

Remember the population crisis? Until fertility fell abruptly in the 1970s, Americans wondered if large families were here to stay and worried about the impact of a rapidly growing population on America's resources and quality of life. Population activists wrote scary books, and the government formed a distinguished commission to study this unprecedented population boom. But when fertility fell, it became clear that the baby boom was not a never-ending cascade of births that would swamp society, but a tidal wave instead, inundating a generation but then receding.

Instead of a population crisis, America today faces slowing population growth. Population growth in the 1970s was even lower than the 13.4 percent in the 1960s, which itself was lower than the unprecedented (in this century) 18.5 percent of the 1950s. For 1985, the Census Bureau estimates a population of 239 million Americans, and for 1990, 250 million—just 9.7 percent more than in 1980. By the turn of the century, there should be 268 million Americans, 7.3 percent more than in 1990.

The population is still growing, of course, but at only about half the rate of the 1950s. Women today average only 1.8 births. It takes an average of 2.1 children per woman for the population to replace itself over the long run (the extra one-tenth child is necessary to compensate for the death of some children before they reach the childbearing years). At today's rates, America's total population would level off around the middle of the next century if there were no immigration.

No one can safely forecast what fertility will be in the future. If today's children decide to have large families when they are adults, a new wave of births could swamp America's age structure once again, lowering the median age. And who is to guarantee they will not make such a decision? Today's children are the product of small families, with fewer siblings, split by divorce, confused by new roles for mothers and fathers. Baby bust followed baby boom, so another boom could follow the baby bust. It is unlikely, but so was the baby boom of the 1950s.

AGE, THE PREDICTOR

Age is a powerful predictor of behavior. Age determines a person's interests and needs more than any other demographic characteristic. The fluctuations in the number of people in different age groups each decade affect nearly all Americans—business executives, government officials, home builders, school planners, and even newspaper reporters who seek to know if today's trends represent a change in the American psyche or simply a change in numbers.

Children need schooling, young people need jobs. Middle-aged adults pursue career, community, and family. Mature couples often find themselves with fewer responsibilities and more discretionary income. Americans in their retirement years have even more free time, but usually lower incomes. Consumption patterns differ by age, from teenagers' tastes in movies to the aged's need for nursing homes. As the number of people in different age groups waxes and wanes, so will the responsibilities of government and the opportunities in business.

Age is among the most predictable of demographic trends. In this, it stands in contrast to other trends. Attitudes toward marriage, child-bearing, and divorce can change rapidly. The ups and downs of the economy affect education, income, and occupation. Changes in women's roles, ethnic identity, and racial integration all reflect complex social forces. Americans' freedom to move across the country creates a sudden boom or bust for different areas. But the millions of people born each year move through life together—demographers call each age group a *cohort* because, like the cohorts of the ancient Roman armies, they move in step.

In the normal course of events, death takes a predictable number of the members of each age group with every passing year. Death rates differ by race, sex, and other demographic characteristics. These things are known. This is why the Census Bureau can predict with near certainty the size of each age group once its members have been born, whereas its predictions of the total size of the population are less certain because they must include predictions of the number of children likely to be born and guesses about future levels of immigration.

When the size of each generation differs markedly from the ones around it, as in America today, it upsets virtually every institution. A surge of youngsters into the schools gave the nation's educational system headaches in the 1960s. A surfeit of young job seekers in the 1970s contributed to rising unemployment, while the campuses were knee deep in protest because the baby-boom generation entered college.

In the 1980s, careers in business and the professions are enjoying a new popularity, while political activism has waned along with college applications. As the peak of the baby-boom generation nears age thirty, yesterday's young rebels are becoming today's middle managers. To-morrow, they will be running the nation's companies and making gov-ernment policy. In the 1990s, as a greater share of the population fills the years when people are married, stay in one place, and become civic-minded, communities may enjoy a new stability. The roots will grow deeper.

The burger franchises of the 1970s could not have succeeded with-out the presence of so many teen-agers. As teen-agers become a propor-tionately smaller share of the population, however, the market for fast food is changing. The franchises have been changing their appeal, offering new foods, breakfasts, and a working-person theme to appeal to the adult consumer. The models in advertisements have grown older. As American companies become increasingly aware of the power of demographic change, many are gearing products and services to those age groups most likely to be increasing rapidly in the years just ahead, and abandoning or cutting back ventures that may have peaked because they appeal to age groups whose size will be shrinking.

Today's business climate demands different strategies than did that of the 1960s and 1970s, when it appeared that the population would continue to grow rapidly. In such an environment, a company's success could be assured simply by providing more of everything. The number of government services also expanded rapidly, following the same assumptions. Now, both business and government have a more difficult task, faced with such fluctuations in the size of age groups.

If the theme of the 1970s was "grow bigger," the theme of the 1980s should be "stay flexible." When its customers are changing, a business must change with them. That goes for even the mighty U.S. government.

Politicians can no longer claim to know their districts without also understanding how the age of the electorate will be changing. Voting behavior varies by age. Americans aged twenty-five to thirty-four composed 23 percent of eligible voters, but they cast only 20 percent of the votes in the 1982 national elections. In contrast, Americans aged forty-five to fifty-four were only 13 percent of all voters, but they were 17 percent of those who actually voted. Elderly Americans also vote in disproportionate numbers; people sixty-five or older were 15 percent of the voting-age population, but were 19 percent of voters in 1982.

Age is the most important predictor of family status. Over half of American families headed by someone aged twenty-five to thirty-four contain at least one child under the age of six. But less than 4 percent of those headed by a forty-five- to fifty-four-year-old contain young children. Virtually no families whose head has reached the age of sixty-five have young children.

Income, too, varies markedly by age. Median household income for the forty-five to fifty-four group was $27,985 in 1982; for those sixty-five and over, it was only $11,041. The generation aged forty-five to fifty-four contains the highest share of homeowners, high-income households, and people at the peak of their careers.

In 1980, the census counted 226.5 million Americans, 11.4 percent more than in 1970. But the sixty-five-plus age group increased nearly two and a half times as fast, rising 27 percent. The number of Americans in their forties declined by 6 percent as the Depression generation filled these years. In contrast, the number of thirty to thirty-four-year-olds soared 54 percent—more than any five-year age group in any decade during this century—as members of the leading edge of the baby-boom generation turned thirty. But the number of children aged five to nine declined 16 percent, as the baby-bust generation followed the baby-boomers in the childhood years.

Because age influences so many aspects of American life, the past fluctuations in birthrates will have their effect on society for years to come. As the size of the different age groups ebbs and flows each decade for the lifetime of today's Americans, America's interests—and even its fortunes—may rise and fall with the tide.

THE BABY BOOM'S IMPACT

Because the attitudes and behavior of the baby-boom generation determine the nation's dominant moods, understanding its ups and downs has become important. In some ways, the baby-boom generation is different from other Americans. Its members are better educated than the older generation, baby-boom women are more likely to be in the labor force, and men and women of the baby-boom generation are more likely to have similar attitudes toward family and career. In contrast to the conformity that marked the 1950s, individualism has become a strong value today—as baby-boom men and women try to stand out from the crowd.

What will the future be like as the baby-boomers age? By the year 2000, the baby-boom generation will be aged thirty-six to fifty-three; as a result, there may be more attention paid to investments, affluent life-styles, and community affairs. These are among the traditional interests of middle-aged Americans.

Middle-aged people are in their most productive years. The forties and fifties are the years when earnings and discretionary income peak. Interest in recreation, travel, and luxury consumer goods should grow for the remainder of the century. Because the average couple will have fewer children, while relatively more families contain two earners, a higher share of income will be available for adult-oriented goods, and people will be willing to spend for convenience and for products and services that help them assert their individuality.

Baby-boomers are not traditional in their beliefs, and though they may soon be middle-aged, they are unlikely to return to the conformity that marked the 1950s. A study of the attitudes of the baby-boom generation by the American Council of Life Insurance (ACLI) found "a new brand of traditionalism" among baby-boomers. Reported in

American Demographics magazine, the ACLI study found "a distinct longing for more traditional values in some areas, hard work, strong family and religious ties and respect for authority, coupled with an increasing acceptance of nontraditional ideas in others—a tolerance of changing sexual mores and a desire for less materialism."

Three out of four baby-boomers surveyed by the ACLI said the most appealing life-style was one of shared responsibility between men and women. Although the women of the baby-boom generation were much more likely than the older generation to postpone marriage and delay childbearing, they expressed fairly traditional views about raising children. Some 60 percent believed that a woman should not go to work until her children started elementary school. Nonetheless, nearly half of women with preschool children are in the labor force.

The ACLI found that "baby boomers stand apart from older generations in their high degree of optimism about their financial future." However, they were less optimistic about the future of their own children; only about one in three thought that their children would fare better financially, a finding that differs significantly from the attitudes of older generations, who envisioned each generation as being better off than the previous one.

The attitudes of the baby-boom generation during the 1970s, when its members were in school, reflected the same ironies. Even as that generation took greater advantage of opportunities for higher education than any generation before it, its members wanted to change the system. Now, two thirds of the generation say they would like to see less emphasis on making money, but their attitudes firmly support the work ethic and the pursuit of affluence. Similarly, in family life, this generation has radically changed the traditional family, but its members still express support for family ties.

OLD FOLKS, NEW WAVES

The elderly are America's newest wave. Among the most agreeable of demographic trends has been the steady rise in life expectancy thoughout this century. In 1900, a newborn American could expect to live to age forty-seven. Eighty-four years later, life expectancy had risen to seventy-four and a half—fully a quarter century longer. If life expectancy continues to rise as it has since 1968, a person born in the year 2000 could expect to live to the age of eighty, a thirty-three-year increase over American life expectancy a century earlier.

For most of this century, gains in life expectancy were made by eradicating childhood diseases and improving the living conditions that contributed to high infant mortality. The gains for older Americans were slight. In the past decade, however, more than two thirds of the increase in life expectancy has resulted from a decline in deaths from heart disease, which has been the leading killer of older Americans. Americans' interest in health and fitness and continued attention to the prevention of heart disease, cancer, and other causes of death among the elderly could result in further life expectancy increases.

The number of Americans who had reached the ripe old age of eighty-five by Census Day 1980 was a dramatic 48 percent more than the number a decade ago. Only one quarter of us live until our eighty-fifth birthday, however, so the boom among the elderly is one of degree only. Still, it is an important change. The gains in life expectancy among the elderly have been so dramatic that the number of Americans aged sixty-five or older has risen faster than the total population in every decade of the twentieth century—a rise of 729 percent since 1900, to be precise, compared to a 198 percent increase in the total population. And more gains lie ahead.

In 1940, when the Social Security System was in its infancy, people who had reached age sixty-five were considered elderly, ready for the rocking chair, their productive years behind them. In 1940, only 9 million Americans were aged sixty-five or older. Today, there are 28 million. People in their sixties and seventies can still be productive and healthy. No longer can older Americans be treated as a mass, as "seniors" in terminology, as "65-plus" in statistics, as mere footnotes in marketing plans, or as candidates for government support. The stereotype of the older American is giving way before the new vigor and longer life expectancy of people in the advanced age groups.

Because of women's longer life expectancy, the great majority of the elderly are women. The median age of men recorded by the 1980 census was 28.8 years, but for women it was 31.3 years, two and a half years older. More male babies are born than female babies, and until the age of 28, men outnumber women. But then, in one of nature's remarkable turnarounds, women begin to outnumber men. At every age beyond 28, women outnumber men by an increasing margin. Over age 64, only 67 men are alive for every 100 women.

Until 1950, men outnumbered women in America, not because of a different life expectancy but because the Land of Opportunity attracted more men than women. Even today, in a few states that are off the beaten track, men still outnumber women. The 1980 census found more men than women in Alaska, Hawaii, Nevada, North Dakota, and Wyoming. But overall, life expectancy has risen more for women than men, and so the numerical gap between the sexes has been widening. Women now outnumber men by 6.3 million in America, some 1.2 million more than a decade ago. An older America is becoming a more female America.

The 1980 census counted exactly 32,194 Americans who claimed to be at least 100, but the actual number of centenarians is anybody's guess. The Census Bureau's best estimate of the real number of centenarians at the time of the 1970 census was 4,800, up from an estimated 3,300 in 1960. The number could not have increased tenfold in only twenty years. But if you trust the Census Bureau's long-range age projections, nearly 2 million Americans born this year will still be alive a century from now.

AGE, BY STATE

Because Americans typically live near people like themselves— whether on a Utah Indian reservation or in a Florida retirement condominium—there are wide variations in age among America's counties, metropolitan areas, and states. To nobody's surprise, the 1980 census found that Florida has the nation's greatest number of old folks. Florida's median age of 34.7 years is more than 10 years higher than Utah's 24.2 years, the state that has the lowest median age in the country. The Mormon religion favors large families as much as old folks favor Florida. Nearly one quarter of Utah's residents are under age 10; and some 17 percent of Floridians are age 65 or older.

Table 1 MEDIAN AGE

United States Total, 30.0 Years

States		Cities	
1 Florida	34.7	1 Miami Beach, FL	65.7
2 New Jersey	32.2	2 Pompano Beach, FL	50.6
3 Pennsylvania	32.1	3 Largo, FL	47.7
4 Connecticut	32.0	4 Clearwater, FL	44.1
5 New York	31.9	5 Hollywood, FL	43.2
6 Rhode Island	31.7	6 St. Petersburg, FL	42.2
7 Massachusetts	31.1	7 Union, NJ	42.1
8 Missouri	30.8	8 West Hartford, CT	41.8
9 Arkansas	30.6	9 Skokie, IL	41.0

States		Cities	
10 West Virginia	30.4	10 San Leandro, CA	40.3
11 Maine	30.4	11 Clifton, NJ	39.9
12 Maryland	30.3	12 Walnut Creek, CA	39.7
13 Nevada	30.2	13 Bethesda, MD	39.7
14 Oregon	30.2	14 Irondequoit, NY	39.6
15 Oklahoma	30.1	15 Towson, MD	39.2
16 New Hampshire	30.1	16 Stratford, CT	38.1
17 Kansas	30.1	17 Lower Merion Township, PA	38.1
18 Tennessee	30.1	18 Miami, FL	38.0
19 Iowa	30.0	19 Abington Township, PA	36.8
20 Ohio	29.9	20 Wauwatosa, WI	36.8
21 Illinois	29.9	21 Dearborn, MI	36.6
22 California	29.9	22 Euclid, OH	36.6
23 Washington	29.8	23 Newport Beach, CA	36.4
24 Virginia	29.8	24 Fort Lauderdale, FL	36.4
25 Nebraska	29.7	25 Cranston, RI	36.4
26 Delaware	29.7	26 Hialeah, FL	36.3
27 North Carolina	29.6	27 Scranton, PA	36.3
28 Vermont	29.4	28 Wilkes-Barre, PA	36.3
29 Wisconsin	29.4	29 Oak Lawn, IL	36.1
30 Minnesota	29.2	30 West Palm Beach, FL	36.0
31 Indiana	29.2	31 Asheville, NC	36.0
32 Arizona	29.2	32 Scottsdale, AZ	35.9
33 Alabama	29.2	33 Glendale, CA	35.8
34 Kentucky	29.1	34 Bayonne, NJ	35.8
35 Montana	29.0	35 Burbank, CA	35.7
36 Michigan	28.8		
37 South Dakota	28.8	*The Bottom Ten*	
38 Georgia	28.6	454 North Charleston, SC	23.5
39 Colorado	28.6	455 Laredo, TX	23.5
40 Hawaii	28.3	456 Bloomington, IN	22.8
41 North Dakota	28.1	457 East St. Louis, IL	22.7
42 Texas	28.0	458 Compton, CA	22.6
43 South Carolina	28.0	459 Provo, UT	22.2
44 Mississippi	27.6	460 West Valley, UT	21.7
45 Idaho	27.5	461 Orem, UT	21.5
46 New Mexico	27.3	462 East Lansing, MI	21.4
47 Louisiana	27.3	463 Sandy City, UT	20.2
48 Wyoming	27.0		
49 Alaska	26.0		
50 Utah	24.2		

Source: 1980 census.

The population of Charlotte County, Florida, has the oldest median age of any county in the United States, 57.3 years. San Juan County, Utah, has the youngest, 19.4 years. San Juan is part of a Navajo Indian reservation. Almost three quarters of all families there have a child at home under the age of eighteen. Fewer than one quarter of families in Charlotte County, on the Gulf Coast between Sarasota and Fort Myers, have a child under eighteen living at home.

Outside Florida, the populations with the nation's highest median ages are in the Northeast. New Jersey, with a median age of 32.2 years, ranks second, followed by Pennsylvania at 32.1 years and Connecticut at 32. New York, the nation's second largest state, has a median age of 31.9 years, two years above the largest state, California, where the median age is 29.9 years. The western states have the youngest median ages: Alaska, 26.1; Wyoming, 27.1; New Mexico, 27.4; and Idaho, 27.6.

Like the states, metropolitan areas across the country display important differences in median age. Among the nation's 318 metropolitan areas at the time of the 1980 census, the population of Sarasota, Florida, had the highest median age. The census found as many Sarasotans over the age of fifty as below that age. In Jacksonville, North Carolina, the median age is only twenty-two, because the area contains a military base and has a high proportion of blacks, whose median age is lower than that of whites. Appropriately, the 1980 census found that the median age of the metropolitan area that contains the nation's capital is almost exactly equal to the nation's: 30.1 years for Washington, D.C., versus 30 for the nation.

To some extent, localities differ in median age because of differences in the age profile of America's racial and ethnic groups. The median age of Hispanic Americans is only 23.2 years, the 1980 census reported. The median age of America's 3.5 million Asians and Pacific Islanders is 28.7 years. The median age of these groups is lower than that of whites because young people are most likely to pack up and move to a new country, and Hispanic and Asian immigration is more recent than is European immigration.

Black Americans have a median age of 24.9 years compared to 31.3 for the white population, because the average black woman bears more children and starts at an earlier age than the average white woman, and blacks have a shorter life expectancy than whites. For the 1.4 million American Indians, Eskimos, and Aleuts as a group, the median age is just 22.8 years. These racial groups also have higher fertility than whites and a shorter life expectancy.

Eleven percent of Americans counted by the 1980 census have reached the age of sixty-five, and 28 percent are under eighteen. In twenty-four counties, however, more than one resident in four is sixty-five or older. Eight of these counties are in Florida. The county with the highest median age, Charlotte, also has the highest share of people sixty-five and older—more than one third of the county residents. Other counties with high median ages are all in remote rural areas—Sierra County, New Mexico; Furnas County, Nebraska; Llano County, Texas.

Table 2 PERCENT AGED 65 PLUS

United States Average, 11.3 Percent

States		Cities	
1 Florida	17.3%	1 Miami Beach, FL	51.8%
2 Arkansas	13.7	2 Pompano Beach, FL	29.8
3 Rhode Island	13.4	3 Largo, FL	29.5
4 Iowa	13.3	4 Clearwater, FL	26.0
5 Missouri	13.2	5 St. Petersburg, FL	25.7
6 South Dakota	13.2	6 Hollywood, FL	25.1
7 Nebraska	13.1	7 Daytona Beach, FL	21.5
8 Kansas	13.0	8 West Hartford, CT	20.2
9 Pennsylvania	12.9	9 West Palm Beach, FL	20.2
10 Massachusetts	12.7	10 Walnut Creek, CA	20.0
11 Maine	12.5	11 Fort Lauderdale, FL	19.0
12 Oklahoma	12.4	12 Towson, MD	19.0
13 North Dakota	12.3	13 Brookline, MA	19.0
14 New York	12.3	14 Scranton, PA	18.8
15 West Virginia	12.2	15 Wilkes-Barre, PA	18.7
16 Wisconsin	12.0	16 Union, NJ	18.6
17 Minnesota	11.8	17 Santa Barbara, CA	18.3
18 Connecticut	11.7	18 Binghamton, NY	18.3
19 New Jersey	11.7	19 Asheville, NC	18.1
20 Oregon	11.5	20 Wauwatosa, WI	17.9
21 Mississippi	11.5	21 Utica, NY	17.9
22 Vermont	11.4	22 Reading, PA	17.8
23 Arizona	11.3	23 Lower Merion Township,	
24 Alabama	11.3	PA	17.7
25 Tennessee	11.3	24 St Louis, MO	17.6
26 Kentucky	11.2	25 Quincy, MA	17.1
27 New Hampshire	11.2	26 Huntington, WV	17.0
28 Illinois	11.0	27 Miami, FL	17.0
29 Ohio	10.8	28 Clifton, NJ	16.9
30 Montana	10.7	29 San Leandro, CA	16.9
31 Indiana	10.7	30 Euclid, OH	16.8
32 Washington	10.4	31 Schenectady, NY	16.8
33 North Carolina	10.3	32 Irondequoit, NY	16.7
34 California	10.2	33 Portland, ME	16.6
35 Delaware	10.0	34 Fall River, MA	16.6
36 Idaho	9.9	35 Altoona, PA	16.6
37 Michigan	9.8		
38 Texas	9.6	*The Bottom Ten*	
39 Louisiana	9.6	454 Irvine, CA	3.6
40 Georgia	9.5	455 East Lansing, MI	3.6

States		Cities	
41 Virginia	9.5	456 Simi Valley, CA	3.4
42 Maryland	9.4	457 Westminster, CO	3.3
43 South Carolina	9.2	458 West Valley, UT	2.9
44 New Mexico	8.9	459 Columbia, MD	2.8
45 Colorado	8.6	460 Plano, TX	2.6
46 Nevada	8.2	461 Cerritos, CA	2.2
47 Wyoming	7.9	462 Sandy City, UT	2.1
48 Hawaii	7.9	463 Anchorage, AK	2.0
49 Utah	7.5		
50 Alaska	2.9		

Source: 1980 census

In thirty counties, more than 40 percent of residents have yet to reach the age of eighteen. In San Juan County, Utah, which also holds the record for the youngest median age, fully 47 percent of the population is younger than eighteen. Like San Juan, many other counties with young populations are Indian reservations—with names like Apache (Arizona), Sioux (North Dakota), and Buffalo (South Dakota). So diverse is the sprawling state of Texas that it finds room for seven of the oldest counties and for four of the youngest.

Fewer than 3 percent of Alaska's residents are sixty-five or older —that state has yet to be discovered as a retirement haven. Only 8 percent of Hawaii's people are of retirement age, despite the appeal of that state's climate. After Utah, the highest proportions of the under-eighteen group are found in Alaska, Idaho, Mississippi, and New Mexico—all over 32 percent. The lowest proportions of the young, outside of Florida, are in Connecticut, Massachusetts, New York, and Pennsylvania—all under 27 percent—and in Rhode Island, the only state besides Florida in which fewer than 26 percent of the people are under the age of eighteen. The nation's smallest state has the largest share of the elderly of any state but Arkansas (13.7 percent) or Florida (13.4 percent) because it is an urban state that attracted European immigrants, early in the century, who have become today's elderly.

The Northeast has a smaller than average proportion of people below age forty-five, but above average for ages forty-five and above. The pattern in the West is the opposite. Of all the regions, the West has the most favorable ratio of working-age people to dependents, people under eighteen and over sixty-four. The West can claim a healthy age structure, whereas the Northeast must worry about an aging population.

Like archaeologists sifting through the strata of a lost civilization to uncover clues about its people's way of life, those who sift through census age data can find the forces that moved Americans. The age differences uncovered by the census reflect the flow of Americans out of the Northeast and into the West and South, out of big cities and into areas that are not so densely settled, and are compounded by differences in birthrates and death rates of the movers and those who do not move.

Table 3 PERCENT UNDER AGE 18

United States Average, 28.1 Percent

States		Cities	
1 Utah	37.0%	1 Sandy City, UT	47.6%
2 Alaska	32.5	2 Orem, UT	44.0
3 Idaho	32.5	3 West Valley, UT	43.1
4 Mississippi	32.3	4 East St Louis, IL	41.1
5 New Mexico	32.1	5 Compton, CA	39.7
6 Louisiana	31.6	6 Laredo, TX	39.4
7 Wyoming	31.0	7 Brownsville, TX	39.3
8 Texas	30.3	8 Plano, TX	37.8
9 South Carolina	30.2	9 Baldwin Park, CA	37.8
10 Georgia	30.1	10 East Los Angeles, CA	37.3
11 Alabama	29.8	11 Simi Valley, CA	37.0
12 South Dakota	29.8	12 Camden, NJ	36.9
13 Michigan	29.7	13 McAllen, TX	36.6
14 Kentucky	29.6	14 Cerritos, CA	36.2
15 Montana	29.5	15 Rancho Cucamonga, CA	35.9
16 Indiana	29.5	16 El Monte, CA	35.2
17 Arkansas	29.4	17 Kenner, LA	35.2
18 North Dakota	29.3	18 El Paso, TX	35.0
19 Arizona	29.1	19 Columbia, MD	35.0
20 Wisconsin	28.9	20 Gary, IN	34.9
21 Minnesota	28.7	21 Carson, CA	34.6
22 West Virginia	28.7	22 Mesquite, TX	34.5
23 Ohio	28.7	23 Sterling Heights, MI	34.4
24 Maine	28.6	24 Mission Viejo, CA	34.3
25 Hawaii	28.6	25 Taylor, MI	34.2
26 Nebraska	28.5	26 Newark, NJ	34.1
27 Vermont	28.4	27 Albany, GA	34.0
28 Illinois	28.4	28 Fountain Valley, CA	33.8
29 Iowa	28.3	29 Garland, TX	33.7
30 Tennessee	28.3	30 Pico Rivera, CA	33.6
31 Oklahoma	28.3	31 Pontiac, MI	33.6
32 North Carolina	28.2	32 Grand Prairie, TX	33.5
33 New Hampshire	28.0	33 Oxnard, CA	33.5
34 Delaware	28.0	34 Ontario, CA	33.1
35 Colorado	28.0	35 Westminster, CA	33.1

States		Cities	
		The Bottom Ten	
36 Missouri	27.7	454 Mountain View, CA	16.9
37 Maryland	27.7	455 Arlington, VA	16.4
38 Virginia	27.6	456 Brookline, MA	15.7
39 Washington	27.6	457 Cambridge, MA	15.6
40 Oregon	27.5	458 Santa Monica, CA	15.6
41 Kansas	27.5	459 Berkeley, CA	15.4
42 New Jersey	27.0	460 Pompano Beach, FL	15.2
43 California	27.0	461 Bloomington, IN	13.9
44 Nevada	27.0	462 East Lansing, MI	11.9
45 New York	26.7	463 Miami Beach, FL	8.9
46 Connecticut	26.5		
47 Pennsylvania	26.3		
48 Massachusetts	26.0		
49 Rhode Island	25.6		
50 Florida	24.2		

Source: 1980 census

For the nation as a whole, the thirty to thirty-four age group grew the fastest between 1970 and 1980, rising 54 percent as this age group became inflated with baby-boomers. This age group was the fastest growing in twenty-one states and the District of Columbia. In Wyoming, the twenty-five to twenty-nine age group increased 129 percent —the largest increase of any age group in any state during the decade. The energy boom attracted young adults eager to cash in.

Wyoming was one of just five states in which no five-year age group declined during the 1970s. Arizona, Nevada, Florida, and Utah—boom states all—were the other four.

At the other extreme, the greatest decline for any age group in any state was the 31 percent drop in the number of children between the ages of five and nine in Massachusetts. This age group decreased the most or increased the least in thirty-three states, demonstrating the deflating effect of the baby bust. But this age group decreased most of all in those states that were least able to retain young adults, who are the parents of young children.

In every northeastern state, the number of children aged five to nine declined more than any other age group. The Northeast's 28 percent decline in this age group was almost twice the 16 percent drop for the nation as a whole. The five to nine age group also decreased more than any other age group in most southern and western states, but because these states attracted so many migrants the drop was only half the average national decline.

Between 1970 and 1980, Massachusetts suffered a larger percentage decline than any other state in the number of children under age five —down 28 percent. The size of this age group dropped 5 percent nationally, but it grew in twenty-seven states, principally in the West, the region to which young adults are moving. Every state in the western region gained in number of youngsters under five. Their number grew an enormous 70 percent in Utah. Whereas the Northeast saw a 22 percent decrease in children under age five, more than four times the national decline, the West ended the 1970s with 13 percent more young children than when the decade began.

The big cities of the Northeast used to attract young people seeking jobs and excitement. As these people started families, they created the suburbs that now surround large cities. But as the magnetism of northern cities switches poles, young adults are moving elsewhere. Areas that cannot attract a steady flow of young people to replace those who move out face an increasingly aging population. They will not be producing proportionately as many children as states with younger populations. This is why the states of the Northeast have the nation's highest median age population, following Florida. In the past, fertility rates were high enough to assure a growing population even with a net loss in movers. This is no longer true.

The number of people in their twenties is about to decline, as the baby-bust generation enters adulthood. There may not be enough of them to go around for all states, and certainly not for all cities. Areas that find themselves with a rising imbalance of older people may turn increasingly to young immigrants from abroad to fill the work force and pay the taxes.

FUTURE FLOWS

For the rest of the 1980s and throughout the remainder of this century, America will continue to face unprecedented changes in the size of the various age groups. Some age groups will increase in size enormously, faster than ever before. Others will decline in size for the first time. These changes will affect virtually all of America's institutions, whether school systems interested in the number of school-age children; moviemakers and fast-food chains counting teen-agers; colleges and the armed forces looking for eighteen-year-olds; or manufacturers and marketers sizing up tomorrow's labor force and consumer groups. Social Security planners, who become interested in Americans when they reach their sixties, and nursing-home operators, who care about people in their eighties, will have to pay special heed.

Americans may still think the country has an inexhaustible supply of children, but this is no longer the case. Although the number of children under five should reverse its recent decline and rise rapidly in the 1980s as members of the baby-boom generation will be having children, the under-five population will begin to decline again in the 1990s when the small baby-bust generation reaches its childbearing years. How many children families decide to have, of course, is a matter of conjecture, but so far they are still opting for just one or two, and putting off marriage and childbearing.

Table 4 THE AGE SCORE CARD, 1980–2000

	Population (in millions)			(percentage change)	
	1980	1990	2000	1980–1990	1990–2000
Children					
under 5	16.4	19.2	17.6	16.7	−8.2
5–9	16.6	18.6	18.8	12.1	0.9
Youths					
10–14	18.2	16.8	19.5	−8.0	16.4
15–19	21.1	17.0	19.0	−19.7	11.8
20–24	21.6	18.6	17.1	−14.1	−7.8
Young Adults					
25–29	19.8	21.5	17.4	8.8	−19.2
30–34	17.8	22.0	19.0	23.4	−13.6
Middle-Agers					
35–39	14.1	20.0	21.7	41.6	8.7
40–44	11.8	17.8	22.0	51.8	23.2
45–49	11.0	14.0	19.8	26.5	41.4
Empty-Nesters					
50–54	11.7	11.4	17.3	−2.3	51.9
55–59	11.6	10.5	13.3	−10.1	27.1
60–64	10.1	10.6	10.5	5.0	−1.4
Retirees					
65–69	8.8	10.0	9.1	13.6	−9.0
70–74	6.8	8.0	8.6	17.6	6.6
75–79	4.8	6.2	7.2	29.3	16.4
80–84	3.0	4.1	5.0	36.6	22.3
85–plus	2.3	3.3	4.9	45.9	48.7

Source: Census Bureau

When the number of people of childbearing age fluctuates, but the birthrate remains constant, the number of young children also fluctuates. The number of children aged five to nine, which fell 16 percent during the 1970s, will rise again during the rest of this decade and remain stable throughout the 1990s because the children of the baby-boom parents will be passing through these years.

But teen-agers are becoming scarcer. The number of children aged ten to fourteen will decline during the present decade. Their number will grow rapidly in the 1990s, however, echoing the succession of the baby boom and baby bust in the 1950s and 1960s. The number of teen-agers aged fifteen to nineteen will decline during the present decade, as the baby-bust generation passes through the teens.

If crime and accident rates decline in the 1980s and teen-age unemployment becomes less a serious problem than an inconvenience, the nation's law-enforcement officials and politicians are sure to claim the credit. But the reason for these beneficial shifts will be instead the 20 percent drop in the number of people aged fifteen to nineteen, a group highly prone to accidents, crime, and unemployment. When this age group starts to increase again in the 1990s, as it will by some 12 percent, what will the officials say then?

After soaring 30 percent in the 1970s, the twenty- to twenty-four-year-old age group now faces two decades of unprecedented decline. By 1990, some 14 percent fewer Americans will be between the ages of twenty and twenty-four years than was the case in 1980. By the turn of the century, there will be 8 percent fewer still. Products and services that cater to the young adult will face the diminished demand that products geared to teen-agers face today. The supply of entry-level workers is about to dry up. Hundreds of colleges may no longer exist by the turn of the century, unless they can cater to adults.

The youth market will be shrinking rapidly as the baby-bust generation follows the baby-boom generation. The young-adult age group will be in transition in the 1980s and 1990s. The number of people aged twenty-five to twenty-nine, whose ranks rose 45 percent during the 1970s, will continue to grow during the 1980s. But growth will cease and then decline as the last members of the baby boom leave this age group in the early 1990s. The last baby-boomer will turn thirty in 1994.

More growth is in store for the fast growing thirty- to thirty-four-year-old group. Between 1980 and 1990, this group will increase 23 percent. Then, as the last members of the baby-boom generation reach age thirty-five in 1999, the size of this age group will drop by 14 percent.

By the turn of the century, America will have completed its transition to middle age. The largest generation in U.S. history will have passed from young adulthood to its middle years. As it fills with members of the baby-boom generation in the 1980s, the thirty-five to thirty-nine age group will increase over 40 percent.

In the economy of the year 2000, Americans in their early forties will become the dominant group, and that fact should have a healthy influence on the economy. After declining 3 percent during the 1970s, the size of the forty to forty-four age group will grow faster in the 1980s than it ever has before. It will continue to grow rapidly in the 1990s, as the older members of the baby boom succeed the younger members of the World War II generation in this age group.

The number of people aged forty-five to forty-nine, which dropped 8 percent in the 1970s, has started to rise in the 1980s, and will grow a projected 27 percent between 1980 and 1990. This age group will grow in number at least 40 percent more in the 1990s, as the leading edge of the baby-boom wave strikes it.

The number of Americans aged fifty to fifty-four has started declining, however, for the first time ever, as the small generation born during the late 1920s and the Depression years reaches this age group. In the 1990s, the number will reverse and grow faster than ever before because of the prewar baby bust, followed by the postwar baby boom.

After surging 17 percent in the 1970s, the number of Americans aged sixty to sixty-four is growing more slowly in the present decade than ever before. And, despite all the talk of an aging America, between 1990 and 2000 the number of sixty- to sixty-four-year-olds is projected to decline for the first time in history. As a group, Americans aged sixty-five and over during the 1980s will fail to match their 27 percent growth of the 1970s. The group will grow far more slowly in the 1990s than ever before.

These trends may not fit the image of an aging society, but the size of age groups changes not only because of lower death rates and past fluctuations in fertility, but also because of immigration patterns. The immigration boom around the turn of the century turned to bust in the 1920s. The immigrants who came to these shores as young adults in the early part of this century are nearing the end of their lives. They are followed by a group of Americans whose ranks were not so well augmented by immigrants. Reflecting this trend, the size of the sixty-five to sixty-nine age group will rise 14 percent this decade, but decline 9 percent in the next. The number of seventy-five- to eighty-four-year-olds will grow about 32 percent this decade, then slow to a 19 percent growth in the next.

However, the oldest of the old are increasing the fastest of all. During the 1980s, the eighty-five and older group will increase faster than any other age group—by 52 percent. In the 1990s, it will increase another 48 percent. In the past, the future size of the oldest age groups was unknown because the Census Bureau's projections combined all ages at eighty-five and above. The bureau lumped old folks together because it assumed that few people cared about such distinctions and because these age groups were so small. Now, for the first time, the Census Bureau has made a more precise projection.

According to the bureau's new calculations, between 1982 and 2000 the ranks of Americans aged ninety-five to ninety-nine will increase over 180 percent; those ninety to ninety-four will increase by almost 120 percent; and the eighty-five to eighty-nine set will be 85 percent larger in 2000 than in 1982.

The reasons for these extraordinary percentage increases projected are partly natural but also partly statistical: small numbers change as a percentage more rapidly than large ones. Another reason lies in the aging of America's wave of European immigrants of the early 1900s. By the end of this century they, like the Ellis Island facility that welcomed them, will be only a memory.

Age groups ebb and flow, but the overall trend is toward an older society in the next century. As it was youthful a decade ago, and will soon become middle aged, so will America become even more elderly in time. The number of Americans aged sixty-five and older has already surpassed the number of teen-agers. By the middle of the next century, as many Americans could be eighty-five or older as are sixty-five and older today.

That will be a remarkable society to contemplate. The economy should gain in productivity in the next two decades because a relatively higher share of the population will be of working age than in retirement or childhood. But when the baby-boom generation begins to retire in the next century, these gains will be lost. The ratio of workers to people age sixty-five or older—most of whom are retired—will drop abruptly.

Today, for every person sixty-five or older, five people are between the ages of eighteen and sixty-four. By 2050, fewer than three people will be of working age for each one of retirement age. That will make the burden of supporting the elderly much heavier, unless something is done. Older people may have to retire later, not earlier as is today's trend. More immigration to the United States might become as popular in the next century, as it is unpopular today, to supply enough workers to support America's large retired population.

People born at the end of the baby boom—those in their early twenties today—may not collect their Social Security benefits because the ratio of workers to retirees will have fallen so much. Can we expect today's politicians to solve this problem? Probably not. The first baby-boomer will not turn sixty-five until 2012. The last one will reach that age in 2029. For some thirty years after 2029, baby-boomers will dominate the elderly years. Americans aged sixty-five and older will double in share to 22 percent of the total population by 2050.

The nation has never faced such times. In nursing homes across the country, baby-boomers will be recalling the years of their youth—when an entire nation did their bidding. Will the nation still do their bidding then? Probably so. Their time may have passed, but their influence might remain. Their voting power could be enormous. The baby-boom generation does not act just like other generations because it is so large. Even in retirement, baby-boomers may expect the nation's younger leaders to respect their numbers, if not their age.

TRENDS TO WATCH

– Between now and the year 2000, a growing number of Americans will become middle-aged, a time when people are most likely to be married, have children, pursue careers, and accumulate possessions. Today's muppies will become tomorrow's corporate leaders.

– America's attitudes are likely to continue shifting away from the youth culture that dominated the 1960s and 1970s toward a middle-aged culture. But individuality has replaced conformity as a powerful force in society as the large baby-boom generation grows up.

– As life expectancy increases, while fertility remains low, a growing share of the population will consist of older people, and the great majority of them will be women, because women live longer than men.

– Dramatic shifts in the size of age groups will continue to occur in coming years because the baby-boom generation is flanked on each side by much smaller generations. As a result, the size of consumer markets, political constituencies, the labor force, school enrollments, and the retirement population will be fluctuating for decades to come.

3 | Splitting the Nuclear Family

"Like biologists discovering new species, demographers have turned up varieties of American relationships they scarcely knew existed."

Divorces doubled in number during the past decade; singles surged; couples cohabited. Families fell on infertile soil, and children were fewer and farther between than ever before.

The American family did not die during the 1970s, and it lives on in the 1980s. Most people still marry and have children, and the preferred number of children is still two. But the family is no longer the central unit of society.

More than ever before, Americans move in and out of marriage. There is less pressure for married couples to have children. People can live alone, or live with someone of the opposite sex outside of marriage. A snapshot of living arrangements still shows that a majority of Americans live in traditional families. But to follow the family members through life would reveal relationships as complex as those on an afternoon soap opera. Like biologists discovering new species, demographers have turned up varieties of American relationships they scarcely knew existed.

Behind the new life-styles are the members of the baby-boom generation. Americans typically marry and start their childbearing in their twenties, but when the young Americans of the baby-boom generation reached the household formation years in the 1970s, they did not follow in the footsteps of the older generation. They have been forging new paths instead, and many of the older generation have joined them.

These are turbulent times. Families may still be nuclear, but the atoms are splitting. Old patterns are fragmenting, but new ones are not yet firmly in place. As more women pursue higher education and career, sex roles are changing, but attitudes about these new roles have not been changing uniformly. When husband and wife disagree over their respective roles, a divorce often results.

High divorce rates mean that children today grow up with multiple sets of parents, grandparents, live-in friends, and other untested arrangements. The number of households containing a married couple with their children declined during the 1970s. As divorce divided husband-wife families, the fastest-growing family type was the single-parent family, usually a woman living alone with her children.

Young people leave their parents' home sooner than they used to, but they marry later after living alone or with friends for a few years. Divorce typically creates two households where there was only one, and at least one of the new households does not constitute a family. After older Americans become widows or widowers, they are more likely than in the past to live alone instead of moving in with relatives.

These forces have meant slow growth in the number of family households and fast growth for nonfamily households. As a result, the average number of people per household has been shrinking. The people living under one roof make up a single household if they take their meals together, according to the Census Bureau. One housing unit can contain several households if the residents eat separately or have separate entrances.

The 1980 census was the first census in history to record an average household size of fewer than three people. In 1983, there were almost 84 million households in the United States, one for every 2.7 people.

When Americans think of a family, they still visualize four people: husband, wife, and two children. Businesses create and market products for this stereotypical family; the government still publishes reports showing the effects of its policies on such a family. But these images are out of date. In 1970, the average family consisted of 3.6 people. By 1983, the average had fallen to just 3.3 people. By 1990, the typical American family—if it is still possible to speak of a typical family—probably will consist of only 3 people.

Not only changes in life-style, but also extraordinarily favorable housing conditions encouraged the formation of separate households in the 1970s. When housing was the best investment a person could make, the cost of establishing a separate household was low. Changing life-styles created a demand for more housing, but housing was a bargain. As housing costs have risen in recent years, young people have found it more difficult to establish separate households, while married couples may think twice about the economics of splitting up. These new circumstances may show up as future demographic trends.

Because a household is defined as an occupied housing unit, the number of housing units and the number of households are closely related. The 1980 census found 88 million housing units and 80 million households. The number of vacancies was up from the previous decade, despite the rapid rise in the number of households, partly because the Census Bureau began counting unoccupied mobile homes as vacant units for the first time. The population grew 11 percent during the 1970s, but the number of households rose 27 percent, two and a half times faster. Virtually every area of the country enjoyed a housing boom, which cushioned the economic impact in areas that lost population or had slower-than-average growth.

The decline in household size occurred with striking sameness throughout the country because the trends behind the changing American household became nationwide. Different areas of the country grew at different rates during the 1970s, and they contain vastly different numbers of households today, just as the size of their population is different. But average household size is more uniform across the country in 1984 than in 1970.

The median number of households per U.S. county in 1980 was 7,492, which means that as many of the nation's counties had fewer than 7,492 households as had more. The range was from just 34 households in remote Loving County, Texas, to 2.7 million households in Los Angeles. However, 84 percent of all counties, large or small, have an average household size of between two and three people.

Only the counties of New York, New York, and Kalawao, Hawaii, have an average household size below two people. New York County is Manhattan, an island of apartment dwellers, and Kalawao, on the island of Molokai, hosts a leper colony. Just nine counties in the whole nation, mostly Indian reservations, have an average household size above four people. Seven states have not a single county in which average household size is above three people. Small households have been sweeping the nation. For the first time in history, households containing only one or two people have become a majority of all the households in the country.

UNDERSTANDING HOUSEHOLDS

Households, by census definition, are of only two basic types—family or nonfamily. Family households are not only married couples, who may or may not have children, but also single parents living with children or relatives living together—two sisters sharing a household, for example. To the Census Bureau, any household that contains people who are related to the householder by blood, marriage, or adoption is a family household.

Nonfamily households are all other types of living arrangements—either people who live alone or people who live with someone other than a relative. Of the 21.5 million nonfamily households in 1980—27 percent of all households—18 million contained a person living alone. Of these, 11 million were women. Among the nonfamily households in 1980 were 1.6 million unmarried couples—a household type the Census Bureau calls "Persons of the Opposite Sex Sharing Living Quarters," or POSSLQ. Unmarried couples attract public attention disproportionate to their numbers.

Although 221 million Americans live in the nation's 80 million households, nearly 6 million do not. Instead, they live in college dormitories, prisons, military camps, mental hospitals, and nursing homes. The Census Bureau refers to such institutional living arrangements as group quarters. There are more than three times as many group-quarter residents as there are unmarried couples, but residents of group quarters receive public attention only when they escape or graduate.

About 59 million households in 1980 contained families—73 percent of all households. Among family households, 41 percent are married couples with children under the age of eighteen living at home. This traditional type of household comprises about 30.2 percent of all households. Close behind, at 30 percent of all households, are married couples without children living at home. In all, over 48 million American households contain married couples—60 percent of all households.

For all the changes in family structure, America is still a land of married couples. They occupy a majority of the households in every state. The state with the highest share of married-couple households is Utah—69 percent of all households; New York State has the lowest share—54 percent.

Eight million family households—10 percent of all households—contain a woman living without a husband, but with children or relatives. Finally, some 2 million family households contain a man living without a wife, but with children or relatives.

The woman's movement was largely responsible for the American family losing its head between the 1970 and 1980 censuses. America's households no longer have heads, statistically speaking. Instead they have *householders.* This term means almost the same thing as household head, but the Census Bureau considers it more egalitarian, since in the past the government's assumption was that a man was always the head of household. Now, the householder is the person in whose name a housing unit is owned or rented. If the house is jointly owned, the householder is whoever's name appears in the first column of the census questionnaire, or the *PICO,* for "person in column one." This book uses the terms *householder* and *head* interchangeably, but stops short of *PICO.*

The share of Americans who live in families has been dropping. Among families, there are fewer married couples. And among married couples, fewer contain children. Family households grew only 19 percent, while nonfamily households surged 89 percent between 1970 and 1983. Among family households, the number of married couples grew only 12 percent between 1970 and 1983; the number of married couples with children declined 5 percent; and the number of couples without children increased 33 percent.

Table 5 HOUSEHOLDS, BY TYPE, 1983

Households (U.S. total)	Number (in millions) 80.4	Percent 100%
Family Households	58.9	73.2
Married couples, no children under 18	24.1	30.2
Married couples, children under 18	24.3	30.0
Female head (no spouse)	8.4	10.5
Male head (no spouse)	2.1	2.6
Nonfamily Households	21.5	26.8
Women living alone	11.0	13.7
Men living alone	7.2	9.0
Other	3.3	4.1

Source: Census Bureau

The number of female-headed families rose 72 percent. Two-thirds of families headed by a woman are women living with their children, but not with a husband. This type of family doubled in number between 1970 and 1983. The number of male-headed families with children but without a wife more than doubled, up 116 percent.

The male-headed family, despite the attention it receives, is by far the least common household type. In 1983, the Census Bureau estimated that there were about 700,000 single-parent families headed by a man—less than 1 percent of all households. In contrast, almost 6 million single-parent families had a woman at the head—some 7 percent of all households.

Nonfamily households headed by a man have been the fastest-growing household type. Between 1970 and 1983, they soared 134 percent. Almost 10 million men live in such households, 7.5 million of them living alone. But even more households contain a woman living alone—some 12 million in 1983, 61 percent more than in 1970.

Table 6 CHANGING HOUSEHOLDS, 1970–1983

Households	Percent of Change, 1970–83
Family Households	19.3
Married Couples	11.6
With own children	−4.6
Female-headed (no spouse)	72.2
With own children	100.1
Male-headed (no spouse)	64.2
With own children	116.1
Nonfamily Households	88.6
Female-headed	65.1
Living alone	61.2
Male-headed	134.2
Living alone	111.0
Total	32.4

Source: Census Bureau

LOVE AND MARRIAGE

Americans still follow an age-old pattern: Children grow up and leave their parents. Eventually, they marry and have children of their own. But the timing has changed. Before they plunge into marriage, young people today may test the water by living with someone for a few years outside marriage. The number of couples who live together outside marriage doubled in the past decade.

Although the number of people in such relationships is small, cohabitation is fast becoming a new stage in the life cycle. Many people now spend most of their twenties going to school and starting careers rather than forming families, and this trend has fostered the trend to living together outside marriage. Slightly fewer than half of all cohabitants have been married at one time or another. Of those who have never married, almost all are young people. Cohabitation is rising faster among young people than older people.

Whether they are young or old, men and women who live together are close to each other in age. Over 95 percent of cohabiting men between the ages of twenty-five and thirty-five were living with a woman in the same age group or younger in 1981. Cohabitation is rare among people aged sixty-five and older; less than 6 percent of cohabiting couples in 1982 contained a person over age sixty-five. The number would probably be greater if the sex ratio were not so unbalanced among older people. It is hard for older women to find partners.

Almost three quarters of all households of cohabiting couples in 1982 contained no children. But the number with children has been growing faster than those without children, as divorce breaks up marriages that contain children and the partners ease into new relationships. In 1982, over 300,000 Americans were married to someone other than the person they were living with. Usually their partners were divorced or had never married.

Cohabitation has not become a replacement for marriage. Most such relationships are short-term. Of the 30 million Americans who were aged eighteen to twenty-four in 1982, for example, fewer than 1 million lived as cohabitants. In contrast, 7.4 million were married.

MARRIAGE AND DIVORCE

The ranks of the unmarried have been growing rapidly. In 1982, almost 59 million American adults were unmarried, 21 million more than in 1970. The unmarried include three different groups: those who have never married, those who have divorced but not yet remarried, and those who are widows or widowers. The proportion of widows and widowers has remained relatively constant over the years—between 8 percent and 9 percent of all Americans.

The number of people aged eighteen and over who have never married has risen rapidly—from 21 million in 1970 to 34 million in 1982. Americans are postponing marriage. The social acceptance of cohabitation means there is no reason to rush into marriage. It also has become more acceptable to live alone. Households that contain only one person have been growing more than twice as fast as households in general. Today, about one quarter of all households are occupied by one person only—some 19 million Americans. Fewer than 11 million people lived by themselves in 1970.

Nearly two thirds of single-person households contain a woman; only one third a man. More than half of all men who live alone are younger than forty-five; more than half of the women who live alone are age sixty-five or older. Men who live alone may fit the image of the swinging single, but the majority of lone women are widows.

Almost half of men who live alone have never been married, compared to less than one quarter of the women. The number of people living alone who have never married rose from 2.8 million in 1970 to 6 million in 1982, more than double, as the baby-boom generation reached young adulthood. The median age at first marriage for women rose from 20.8 years in 1970 to 22.5 years in 1982. For men, it rose from 23.2 years to 25.2 years.

Table 7 MARRIED-COUPLE HOUSEHOLDS

U.S. Average, 60.2 Percent

States		Cities	
1 Utah	68.9%	1 Sandy City, UT	85.6%
2 Idaho	66.9	2 Cerritos, CA	81.9
3 West Virginia	65.4	3 Plano, TX	79.8
4 Kentucky	65.4	4 Orem, UT	79.2
5 Wyoming	65.2	5 Mission Viejo, CA	78.6
6 Arkansas	64.7	6 Levittown, NY	78.4
7 North Dakota	64.7	7 Livonia, MI	78.2
8 Iowa	64.3	8 Cherry Hill, NJ	77.8
9 Indiana	64.0	9 Simi Valley, CA	77.1
10 South Dakota	63.6	10 Middletown, NJ	77.1
11 Tennessee	63.4	11 Rancho Cucamonga, CA	76.9
12 Kansas	63.4	12 West Valley, UT	75.6
13 Oklahoma	63.4	13 Sterling Heights, MI	75.3
14 Hawaii	63.2	14 Florissant, MO	74.8
15 Alabama	63.0	15 Fountain Valley, CA	74.7
16 North Carolina	63.0	16 Mesquite, TX	74.0
17 Montana	63.0	17 Richardson, TX	73.8
18 Nebraska	63.0	18 West Seneca, NY	72.6
19 New Hampshire	62.9	19 Penn Hills, PA	72.5

States		Cities	
20 Maine	62.8	20 Garland, TX	72.3
21 South Carolina	62.8	21 Skokie, IL	72.1
22 Texas	62.7	22 Redford Township, MI	72.1
23 Wisconsin	62.6	23 Bristol Township, PA	71.8
24 New Mexico	62.2	24 Woodbridge Township, NJ	71.8
25 Minnesota	62.1	25 Arlington Heights, IL	71.7
26 Arizona	62.2	26 Edison, NJ	70.5
27 Mississippi	62.1	27 Chesapeake, VA	70.1
28 Ohio	62.0	28 Carson, CA	70.1
29 Missouri	61.7	29 Thousand Oaks, CA	69.8
30 Virginia	61.6	30 Arvada, CO	69.8
31 Connecticut	61.1	31 Overland Park, KS	69.7
32 Alaska	61.1	32 Haverford Township, PA	69.6
33 Michigan	61.0	33 Dearborn Heights, MI	69.6
34 Pennsylvania	61.0	34 Farmington Hills, MI	69.5
35 New Jersey	61.0	35 Kenner, LA	69.3
36 Georgia	60.8		
37 Delaware	60.8	*The Bottom Ten*	
38 Vermont	60.7	454 Atlanta, GA	35.3
39 Louisiana	60.3	455 Harrisburg, PA	35.2
40 Oregon	59.8	456 Hartford, CT	34.7
41 Washington	59.4	457 Boston, MA	34.7
42 Florida	59.4	458 San Francisco, CA	34.4
43 Maryland	59.1	459 East St. Louis, IL	33.6
44 Colorado	58.9	460 Santa Monica, CA	32.5
45 Rhode Island	58.8	461 Cambridge, MA	31.9
46 Illinois	58.8	462 Washington, DC	30.5
47 Massachusetts	56.7	463 Berkeley, CA	30.1
48 Nevada	55.7		
49 California	55.2		
50 New York	54.4		

Source: 1980 census

But the increase in the number of Americans who have never married may not represent the dramatic change in life-style it is often thought to represent. The rising ranks of the never married also reflect the presence of more people in the young age groups, when it is common not to be married. The baby-boom generation's arrival at adulthood means that there are more of all kinds of relationships associated with young adults: more marrieds, more unmarrieds; more divorces, more remarriages; more cohabitants, more singles.

Nearly two thirds of all Americans eighteen years old or older who have never been married are under age twenty-five. But only 7 percent of Americans thirty years old or older have never been married. During the past twelve years, the number of people aged eighteen to twenty-four increased by one third as the baby-boom generation filled this age group, pushing upward the share of Americans who were not yet married.

As the baby-boom generation approaches its thirties, the number of marriages has also been rising. From 2.2 million marriages in 1975, the number rose to 2.5 million in 1982, and then fell slightly to 2.4 million in 1983. As the baby-boom generation moves into its thirties throughout the rest of this decade and into the 1990s, the proportion of Americans who have never married should start dropping again.

DIVORCE AND REMARRIAGE

Breaking up is hard to do, but millions have been doing it. Americans obtained nearly 10 million divorces as opposed to 22 million marriages during the 1970s. The divorce rate rose from nine divorces per 1,000 married women in 1960, to twenty-three in 1980. Divorce has become so common that at its current rate, half of all marriages formed today will end in divorce. One person in five will become divorced twice before reaching the age of seventy-five.

Because Americans are marrying later and marriages formed when a couple is mature are more durable than those formed between younger people, this trend might reduce the divorce rate in the future. On the other hand, most divorces occur within a few years of marriage. Because the number of marriages is rising, the number of divorces may soon rise too, given current divorce rates.

Divorce is not a rejection of the institution of marriage. It just means that at least one of the partners wants to do better. Americans still prefer being married to not being married—even if they may prefer not to be married to their current spouse. Fully 70 percent of the women under age forty-five who divorce remarry within five years. Divorced men are even more likely to remarrry.

Ironically though, the high remarriage rate means that the divorce rate is also likely to remain high, because remarriages carry a greater risk of divorce than do first marriages. Because divorce occurs so frequently, it has become all the more acceptable. In 1970, only 8 percent of women between the ages of twenty-five and fifty-four were currently divorced or separated. By 1981, the figure had more than doubled, to 17 percent. These days, nearly half of the marriages each year are remarriages for at least one of the partners. The proportion of all marriages that are first marriages for both partners has dropped from 69 percent in 1970 to 55 percent in 1981, the latest year studied by the National Center for Health Statistics.

A couple faces the highest risk of divorce in their early years of marriage. At today's divorce rates, about 20 percent of new marriages will end in divorce before the fifth anniversary; 33 percent before the tenth; 40 percent before the fifteenth; and 47 percent before the twenty-fifth.

The next twenty-five years come more easily. To say that half of all marriages end in divorce is also to say that half remain intact. One in eight married couples celebrate their fiftieth wedding anniversary. Whether the rough edges are smoothed or only the fittest survive, marriages that last have increasingly favorable odds of lasting longer. Of marriages that last at least twenty years, for example, only 11 percent eventually end in divorce. Just 7 percent of those that survive the first twenty-five years will end in divorce.

The average marriage lasts twenty-three years, before either divorce or death dissolves it. The odds for first marriages are a few years more than this, whereas the odds for remarriages are five to ten years fewer. The average marriage does not last as long as it used to, however. Although people are living longer, the divorce rate has risen so much that since 1965 almost seven years have been shaved off the length of the average marriage. In 1965, the average marriage lasted thirty years.

Another reason for the decline in the average length of marriage is that remarriages make up a higher share of all marriages now than in 1965. Paradoxically, yet another reason divorce has risen is that people are living longer. A century ago, the average marriage lasted only twenty-eight years before death took one of its members. Divorce was rare. By 1977, the average marriage that ended in the death of one of the partners lasted fully forty-three years—fifteen years longer—because life expectancy had increased. No longer can spouses count on the arrival of the Grim Reaper to end an unhappy marriage. Nor do they have to. They can divorce.

THE HOUSING BOOM

Households could not have grown more than twice as fast as the population in the 1970s without a boom in housing. It is no mere coincidence that the past decade has been called both the decade of divorce and the decade of housing. Housing conditions in the 1970s made it possible for young people to leave their parents' home and put down roots of their own. Couples could divorce and afford two separate homes with the money from the sale of their old home. Older Americans could continue living alone after the death of their spouse because the equity in their home was a new source of financial security. A mid-life professional could afford to drop out of a career and start anew with the money from selling his or her home.

The surge of baby-boomers into the household-formation years had home builders building units as fast as they could. To accommodate all the new kinds of households, people added apartments to their homes, the number of mobile homes grew 113 percent, and rapidly growing areas were adding almost as many housing units as people.

Had the coming of age of the baby-boom generation in the 1970s not coincided with such favorable housing conditions, America would be different today. But would the divorce rate be any lower? Would young people marry earlier? Would more elderly women move in with relatives? Would young people remain at home with their parents? Or would so much pressure have built up instead that politicians, bankers, and builders would have had to act—somehow—to supply the needed housing?

Simply to keep pace with a growing population, America would have had to add more than 7 million new housing units during the 1970s. But instead, for every new American in the 1970s there was nearly one new housing unit. Between 1970 and 1980, the nation gained 23 million people and 20 million housing units. Such demographic trends as rising divorce rates, increasing longevity, and delayed marriage combined with favorable economic conditions to stimulate the building of some 13 million more housing units than would have been needed had average household size not declined.

Even though the population grew more slowly than at any time since the Depression, housing grew faster than in any decade since the turn of the century. It was the first decade in which the population growth rate slowed while the housing growth rate accelerated. Even most of the areas that were losing population were gaining households. Only fifty-eight counties in the entire nation did not gain housing units. Among these few losers, a drop in the number of housing units in the core areas of New York City's urban blight accounted for some 80 percent of the total housing decline.

So attractive was the incentive to buy a home throughout most of the 1970s that the proportion of American households that owned a home rose in spite of the rapid growth of young householders and of single-person households, who are more likely to rent. The number of married couples who rent dropped during the decade. The share of young married householders who own rather than rent rose from about one half in 1970 to nearly two thirds in 1980. About two thirds of all householders today own their home.

The gap between the income of renters and owners widened. Between 1970 and 1980, the median income of renters dropped to only 67 percent of the U.S. average, while that of homeowners rose to 125 percent. It made so much economic sense to buy a home in the 1970s that only those not in a position to do so, either because their income was too low or their family status too uncertain, did not cash in. Households headed by women are less than 25 percent of all households, for example, but 40 percent of all renters. The median income of homeowners in 1980 was $19,800, versus only $10,500 for renters.

Table 8 OWNER-OCCUPIED HOUSING

U.S. Average, 64.4 Percent

States		Cities	
1 West Virginia	73.6%	1 Redford Township, MI	91.4%
2 Michigan	72.7	2 Livonia, MI	90.2
3 Idaho	72.0	3 Levittown, NY	89.9
4 Iowa	71.8	4 Cerritos, CA	86.5
5 Indiana	71.7	5 Dearborn Heights, MI	85.8
6 Minnesota	71.7	6 Middletown, NJ	85.5
7 Mississippi	71.1	7 St. Clair Shores, MI	84.1
8 Maine	70.9	8 Haverford Township, PA	84.0
9 Utah	70.7	9 Sandy City, UT	83.6
10 Oklahoma	70.7	10 Florissant, MO	82.9
11 Arkansas	70.5	11 Simi Valley, CA	80.8
12 Kansas	70.2	12 Penn Hills, PA	80.7
13 South Carolina	70.2	13 Warren, MI	80.2
14 Alabama	70.1	14 Rancho Cucamonga, CA	80.2
15 Kentucky	70.0	15 Sterling Heights, MI	80.2
16 Pennsylvania	69.9	16 Cherry Hill, NJ	80.1
17 Missouri	69.6	17 Irondequoit, NY	79.0
18 South Dakota	69.3	18 Stratford, CT	78.8
19 Wyoming	69.2	19 Abington Township, PA	78.5
20 Delaware	69.1	20 Roseville, MI	78.1
21 North Dakota	68.7	21 Fountain Valley, CA	77.9
22 Vermont	68.7	22 Carson, CA	77.4
23 Tennessee	68.6	23 Mission Viejo, CA	77.2
24 Montana	68.6	24 Union, NJ	76.7
25 North Carolina	68.4	25 Parma, OH	76.7

States		Cities	
26 Ohio	68.4	26 Oak Lawn, IL	76.5
27 Nebraska	68.4	27 Bristol Township, PA	76.0
28 Arizona	68.3	28 West Seneca, NY	75.6
29 Florida	68.3	29 Woodbridge Township, NJ	75.0
30 Wisconsin	68.2	30 Des Plaines, IL	74.9
31 New Mexico	68.1	31 Dearborn, MI	74.9
32 New Hampshire	67.6	32 Tonawanda, NY	74.5
33 Washington	65.6	33 Skokie, IL	73.8
34 Virginia	65.6	34 Lakewood, CA	73.1
35 Louisiana	65.5	35 West Valley, UT	72.3
36 Oregon	65.1		
37 Georgia	65.0	*The Bottom Ten*	
38 Colorado	64.5	454 Passaic, NJ	25.2
39 Texas	64.3	455 Boston, MA	24.6
40 Connecticut	63.9	456 East Orange, NJ	22.8
41 Illinois	62.7	457 Miami Beach, FL	22.3
42 New Jersey	62.0	458 New York, NY	22.1
43 Maryland	62.0	459 Cambridge, MA	21.5
44 Nevada	59.6	460 Hartford, CT	21.3
45 Rhode Island	58.8	461 Santa Monica, CA	20.9
46 Alaska	58.3	462 Newark, NJ	19.2
47 Massachusetts	57.5	463 Union City, NJ	18.8
48 California	55.9		
49 Hawaii	51.7		
50 New York	48.6		

Source: 1980 census

Midwesterners are most likely to own the home they live in. The list of the top states in homeownership includes the likes of Michigan, Iowa, Indiana, and Minnesota, all over 70 percent. But the top ten also includes Idaho, Mississippi, Maine, and Utah. West Virginia is the state with the highest share of homeowners—74 percent. New York State, influenced by New York City's households, is the only state in which fewer than half of households are owner occupied. Other states near the bottom include those in which a high proportion of residents live in metropolitan areas—Rhode Island, Massachusetts, Nevada, Maryland, and New Jersey.

Homeowners made the rising value of housing and the low mortgage rates of the 1970s work for them, whereas renters were on the other end. Homeowners became wealthier in the 1970s as the value of their homes soared. The median value of single-family homes rose 178 percent in the 1970s—to $47,200 in 1980. In boom areas, housing values rose much more. In every western state, housing values rose over

200 percent. Owners in Wyoming enjoyed the most rapid growth—up 291 percent. New York's homeowners, where housing value rose the least, had to settle for a mere 103 percent appreciation.

Land-scarce Hawaii was the only state with a 1980 median housing value greater than $100,000, leading the nation with a median of $118,100. After Hawaii, states with the highest median housing value were California, $84,500; Alaska, $76,300; and Nevada, $68,700. At the bottom end of the scale were Mississippi, $31,400, and Arkansas, $31,100.

Among cities of 50,000 people or more, those in California dominate the upper ranks of housing value. With the exception of Honolulu, Hawaii, and Bethesda, Maryland, California cities monopolize the top ten, led by Newport Beach, where the average housing value in the 1980 census was $218,180; second-place Santa Monica's average home was worth $187,326. The lower ranks are filled by a more diverse group of cities, including Camden, New Jersey, at the bottom with a median housing value of just $16,092; Harrisburg, Pennsylvania; Detroit, Michigan; Buffalo, New York; and Terre Haute, Indiana.

America's housing conditions are improving, the census shows. The number of year-round units with air conditioning almost doubled during the 1970s. The share that lack private plumbing was cut in half. Fewer than 3 percent of all housing units now lack plumbing. Still, in more than 100 rural counties, 20 percent of homes lack plumbing. But it is hard to find a house anywhere that does not have complete kitchen facilities.

The average number of rooms per home rose by 0.3, or nearly one-third of a room in the past decade. As a result, the average person may have a bit more privacy. The increase in rooms per person between 1970 and 1980 was equivalent to the entire increase in the thirty years between 1940 and 1970. The state with the highest proportion of people per room is Hawaii, where 15 percent of households, five times the national average, have more than one person per room. In Nebraska and Iowa, with land to spare and a much slower population growth than Hawaii, only 2 percent of homes have more than one person per room.

Condominiums emerged in the 1970s as a way of providing the benefits of home ownership to the millions of the young people of the baby-boom generation who were eager to form households of their own, but who could not afford the traditional single-family home. The splintering of the traditional family also encouraged the growth of alternative kinds of housing. Smaller households require smaller housing units.

More than 350,000 apartments were converted to condominiums during the 1970s, about 80 percent of them in metropolitan areas. Almost half of their owners are under thirty-six years old, and 57 percent are single persons. Over 60 percent earn more than $20,000 per year, and 66 percent are professionals or managers. The 1980 census reported 2.1 million condominiums, 92 percent of them in metropolitan areas. Condominium residents fit the profile of Americans who are likely to pair off, have children, and move into single-family homes. Most of them probably bought a condominium as a first step toward owning a single-family home. But as housing conditions have changed in the 1980s, many may now find the cost of single-family housing permanently beyond their reach.

Demand for housing does not guarantee supply. The country is unlikely to see a repeat of the housing conditions of the 1970s. Because the baby-boomers' demand for housing should be even greater in the 1980s than the 1970s, however, something may have to give. Americans in the past have adjusted their life-styles to fit tight housing conditions, but the baby-boom generation is too important a group of customers for the housing market and too potent a political force quietly to accept the frustration of the American Dream.

THE FAMILY'S FUTURE

Trends that have led to smaller households in the 1970s may begin to lead in the other direction in the years ahead. As the baby-boom generation grows older, reaching their thirties this decade, young families will be in evidence.

Data Resources, Inc., a private forecasting firm, anticipates an increase of only 21 percent in the total number of households between 1980 and 1990, less than during the 1970s because the rate of population growth has slowed.

The young-person household is becoming scarcer. After soaring by more than 50 percent during the 1970s, the number of households headed by people under age twenty-five should decline as much as 18 percent in the 1980s. However, households headed by Americans aged twenty-five to forty-four will grow 36 percent because the baby-boom generation will be in this age group. These are the years when people are most likely to be raising families.

The dominant households of this decade will be headed by Americans born near the peak of the baby boom, those in the twenty-five to thirty-four age group. By 1990, they will head about one household in four. This is the age group in which families make home improvements and buy life insurance, appliances, furniture, and children's clothing. The rise in the cost of housing has made it more difficult for young families to settle down. The trend toward two-income families results not only from women's changing attitudes toward a career, but also from the need many of these families have for extra income to realize their goal of home ownership.

Data Resources projects that households containing a head between the ages of forty-five and sixty-four years old will grow only 8 percent in the 1980s. But within this age group, those with a head aged forty-five to fifty-four will grow 18 percent, after declining 2 percent in the 1970s because members of the small generation born during the Depression were in this age group. Households headed by people in the fifty-five to sixty-four group will decline in the 1980s because the Depression-born generation is arriving in these years now.

Households headed by people aged sixty-five or older should continue their above-average growth, if Americans live longer and widows continue to live alone rather than moving in with relatives. By 1990, almost 21 million households could contain a householder who has reached the age of sixty-five—more than one household in five.

These trends mirror the changes in the size of the country's different age groups. But projecting the number of households is more difficult than projecting the number of people who will be in different age groups. People may march in step through the age groups, but when it comes to marriage, divorce, living alone, or living together, people have a mind of their own. Demographers cannot read minds, but knowing the future number of households headed by people in different age groups is even more important than knowing the number of individuals.

Most consumer purchasing is done on behalf of households rather than individuals. Government policy usually is directed to households. Telephone service and mail service go to households. A surge of individuals into the family years will give the nation more of a family atmosphere. The decisions people make about their living arrangements affect the fortunes of the housing and real estate industries, the obligations of local governments, and the planning of all those businesses that direct their products to the home.

Because a smaller share of households contains families, because fewer couples have children, and because the average couple has fewer children, priorities for spending the household budget are different from what they used to be. Instead of buying bunk beds and braces for their offspring, and saving for their children's future, more couples are free to spend money on themselves. A higher share of their income goes to discretionary purchases: luxuries, travel, and automobiles. They have more money but less reason to save.

Other new kinds of households are not so fortunate—elderly women who live alone, young people setting out on their own alone, and divorced women who are single parents. These groups have lower incomes. The growing number of baby-boom marrieds in the prime of life may obscure the needs of these other types of households as the dominant group bustles to raise a family, earn a living, and advance a career.

Divorced, living alone, cohabiting, single parent, and extended families have become so common that they can no longer be viewed as odd. In some communities, the traditional family household is even less in evidence than other kinds of living arrangements. In many other communities, there have been fewer changes. Overall, millions of children are growing up in circumstances that have no precedent. If, as adults, they reject the values of the current generation, it could lead to renewed popularity for lifelong marriages and large families.

But today's living arrangements reflect life-styles that are unlikely to be reversed. Women are not going to trade their gains in education, employment, and income for the oven and the kitchen sink, if that is the price of tradition. Couples are having small families, not because the previous generation had large families but because they have other interests.

Marriage and childbearing remain the American ideal, but the ideal is less likely to be achieved. More than half of all children born in the early 1980s will become part of a single-parent family before they reach the age of eighteen. The 1980s are likely to see slower-than-average growth for family households and above-average growth for nonfamily households.

One hundred years ago, families were fragmented by early death and economic hardship. In 1900, over one third of Americans had never married. Now the share is less than one fourth. When advocates of the traditional family yearn for a return to the past, the past they imagine is not the past that actually occurred in America. The 1950s were unusual, a time of abnormally high marriage rates, when a whole society, reacting to the hardship of the Depression and World War II, married at earlier ages than before, and created a family-centered era.

Families in America's formative years were often as fragmented as those of today, but for different reasons. There were many births because many children died. Death divided couples at an early age. Then, there was little choice. There may be too much choice for some in the 1980s, but Americans value their freedom more than tradition. The word *life-style* implies the liberty not to follow the trodden path, but it does not guarantee a direction. So the future of the family may contain surprises.

TRENDS TO WATCH

— The family is no longer the nucleus of society, although it remains an important institution. People today are more free to choose their own life-style, rather than have it dictated to them by social custom.

— The divorce rate has risen to record levels; people live together in unmarried relationships; the average person marries at a later age; couples postpone childbearing; and a greater number of people live alone.

— Married couples are still the largest share of all households, but other types of households have been growing faster, and they should continue growing faster in the future.

— The proportion of adults who remain single throughout their lifetime could be three times as large as in their parents' generation.

New Women, New Men

"Women are no longer defined by their relationships with men. They have become learners, earners, career-seekers, and household heads in their own right."

It's getting harder to tell the sexes apart. Women still have primary responsibility for children and they still do most of the housework. Men are still expected to be the primary breadwinners. But, in some ways, young women now resemble young men more than they resemble older women.

The revolution in women's roles has been a young women's revolution. Younger women are much more likely than older women were to postpone marriage and childbearing, attend college, and develop a commitment to the labor force. Women today marry almost two years later than they used to. Between 1950 and 1982, for instance, the proportion of women aged twenty to twenty-four who had never been married rose from about one third to over one half.

In 1982, over one third of women aged twenty-five to twenty-nine were childless, and almost one quarter of women aged thirty to thirty-four. In 1960, by contrast, a mere 13 percent of women in the twenty-five to twenty-nine age group were childless, and only 10 percent of women aged thirty to thirty-four. The average woman today spends much less of her lifetime caring for children.

Freed from the responsibilities of caring for children, women are better able to pursue education and career. Labor force participation rates for married women have increased much more than those for single women or for those who are divorced, separated, or widowed. Among married women aged twenty-five to thirty-four, the rates jumped from 28 percent in 1960 to 63 percent in 1983. That, in one statistic, shows the difference between the mothers who produced the baby boom and their baby-boom daughters. If they remain married, couples today can expect to live together without children for thirty years. By comparison, two centuries ago in the early years of the American Republic, American couples averaged only seven child-free years of marriage together before one of the couple died.

The men and women of the baby-boom generation are pioneers. Now passing through their childbearing years, the largest group of American women ever in their twenties and thirties, they are setting a new example. To many, education and career mean as much as marriage and childbearing. In a single generation, as if on cue, America's women have decided that being a housewife is not what life is all about. In 1960, if her husband worked, less than one wife in three was also in the labor force. But by 1982, in six of every ten married couples with earners, both the husband and the wife were in the labor force.

Young women are much more likely than older women to have a college education. As a group, only 14 percent of women are college graduates, versus 22 percent of men. But there are important differences by age. More than one woman in five aged twenty-five to thirty-four have completed college, but less than one in ten women aged fifty-five and over. College enrollment rates for women aged eighteen and nineteen exceeded those for men of the same age in 1982. Women now outnumber men in college, and 45 percent of graduate students are women. In 1972, for every 100 men in college, there were just 74 women. By 1982, there were 109 women per 100 men.

College enrollments soared in the late 1960s and 1970s as the baby-boom generation started turning eighteen. But while men's enrollment increased only 13 percent between 1972 and 1982, women's soared 65 percent. Baby-boom women, like many upwardly mobile groups before them, understand that education is a key to success. They are obtaining business and professional degrees. In 1970, only about 5 percent of law degrees and 8 percent of medical degrees went to women. Today, women receive one third of all law degrees and one fourth of medical degrees. If the average woman did not marry earlier than the average man, these percentages might be higher still.

Older women are catching up in schooling. Today, one college student in five is a woman aged twenty-five or older. The number of women aged thirty-five or older in college is almost double the number of older men who are enrolled. Women's educational attainment seems certain someday to equal that of men.

Similarly, younger women are more likely than older women to be in the labor force. Over 70 percent of women in their twenties are working or looking for a job, compared with fewer than 45 percent of those aged fifty-five to sixty-four. The older generation is giving way to the new, which expects women to work. When people attend college and find jobs, they see the world differently. Role models for women are appearing in politics, business, government, the universities, and sports.

Women's gains in education and work experience are altering their voting behavior. In 1980, for the first time, an equal share of women and men reported voting. Women are 52 percent of the voting-age population. As more of them exercise their right to vote, politicians will find them to be a formidable influence. Some day America probably will have a woman president. The revolution in women's roles is just beginning.

New roles for women mean new roles for men. Today's men not only toil in the labor force, they are also more likely to be working at home, doing dishes, cooking meals, going shopping, even moving if their wives' careers require it. Over 400,000 men even told the Census Bureau in 1983 that they were not in the labor force because they were keeping house.

The young men who live alone, who head families without a wife, or who live with someone outside of marriage have roles as different from their fathers' as the young women who combine raising children with pursuing a career are different from their mothers. The number of men who live alone has nearly doubled since 1970 to 7.5 million. Like women's, men's median age at first marriage has risen two years since 1960, and is now nearly twenty-five, its highest point since 1900. Then, men could not afford to marry young; now, they don't want to.

The share of men aged twenty to twenty-four who have never been married rose from 55 percent in 1970 to 72 percent in 1982. The proportion of never-married men between the ages of twenty-five and twenty-nine rose from less than one in five in 1970 to more than one in three in 1982. Among men aged thirty to thirty-four, only 9 percent had not married in 1970; by 1982, the share had nearly doubled to 17 percent. Rising divorce rates, too, have caused more men to learn the rules of domestic survival. A growing share of men are having to learn something about keeping house, whether or not they like it.

Although the number of years women work has increased, men are spending a smaller portion of their lives at work. Even though men's life expectancy increased 2.2 years between 1970 and 1977, for example, the average number of years a man spent in the labor force did not increase. Men gained over two years of retirement. The average woman, on the other hand, added 2.3 years to her life, but her work-life expectancy rose by fully 5 years. A man who turned sixteen in 1977 could expect to spend 39 years in the labor force, compared to 28 years for a sixteen-year-old woman.

Apart from the childbearing years, the work experiences of men and women have become similar. In 1982, 77 percent of all men were in the labor force, a rate much higher than women's 53 percent, but women's rates are still rising while men's rates have declined. Women today make up 43 percent of the labor force, up from just 38 percent in 1970. Some 48 million women are working or looking for work.

WOMEN AND CHILDREN

Not counting married couples, with either husband or wife as head, or householder, women today head more households than do men. In 1950, among women twenty-five and older, just one woman in seven was the head of a household. Today, the share is approaching one in three. Women who live alone outnumber men who live alone by more than 4 million. Because of their longer life expectancy, almost half of all women aged sixty-five and over head their own household, but younger women, too, often have the sole responsibility for running a household. One woman in five between the ages of twenty-five and thirty-four lives without a husband and heads her own household.

In the past, virtually all women expected to marry in their early twenties and begin having children. Women today also play important roles as earners. When they become mothers, women fit two sharply contrasting profiles depending on the age at which they begin childbearing. Women aged thirty and older who gave birth in 1983, for example, were better educated and had higher incomes than those under age thirty who became mothers.

Half of new mothers aged thirty and older in 1983 had completed at least one year of college; 40 percent were employed, and 34 percent of the employed worked as professionals. Over 46 percent lived in families with incomes of $25,000 or more. However, among new mothers under age thirty, just over one quarter had completed at least one year of college, only 33 percent were employed, and of the employed, just 17 percent worked as professionals. Just 26 percent lived in families with incomes of $25,000 or more.

Women who have delayed childbearing into their thirties are now having children. Birthrates for women aged thirty to thirty-four began to rise in the 1970s and have continued to rise in the 1980s. Between 1980 and 1983, although fertility showed no significant increase for women younger than thirty, it rose for women aged thirty and older. The women who have put off having children until their thirties are the force behind America's growing affluent two-income couples, but those women who become mothers earlier are more likely to be poor. These women may be in the labor force, but they are not pursuing a career. Many hold low-status jobs.

Female household heads of the 1980s, on average, are younger than those of the 1950s; they are more likely to be divorced than widowed, and they are more likely to have children. Birthrates have fallen for women in general in recent years, but they have fallen less for teen-agers than for other women. Thus, teen-age births have risen as a share of all births. As Americans became more tolerant of sexual relations outside marriage, the proportion of never-married women aged fifteen to nineteen who reported having intercourse rose steadily during the 1970s. From 28 percent in 1971, the figure rose to 46 percent—nearly half—in 1979. Among blacks the 1979 figure was 65 percent—nearly two thirds.

Although some of this increase may result simply from teen-agers' greater willingness to tell interviewers about their sex lives, the pregnancy figures speak for themselves. In 1971, 8 percent of teen-age women became pregnant before marriage. By 1979, the percentage had doubled to 16 percent. Among blacks, the 1979 figure was 30 percent. In 1971, nearly 33 percent of these pregnant teen-agers got married before giving birth; in 1979, only 16 percent got married, only about half that percentage.

Until the 1960s, out-of-wedlock births to women at all ages remained at about 4 to 5 percent of all births. By 1981, however, they had soared to 19 percent of all births. Out-of-wedlock births were 12 percent of all births to whites in 1981, but over half of all births to blacks, 56 percent. Among black teen-agers, a remarkable 87 percent of births in

1981 were to unmarried women, versus 35 percent for whites.

Fertility has dropped for all economic groups, but it is still true that the rich get richer and the poor get pregnant. To the extent that education, career, and a higher income go with lower fertility, today's fertility trends mean that a growing share of all births will be to less educated, less affluent Americans. The typical woman who chooses not to have a child is white, highly educated, employed, and urban.

Thirty-eight percent of all women between the ages of eighteen and forty-four are childless, but there are sharp differences according to race, education, and labor-force status. Fully 48 percent of women professionals have no children. Half of women with at least four years of college are childless, but just 24 percent of those without a high school degree. Only about 11 percent of all childless women aged eighteen to thirty-four expect never to have children. But their expectations differ by education. Over 18 percent of women with at least five years of college say they do not plan to have children. Given today's birthrates, however, as many as 30 percent of women might never have children.

High-income couples are more likely not to have children than are low-income couples. A remarkable relationship exists between fertility and income—the lower a family's income, the higher its fertility, on average. Women with family incomes under $10,000 in 1983 had twice as many births to date as women in the $35,000 and over bracket.

As young women combine childbearing with employment, the number of children who have working mothers is soaring. Half of all women with preschool children are in the labor force. Just a generation ago, the share was only 11 percent. For women with school-age children, the proportion in the labor force has risen from about one in four immediately after World War II to two out of three today.

In 1981, 32 million children under the age of eighteen had mothers in the labor force, up from 26 million in 1970. The number of children whose mothers work outnumbers the children of nonworking mothers by some 5.5 million. Among children aged six to seventeen, 24 million have working mothers, compared to only 16 million whose mothers do not work. There are still more preschool children whose mothers do not work than those whose mothers do work, but this will probably not be true much longer.

Twenty percent of children today live with their mother only. More black children live with just their mother than with two parents. Of the more than 30 million children whose parents work, nearly one in four is living in a single-parent family. There may be as many as 2 million children on an average day who come home from school to empty houses—the so-called latchkey children because they must take care of themselves until a parent arrives.

Child care remains an obstacle that sets women apart from men. As more women go to work, fewer relatives and friends remain available at home to care for the preschoolers whose mothers are in the labor force. A lack of child-care arrangements may be one reason that a growing share of working married women are working part time rather than full time. About 67 percent of working married women who had children under eighteen worked full time in 1981, and one-third part time. In 1960, 71 percent worked full time.

In the past, when mothers worked, they typically left their preschool children in the care of a relative, often in the child's own home. By 1982, however, fewer than one working mother in three cared for her preschooler at home, whereas over 40 percent sent their children to someone else's home. Fifteen percent used group day care. Working mothers still shoulder most of the responsibility for child care, but the father's help has always been more important than people recognize. In 1982, for 14 percent of working women, the father of the preschooler provided the child care while the women worked.

DIFFERENCES OF SEX

Nature has yet to adjust its rhythms to the revolution in men's and women's lives. A fundamental difference remains between the sexes: Women live longer than men—and by a growing margin. In 1920, there was a one-year gap in life expectancy between the sexes. Now the gap has risen to over seven years. Life expectancy at birth is 78 years for a woman, but only 71 years for a man. As a result, the average American woman is older than the average man. In 1984, the median age for women was 32.5 years. For men, it was 29.9.

More boys are born than girls—over 90,000 more in 1980. But in the same year among Americans aged eighty-five and over, fully 892,-000 more women than men were still alive. Under age ten, there were 105 boys for every 100 girls, but at age eighty-five and above, only 44 men remained per 100 women.

By 1990, the difference between the number of women and men in America will rise to some 7 million. In every five-year age group between sixty-five and eighty-four, women will outnumber men by at least

1 million. In the eighty-five and over group, the gap will be an enormous 1.5 million. The elderly population, most of whom are women, has been growing faster than the number of children. This trend will create an even wider gap between the sexes in the future, unless nature learns to fine-tune births and deaths better by sex.

In 1970, the number of men and women became equal between the ages of eighteen and nineteen—just in time for couples to pair off. But the age at which women switch from being a minority to a majority is rising as death rates for young men decline to approach the lower rates of young women. Today, women do not begin to outnumber men until the age of twenty-eight. If male mortality continues to fall until the turn of the century, as the Census Bureau projects, women will not begin to outnumber men until the age of forty-one.

In an era in which young women and men are behaving increasingly alike, but women still live longer, it is a mystery why younger women persist in marrying older men (or do older men persist in marrying younger women?). As women delay marriage, they face decreasing odds of finding an older partner. Women aged eighteen and nineteen are three times more likely to be married than are the men of that age. But by age thirty-five, women are less likely than men to be married. Typically, brides are two and a half years younger than their grooms. A woman's odds of marrying a man a few years older than herself diminish rapidly over age thirty, as women increasingly outnumber men.

Women face not only a marriage squeeze as young adults, but also a bereavement gap in old age. The number of widows has risen from fewer than 6 million a generation ago to more than 10 million today, while the number of widowers has scarcely changed. Since 1940, in fact, the number of widowers has fallen 10 percent, but the number of widows has risen 80 percent.

Between the ages of sixty-five and seventy-four, men's death rates are twice as high as women's. At age sixty-five, women can expect to live another nineteen years, but men just fourteen more years. Even when the husband is the same age as the wife, the average sixty-five-year-old married woman faces a five-year sentence of widowhood because of differences in life expectancy. But because many women marry older men, the sentence is lengthened. And because so few older men are available as marriage partners, the sentence is usually for life.

Although the average age difference between husband and wife has remained relatively unchanged in the past generation, a greater proportion, nearly half, of all marriages now are remarriages. In remarriages, the average age between husband and wife is four years, twice the age gap in first marriages. As a result, the average age difference for all marriages has widened from 2 years in 1970 to 2.3 years today.

Among marriages for men aged forty-five to fifty-four, many of which are remarriages, more than 20 percent are to women under age thirty-five. More than 10 percent of all marriages involving men who are fifty years old are to women aged thirty or younger.

Young adults marrying today have a 50 percent chance of ending their first marriage in divorce, and 80 percent of all divorced people remarry. Therefore, the odds are rising that more marriages in the future will unite older men and younger women. The bereavement gap will widen.

To narrow the gap, women should be marrying men who are, on average, seven years younger than themselves. About 14 percent of forty-year-old women do marry men aged thirty-three or younger. But fewer than 5 percent of forty-year-old men marry women who are forty-seven or older. Given that most older people would rather not live by themselves for long (most widowers quickly remarry), marriages pairing older women with younger men make a lot of sense. But Americans still regard them as strange.

There will always be demographic differences between men and women because there are biological differences. But women are no longer defined by their relationships with men. They have become learners, earners, career-seekers, and household heads in their own right. In school, the workplace, the political arena, and the home, women's move toward equality with men is likely to accelerate.

TRENDS TO WATCH

— Society's attitudes toward women have changed radically, and more married women expect to work full time, to run for political office, and to pursue a career.

— Women still have primary responsibility for raising children, whereas men are still the chief breadwinners, but these differences are likely to diminish in the years ahead as women continue to make gains in education and income, while men fill new roles in the household.

5 Balancing the Regions

"At a time when national population growth has slowed, the growth of some parts of the country comes at the expense of other parts. . . . interstate migration increasingly becomes a zero-sum game. . . . "

Americans are free to cross state borders as they please, and they continually surprise the forecasters. New York State was shocked to learn that it had lost five congressional seats, based on the results of the 1980 census. The state had steeled itself to lose four, but five added insult to injury.

New York State lost over 680,000 of its residents between 1970 and 1980, a loss of 4 percent in a decade in which the rest of the nation gained over 11 percent. That made New York the decade's leading population loser. Rhode Island was the only other state to lose population between 1970 and 1980. New York State lost people because New York City lost people. Two thirds of the state's sixty-two counties gained population, but New York City lost more than 800,000 residents. Where did all these people go?

They went to Florida, and Texas and elsewhere in the South and West. Together, Florida and Texas accounted for one quarter of the national population growth in the 1970s. Adding California, which gained 3.7 million residents, the three states accounted for almost half the nation's population growth. As a whole, the South and West accounted for 90 percent of America's entire population growth in the 1970s.

Florida gained 4 congressional seats, Texas 3, and California 2, giving the three 91 seats in Congress, over one fifth of the total 435. For the first time in history, a majority of Americans live in the South and West. Thus, a majority of the members of the House of Representatives come from states of the South and West. The booming states of California, Texas, and Florida should become more dominant on the national scene at the expense of residents of such big northern states as New York, Pennsylvania, Illinois, and Ohio, where growth has been far slower.

In the 1970s, the population center of gravity—the point at which a map of the United States would balance if each person were represented by an equal weight—moved across the Mississippi River to spend the decade in a field just outside De Soto, Missouri. Starting near Baltimore, where it was located by the first census in 1790, it has been moving gradually westward with each passing decade. The average westward movement per decade until 1970 has been 40 miles and the average southward movement 3 miles. Between 1970 and 1980, however, the center beat the averages. It moved exactly 46.7 miles west and 22.5 miles south, headed toward Houston.

Twenty-two and a half miles may not sound like much in the jet age, but it is almost half the southward distance covered by the population center from 1790 to 1970. Given current trends, the center will never move back across the Mississippi. It is likely to stay in the state of Missouri for many decades to come.

Some states increase in population faster than others because they have a younger population and therefore relatively more births. Others grow slowly because they have more deaths than average, not because they are unhealthier places to live, but rather because they have a higher share of old people. But by far the most important reason for population growth trends in individual states, and therefore in the divisions and regions that contain them, is migration. Together, the nation's Northeast and North-Central regions had a net loss of over 3 million migrants during the past decade.

The Census Bureau divides the country into four regions and, further, into nine divisions. Population trends for these large regions reflect the experience of the individual states within them. Among the four regions, the West increased its population by 24 percent, and the

South 20 percent, whereas the North-Central Region grew only 4 percent, and the Northeast just 0.2 percent in the 1970s.

The West has been the nation's fastest-growing region for many decades, and the South the second fastest in every decade since the 1930s. Since 1950, the population of the West has grown 114 percent, and the South 60 percent. In contrast, the North-Central Region has grown only 32 percent, and the Northeast 24 percent.

The South, already the nation's most populous region by 1940, gained more people than any other region during the 1970s. Its addition of 12.6 million people brought its 1980 census population to 75 million, one third of the national total. The second largest region, the North-Central, gained far fewer residents, 2.3 million, and in 1980 had a total population of 59 million, about one quarter of all Americans.

The Northeast gained only 74,000 people. Its population of 49 million is now 22 percent of the national total. The West's gain of 8.3 million people during the 1970s brought its population total to 43 million, or 19 percent of the national figure. The regional balance is shifting.

Following population growth, the South and West accounted for almost 70 percent of national housing growth in the 1970s. Florida, Texas, and California accounted for 30 percent. The South and West now have a majority of the nation's households, but the increase in the share of households held by these two regions did not match the increase in their share of population because the family fragmentation that occurred across the country created new households in the Northeast and Midwest beyond their population shares.

The number of households in the West increased by 39 percent; the South was close behind at 38 percent. The Northeast and North-Central states added households at a rate well below the 27 percent national average, up 13 percent in the Northeast and 19 percent in the North-Central Region. The four regions rank as follows in the number of households, according to the 1980 census: The South is first, with 26.5 million; the North-Central Region second, with 20.9 million; the Northeast third, with 17.5 million; and the West fourth, with 15.6 million.

BELTS, SUNNY AND NOT SO SUNNY

Impressive gains in population and households for the South and West have given rise to the term *Sunbelt,* an attractive word that appears to summarize recent trends, particularly to northerners in February. The Sunbelt has no precise definition, however, and since there is no official Sunbelt, the only way statistics can back up the claim that Americans prefer living in the Sunbelt is to define the Sunbelt simply as the most rapidly growing states. Some definitions include rainy Washington State, or stretch the Sunbelt as far North as frosty Alaska because that state has been growing at almost three times the national average.

The *Frostbelt* is defined as everything the Sunbelt is not. But not all states in the North are stagnant, and not all states in the South are growing rapidly. New Hampshire grew three times as fast as Alabama from 1970 to 1980. Regional stereotypes reflect the experience of the dominant states of a region. The notion of Sunbelt growth relies heavily on the experience of Florida and Texas. The image of Frostbelt flight stems from the trends in New York City and other aging northern cities.

New York City is so populous that it dominates the statistics, not only of its own state but also of the entire Middle Atlantic Division, which includes Pennsylvania and New Jersey. Together with the New England states, these states comprise the Census Bureau's Northeast Region. New York City contains one fifth of the Middle Atlantic Division's population. The city's dominance explains why the division was the only one among the nation's nine to lose population in the 1970s. Pennsylvania and New Jersey both gained slightly, but as a whole, the Middle Atlantic Division lost 1 percent of its people.

In the 1960s, before the changing economy helped launch a rural renaissance, the three big industrial states of the Middle Atlantic Division gained almost 9 percent in population, following a 13 percent growth in the 1950s. But two of the division's three states have been below the national population growth rate in every decade since the Depression. Only New Jersey was above the national rate, until the 1970s. This trend should not reflect badly on New Jersey, Pennsylvania, or New York. They filled with people long ago—they were the Sunbelt of the first half of this century—and the rest of the country has been catching up.

Demographer Peter Morrison of the Rand Corporation has joked, "Migration South and West is a long overdue correction for the mistake made by European immigrants when they failed to proceed directly to Houston." Had the United States, 300 years ago, been colonized from the West Coast, by Asians instead of Europeans, the Northeast might today be the nation's "Sunbelt" and the West the country's aging industrial heartland.

As history has it, the Northeast and North-Central regions have been below the nation's growth rate for the past fifty years. It has taken half a century of above-average growth for the South and West to obtain a majority of the population.

DIFFERENCES OF DIVISION

The Northeast is sharply divided in its demographics. New England's trends differ from those in the Middle Atlantic Division. The three southern New England states—Massachusetts, Connecticut, and Rhode Island—resemble the states of the Middle Atlantic Division. Their combined population increased just a little over 1 percent during the 1970s. But Maine, New Hampshire, and Vermont have more in common with the fast-growing states of the West than with their southern New England neighbors.

The three northern New England states grew over 17 percent. New Hampshire was the nation's thirteenth fastest growing state. The northern New England states are much less densely settled than their southern neighbors. They, too, are catching up.

The West was the nation's fastest growing region in the past decade, gaining 24 percent in population. The Census Bureau's West contains two divisions: the Pacific States of California, Oregon, Washington, Hawaii, and Alaska; and the Rocky Mountain States of Montana, Idaho, Wyoming, Colorado, New Mexico, Arizona, Utah, and Nevada.

The Rocky Mountain States were by far the country's fastest growing division. The division's population increased 37 percent during the 1970s, almost three and one half times the growth rate of the nation as a whole. It is still by far the nation's least densely settled region, so it should continue to fill with people. The more urban Pacific States Division contains three times the number of people who live in the Mountain States and grew at only half the rate, 19 percent.

Rapid population growth rates come easier when you start small. The Mountain States added only 3 million people; the Pacific States over 5 million. The 1980 census counted just over 11 million people in the Mountain States Division. The New York and Pittsburgh metropolitan areas combined have as many people as live in all of the eight Rocky Mountain States.

The Pacific Division has the distinction of containing both the nation's most- and least-populous states, as well as the northernmost (Alaska) and southernmost and westernmost (Hawaii). So diverse are the Pacific States, stretching from sun-drenched beaches to Arctic ice floes, that their only link is the Pacific Ocean itself.

California dominates the Pacific States Division as New York dominates the Middle Atlantic Division. California surpassed New York as the nation's most populous state in the 1960s, and in the 1970s it added to its margin of leadership. It is hard to imagine California pulling growth averages down, but California's population growth in the 1970s was its slowest ever. California's growth rate slowed to 19 percent, the divisional average, after averaging an astronomical rate of 43 percent per decade for the previous fifty years. Population growth in the Pacific Division as a whole has been downhill since the 1940s, when the division grew 48 percent, a growth rate that has never been surpassed by any census division. Magnet that it is, California now has an average of 151 people per square mile, more than double the average population density for the United States. The Los Angeles area alone now has twice as many people as lived in all of California in 1920.

The eight Mountain States, in contrast, experienced their fastest population growth ever in the 1970s. Although only three of the Mountain States reached their peak growth rates in the 1970s, every state in the division exceeded the national growth rate—a trend matched by no other division. Among the Mountain States, only Montana did not make the list of the ten fastest-growing states during the 1970s; it ranked twenty-seventh.

Nevada was the fastest-growing state of all during the 1970s, increasing 64 percent in population. It also was the fastest-growing state in the 1960s, when it grew even faster. And only Florida's 79 percent surge during the 1950s kept Nevada, with 78 percent growth, from being first in that decade as well. In 1950, however, Nevada had only 160,000 residents among the cactus.

Although the availability of water may limit the number of new residents who can be absorbed by the Mountain States, there still is plenty of room for growth there. Most of Nevada still has fewer than two people per square mile. As a whole, the eight Rocky Mountain States contain less than half the population of California alone. Population density is a mere thirteen people per square mile.

In addition to the Mountain States, Alaska was also among the ten fastest-growing states, placing sixth with a growth rate of 33 percent. Alaska, the nation's least-populous state, had only 402,000 people at the time of the 1980 census.

The Census Bureau divides the South into three divisions, the South Atlantic, the East South-Central, and the West South-Central. The South Atlantic Division contains the states of Delaware, Maryland, Virginia, West Virginia, North Carolina, South Carolina, Georgia, and Florida. The bureau also counts Washington, D.C., as a state and includes it in the totals.

The East South-Central Division contains Kentucky, Tennessee, Alabama, and Mississippi; the West South-Central States, Arkansas, Louisiana, Oklahoma, and Texas. Except for sharing the same region, Delaware has little in common with Texas, or Florida with Maryland. Delaware has fewer than 600,000 people, and its population grew only 8 percent during the 1970s. Texas has 14 million people and grew over three times as fast. Maryland, home to some 4 million people, managed a less than 8 percent gain. Florida has twice as many residents and grew over five times as fast as Maryland.

Although every state in the South except Maryland and Delaware grew faster than the national average, none was remotely as impressive as Florida and Texas. Between them, Florida and Texas contain almost one third of the South's total population. These two boom states affect southern statistics even more than New York City affects those of the Northeast. Both Florida and Texas grew rapidly in the 1970s. In consequence, the West South-Central States, which include Texas, grew 23 percent as a group; the South Atlantic states, which include Florida, grew 20 percent; but the East South-Central States, which include neither Texas nor Florida, grew only 15 percent.

Florida has become the nation's seventh most populous state, and Texas now ranks third. By 1990, Texas could surpass New York to become the second most populous state. Florida may leapfrog over Ohio, Illinois, and Pennsylvania to become number four. Also in the South, North Carolina replaced Massachusetts as the country's tenth most populous state, according to the 1980 census count.

The Census Bureau's North-Central Region, which contains the states of the Midwest, has two divisions; one is America's industrial heartland and the other its breadbasket. The industrial East North-Central States are Ohio, Indiana, Illinois, Michigan, and Wisconsin. The agricultural West-Central States are Minnesota, Iowa, Missouri, North Dakota, South Dakota, Nebraska, and Kansas.

Neither of the two divisions fared well during the past decade, nor any of the states within them. Times have been hard for both farming and heavy industry. The West North-Central States grew 5 percent in population and the East North-Central States less than 4 percent. The fastest-growing state in the North-Central Region, Minnesota, grew only 7 percent, well below the 11 percent national rate. Ohio, the slowest-growing North-Central state, grew less than 2 percent.

Over the years, the states of the Midwest have had their ups and downs. The East North-Central Division grew faster than the national average during the 1950s, but fell below its Depression low in the 1970s. Even in the 1930s, when births were depressed along with the economy, the division grew over 5 percent, largely because the Detroit automobile industry—the high technology of its time—was still on the upswing. In the 1970s, rising energy prices reversed Detroit's fortunes, and laid-off auto workers headed for work in the Texas oil fields.

Each of the five states of the industrial East North-Central Division grew much more slowly in the 1970s than it had in the 1960s. Michigan dropped from more than 13 percent population growth in the 1960s to only 4 percent in the 1970s. Ohio had grown almost 10 percent in the 1960s.

Table 9 1980 CENSUS POPULATION

United States Total, 226,545,805

States		Cities (top 50)	
1 California	23,667,902	1 New York, NY	7,071,639
2 New York	17,558,072	2 Chicago, IL	3,005,078
3 Texas	14,229,191	3 Los Angeles, CA	2,966,850
4 Pennsylvania	11,863,895	4 Philadelphia, PA	1,688,210
5 Illinois	11,426,518	5 Houston, TX	1,595,167
6 Ohio	10,797,630	6 Detroit, MI	1,203,339
7 Florida	9,746,324	7 Dallas, TX	904,074
8 Michigan	9,262,078	8 San Diego, CA	875,538
9 New Jersey	7,364,823	9 Phoenix, AZ	789,704
10 North Carolina	5,881,766	10 Baltimore, MD	786,775
11 Massachusetts	5,737,037	11 San Antonio, TX	785,809
12 Indiana	5,490,224	12 Indianapolis, IN	700,719
13 Georgia	5,463,105	13 San Francisco, CA	678,974
14 Virginia	5,346,818	14 Memphis, TN	646,356
15 Missouri	4,916,686	15 Washington, DC	638,333
16 Wisconsin	4,705,767	16 Milwaukee, WI	636,212
17 Tennessee	4,591,120	17 San Jose, CA	629,442
18 Maryland	4,216,975	18 Cleveland, OH	573,822
19 Louisiana	4,205,900	19 Columbus, OH	564,866
20 Washington	4,132,156	20 Boston, MA	562,994

States		Cities (top 50)	
21 Minnesota	4,075,970	21 New Orleans, LA	557,515
22 Alabama	3,893,888	22 Jacksonville, FL	540,920
23 Kentucky	3,660,777	23 Seattle, WA	493,846
24 South Carolina	3,121,820	24 Denver, CO	492,365
25 Connecticut	3,107,576	25 Nashville–Davidson, TN	455,663
26 Oklahoma	3,025,290	26 St. Louis, MO	453,085
27 Iowa	2,913,808	27 Kansas City, MO	448,154
28 Colorado	2,889,964	28 El Paso, TX	425,259
29 Arizona	2,718,216	29 Atlanta, GA	425,022
30 Oregon	2,633,105	30 Pittsburgh, PA	423,938
31 Mississippi	2,520,638	31 Oklahoma City, OK	403,243
32 Kansas	2,363,679	32 Cincinnati, OH	385,457
33 Arkansas	2,286,435	33 Fort Worth, TX	385,166
34 West Virginia	1,949,644	34 Minneapolis, MN	370,951
35 Nebraska	1,569,825	35 Portland, OR	366,423
36 Utah	1,461,037	36 Honolulu, HI	365,048
37 New Mexico	1,302,894	37 Long Beach, CA	361,334
38 Maine	1,124,660	38 Tulsa, OK	360,919
39 Hawaii	964,691	39 Buffalo, NY	357,870
40 Rhode Island	947,154	40 Toledo, OH	354,635
41 Idaho	943,935	41 Miami, FL	346,865
42 New Hampshire	920,610	42 Austin, TX	345,544
43 Nevada	800,493	43 Oakland, CA	339,337
44 Montana	786,690	44 Albuquerque, NM	331,767
45 South Dakota	690,768	45 Tucson, AZ	330,537
46 North Dakota	652,717	46 Newark, NJ	329,248
47 Delaware	594,338	47 Charlotte, NC	314,447
48 Vermont	511,456	48 Omaha, NE	314,267
49 Wyoming	469,557	49 Louisville, KY	298,455
50 Alaska	401,851	50 Birmingham, AL	284,413

Source: 1980 census

However, five of the seven agricultural West North-Central States increased their population growth rates during the 1970s. Both of the Dakotas lost population during the 1960s, but gained population in the 1970s. Iowa, Nebraska, and Kansas grew more rapidly in the 1970s than in the 1960s. The empty parts of the Midwest are running out of people to lose, and they are beginning to attract new residents, after having lost previous generations to the cities. The farm population may continue to decline, but the seeds of rural resurgence are being sown in the Farm Belt.

ON THE ROAD

Of all Americans who were five years old or over in 1980, nearly half moved during the five years between 1975 and 1980. The 1980 census asked people where they lived in 1975 to track migration trends. Only 10 percent moved from one state to another (not including those who moved out of state and back again or who moved more than once during the five years). Another 10 percent moved from one county to another within the same state, whereas 25 percent moved within the same county.

The 20 million people who were in a different state in 1980 than in 1975 had a dramatic effect on some states. In Nevada, nearly a third of the state's entire 1980 population lived in a different state in 1975. Other states with a high percentage of residents in 1980 who lived elsewhere five years earlier are Alaska, Wyoming, and Arizona. It was such migration that propelled these states to the top ranks in population growth rates. Behind Nevada, Arizona ranked second, up 53 percent; Wyoming fourth, up 41 percent; and Alaska sixth, up 33 percent.

America has few one-way streets. Even states that are growing rapidly lose some people to other states. Among New York State residents in 1980 were 1,348 Nevadans who had moved there between 1975 and 1980. But 11,809 New Yorkers had moved to Nevada. Chiefly, New York's loss was Florida's gain. Of the 1.7 million New Yorkers who moved out of state between 1975 and 1980, 364,000, or more than one in five, found their way to Florida. These former New Yorkers were 20 percent of the 1.8 million people who moved to Florida during those five years. In all, New York lost more net migrants than any other state, while Florida gained the most. But even Florida lost 978,000 residents to other states—and 49,000 of them to New York.

People leaving New York settled in every state, but mainly they settled in the South. Forty-four percent moved South; 29 percent moved to another northeastern state, and 18 percent went West; only 9 percent moved to the Midwest. Florida gained new residents from everywhere, but principally from the Northeast, which provided 42 percent of Florida's new residents. Another 26 percent came from the Midwest and 25 percent from another southern state. Less than 7 percent of Florida's new residents came from the West.

California netted only 94,000 more residents from migration between 1975 and 1980, Texas 574,000. California attracted more migrants from other states than did Texas, but more Californians than

Texans left their home state. Of people who moved to Texas, more than one third came from another southern state. About one quarter came from the North-Central States; some 47,000 people who had lived in Michigan in 1975 were living in Texas by 1980.

Texas has yet to charm the Northeast, however. Only 195,000 of the 3 million people who moved out of the Northeast between 1975 and 1980 settled in Texas. Fewer than 5 percent of displaced New Yorkers chose Texas, but fewer than 2 percent of Texans who moved chose New York.

In the exchange of migrants between 1975 and 1980, twenty-three states and the District of Columbia lost people, while twenty-seven states gained. Among states in the Northeast and North-Central regions, only Maine, New Hampshire, and Vermont gained residents from migration; every other northern state lost them. Every southern state except Delaware, Maryland, and Mississippi had a net gain in migrants between 1975 and 1980. In the West, only Alaska and Hawaii had a net loss. California is no longer the most popular destination for movers. Five states, all much smaller, surpassed it in the number of residents gained—Colorado, Arizona, Nevada, Washington, and Oregon.

Despite its failure to win the migration sweepstakes, all is not gloom and doom for the Northeast. Those who moved into the Northeast between 1975 and 1980, on average, were better educated and more likely to be professionals in their peak productive years than those who moved out of the region. The South, by contrast, gained people with less education and lower job skills. Although 41 percent of migrants to the Northeast had a college diploma, only 24 percent of people moving South, and 33 percent of those heading West, were college graduates. Some 30 percent of people who moved into the Northeast were professional, technical, or managerial workers, compared to only 20 percent of people moving South and 24 percent of people moving West.

Migration trends can change rapidly. The flow of movers changed direction in ten states in the three years following the census. Between 1975 and 1980, New Jersey, North Dakota, Alaska, and Hawaii were losing more residents than they were gaining. In the following three years, all were gaining more than they were losing. Five states that gained migrants between 1975 and 1980 started losing them between 1980 and 1983—West Virginia, Kentucky, Alabama, Arkansas, and Oregon.

Between 1980 and 1983, the New England and Middle Atlantic

divisions continued to lose more residents from migration than they gained. The East North-Central States—Ohio, Michigan, Illinois, Indiana, and Wisconsin—as a group lost so many residents that the division's total population dropped. According to the latest available figures from the Census Bureau, five states have lost population since Census Day: Indiana, Iowa, Ohio, Michigan, and West Virginia. But they could gain again in the future.

Migration trends fluctuate from year to year, affected by the ups and downs of the economy as a river's course is altered by flood or drought. Demographic momentum, however—the river's direction—suggests that the South and West will continue to grow faster than the national average, whereas the Northeast and Midwest will grow more slowly than the national average. Since 1950, the South has increased its share of the nation's population by nearly 3 percentage points, and the West by 6 points. In 1950, these two regions contained 44.5 percent of Americans. In 1983, they contained 53.6 percent. This broad trend is not likely to reverse. Rivers do not flow upstream.

Some people refuse to participate in altering the regional balance. They never move from the state they were born in. Overall, 64 percent of Americans were born in the state the 1980 census found them in, and 29 percent in another state. Six percent were born in another country.

States vary widely in the proportion of native residents. Eighty-one percent of Pennsylvanians were born in Pennsylvania, but only 21 percent of Nevadans are native to Nevada. In eleven states, more of the current residents moved to the state than were born there. The list is a who's who of up-and-coming states: Alaska, Arizona, California, Colorado, Florida, Idaho, Nevada, New Hampshire, Oregon, Washington, and Wyoming. At the other extreme, in nine states at least 75 percent of the residents are native to the state. Besides Pennsylvania, the only state with over 80 percent native-born, these states are Alabama, Iowa, Kentucky, Louisiana, Mississippi, North Carolina, West Virginia, and Wisconsin.

COUNTING COUNTIES

Migration often has a dramatic effect at the local level, on businesses, local governments, and developers. About one quarter of Americans live in counties that lost population during the 1970s. But almost 10 percent live in the ten counties that gained the most new residents. The total population of the fifty counties that gained the most people was over 42 million people in 1980, almost 20 percent of all Americans.

Of the 50 counties that gained the most population during the 1970s, all but four were in the South and West. Florida, Texas, and California accounted for 30 of them, and Florida alone for 12. The top 50 are less than 2 percent of the country's more than 3,000 counties, but they are responsible for 40 percent of the decade's population gain. Together, they gained over 9 million people.

The top ten is a list of the hot spots of the 1970s. Harris County, Texas, which is home to Houston, gained 668,000 people, more than any other county. Maricopa County (Phoenix), Arizona, added 538,000 people, a 55 percent gain. The next three biggest gainers were all in California—Orange County, San Diego County, and Los Angeles County.

Even though Los Angeles County grew only 6 percent, the smallest growth rate of any of the top fifty counties in population gain, its enormous size placed it fifth in the number of people gained. It is the most populous county in the United States, with 7.5 million people. The least populous county, Loving County, Texas, has only 91 people, the 1980 census found. Loving achieved this record by achieving another record: It was the county that lost the highest proportion of its population, dropping 45 percent during the decade.

Except for Maricopa County, every one of the ten counties that gained the most people between 1970 and 1980 are in Florida, Texas, or California. Broward and Dade Counties (Fort Lauderdale and Miami) are in sixth and seventh place; Santa Clara (San Jose) is in eighth, Dallas County is in ninth, and Palm Beach County is in tenth. Together, these ten gained over 4 million people—almost twice as many people as the entire Northeast and North-Central regions combined gained.

The ten counties that lost the most population were scattered all over the map. Even Nevada, the fastest-growing state, had one county, White Pine, that was the nation's fifteenth largest percentage population loser. Only eight states did not have a county that lost population: Arizona, Florida, Hawaii, New Hampshire, Utah, Vermont, Wyoming —and, surprisingly, Delaware. Those states with the greatest number of counties losing population were the farm states of the Midwest. Kansas and Nebraska each had 51 counties that lost population. In all, 557 counties lost population, 18 percent of all counties in the nation.

Despite wide differences in growth rates, America's regional growth is today more evenly distributed than in the past. Fewer counties than ever before lost population, whereas more counties grew than in any other decade of this century, as Americans left densely settled areas. In the 1960s, by contrast, when Americans were still moving from many relatively small rural counties into more concentrated population centers, over 40 percent of all counties lost population. In the 1970s, over 800 counties that had been losing population in the 1960s began to gain, as rural areas became newly attractive.

America's regional differences are fading. Places that were once considered out of the way have become accessible and are more likely to resemble every other place. In an integrated economy, linked by retail chain stores, national markets, and nationwide media, there are few surprises, pleasant or unpleasant. If all areas of the country were to grow at the national rate, Nevada would remain a desert while Manhattan would reach the stratosphere. But the forces that speed the growth of once remote places also speed the day when undeveloped areas will become more like developed areas.

At a time when national population growth has slowed, the growth of some parts of the country comes at the expense of other parts. In the past, rapid population growth and liberal immigration policies provided even areas losing migrants with new sources of population growth. But when the population is not growing noticeably from births or immigration, interstate migration increasingly becomes a zero-sum game, with one state unable to grow because another state is growing rapidly.

This trend encourages regional disharmony. Should the federal government aid the growth of those places to which people are flocking or help cushion the loss of revenues in those places people are leaving? Should it help the Houstons or the New Yorks? What responsibilities do businesses have to the areas in which they are located? As their work force grows older, if they cannot find enough new younger workers, they may have to move. But by moving, they discourage future growth in the area they leave and contribute to its decline. These are new questions for America. A healthy national economy can overcome these strains, but in times of weakness they will be a new force to divide Americans.

PROJECTING THE FUTURE

The freedom to switch residences and to change jobs without permission from authorities is central to the American way of life. In bad times and good, Americans move back and forth across the country.

In the 1980s some forces should increase mobility; others impede it. A growing share of Americans who are in their twenties and early thirties, as the baby-boom generation fills these age groups, should increase regional migration because such people are most likely to move as they finish college, pursue careers, and set up new households. But as the baby-boom generation moves into middle age later on, it could dampen mobility.

The current high cost of housing and high interest rates make it more costly to leave a community. However, the decreasing size of an average household means that the typical move involves fewer people than in the past. That should make moving easier, but a growing share of households contain two earners. It could be more difficult for such couples to move, since they must give up, and find, two jobs. From another perspective, having two earners may make moving easier, since it doubles the odds of finding work. There are forces working in all directions.

The Census Bureau found that mobility had decreased in the year following the census. But mobility could pick up again; Americans will continue to make their own decisions about moving and keep their own counsel. Migration is the most unpredictable of trends. No one will know for certain what the American people have decided in the 1980s until the 1990 census takers finish their job.

The Census Bureau did not do a notably good job before the census of estimating where Americans lived in 1980 because so much migration had occurred during the decade. The 1980 census counted nearly 9 percent more people in the state of Nevada than the bureau had estimated. In Florida, the census count was fully 731,000 people more than the bureau's estimate for 1980. Nationally, the 1980 census counted 5 million more people than it estimated. This may have been only a 2 percent error, but for some local areas the bureau was off by more than 25 percent.

This makes a big difference. The government sends money to local areas on the basis of population estimates between census periods. Because of the gap between the estimates and the census count, by the end of the 1970s some areas were being shortchanged, while others were getting more than their fair share of the federal pie.

Businesses use population estimates as a measure of markets. Some areas may have lost services or products because the estimates portrayed a population smaller than actually existed. Others were targeted for services and goods they could not use. Population estimates are important because ten years is too long to wait for a head count. But

estimates for America's towns, counties, and cities are inaccurate, compared with the census results.

Making population projections, which is a statistical attempt to
foretell the future, is even more perilous than making estimates of the
current population. Demographers can make reasonably accurate estimates of birthrates, death rates, and rates of international immigration
(except for illegal immigration; it is as difficult to estimate the number
of illegal immigrants as it is to catch them). But because people rarely
move precisely in accordance with past patterns, it is hazardous to
project how an area's population—even an area as large as a state—will
change because of migration.

The Census Bureau's state projections for 1990, which are based on
the 1980 census, show little change from the patterns of the 1970s. This
should not be surprising, as the projections are based on the trends of
the 1970s. Still, what other method produces better results? All projections, whether they assume the future will be like the past or use
complex models that simulate the interaction of economic changes with
population movements, are guesses about the future. Some are closer
to the mark than others, but only in retrospect can we tell the hits from
the misses.

According to the bureau's projections, Nevada will once again be
the fastest-growing state in the 1980s. New York City lost more people
during the 1970s than live in all of Nevada, so Nevada still has a long
way to grow. The Mountain States occupy six of the ten slots among
the projected fastest-growing states, with Wyoming, Arizona, and Utah
in the second, third, and fourth positions, and Colorado seventh and
Idaho eighth. But New Hampshire replaces Texas as the nation's tenth
fastest growing state. The only southern state among the top ten is
Florida, in fifth place. Alaska is sixth and Oregon ninth.

Census Bureau projections show only six states growing faster in
the 1980s than in the 1970s—Wyoming, Utah, Oregon, Washington,
Wisconsin, and Rhode Island—but the increases are minor. In all,
seventeen states, mostly in the Northeast and Midwest, should gain less
than 5 percent in population during the 1980s, whereas twelve states,
mostly in the West, should gain more than 20 percent. Because the
nation's largest states are losing people in an exchange with smaller
states, there will be a reshuffling of the most populous states. These
shifts will increase the share of Americans who live in the South and
West, and reduce the share in the Northeast and Midwest.

By 1990, the top ten states in population rank probably will be: (1)
California, with 27.5 million people; (2) Texas, 17.5 million; (3) New

York, 16.5 million; (4) Florida, 13.3 million; (5) Pennsylvania, 11.7 million; (6) Illinois, 11.5 million; (7) Ohio, 10.8 million; (8) Michigan, 9.4 million; (9) New Jersey, 7.5 million; and (10) North Carolina, 6.5 million.

Making projections of households is even more perilous than making population projections. If economists cannot agree on the direction of interest rates from week to week, what hope do demographers have of projecting the number of new housing units that builders will construct five years hence, or how families will form to fill them?

Migration trends often follow the lead of the economy. Jobs have moved out of major metropolitan centers in the Northeast as an industrial nation has become a service society. Southern states have sought businesses, offering competitive wage rates and tax advantages. Northern states, accustomed to population growth in the past, did not foresee the consequences of migration in a new era of slowing birthrates. They took growth for granted, but saw it shift South and West. Now, as growth takes hold in the new boom states, wage rates are rising there, and many businesses are turning overseas for the assembly-line jobs of the future.

The energy crises of the 1970s gave the West a boost in its population growth, but that advantage has turned to uncertainty. The North has awakened from its slumber and is trying to become more competitive. The momentum may shift. Growth begets more growth, but eventually it levels off, and it can turn to decline. The South and West are no more immune to these trends than were the Northeast and Midwest. America is full of surprises.

TRENDS TO WATCH

– Migration trends will produce an increasingly even distribution of population across the country. The least densely settled regions of the country—the South and West will continue to grow faster than the Northeast and Midwest.

– The boom areas of the future are likely to be those in which the economy is growing rapidly, that are attractive and relatively uncrowded places to live in, and whose government and business climate encourage the development of new industries.

– The stagnant areas will be crowded industrial cities that cannot adjust to the changing economy.

Cities, Suburbs, and Beyond

"Today, businesses find it efficient to locate outside metropolitan centers, relying on telephone services, air travel, Express Mail, and computer networks to provide the links that used to require people to work in great commercial clusters and to live near their work."

America's rural areas have come to life again. In the past decade, the population in small towns and villages grew at its fastest rate since the 1890s. And not since the 1870s have rural areas gained as many people as in the 1970s.

It was a sorry decade for urban America. People moved out of large cities in record numbers. The nation's central cities, as a whole, stopped growing. St. Louis lost more than 25 percent of its people, Cleveland almost 25 percent, Detroit 20 percent. Baltimore, Chicago, Philadelphia, and Boston were all down more than 10 percent. New York City lost more residents than the total population of each of eight states.

The suburbs continued to gain residents. The 18 percent population growth in the suburbs in the 1970s was even more than the 15 percent growth in nonmetropolitan areas. But Americans have favored living in suburbs for years. That is not news. The news is that the growth of population in territory beyond metropolitan areas was up sharply, and beyond expectations. This trend is a product of the changing economy and new life-styles.

A metropolitan area is a statistical measure created by the federal government to identify cities of at least 50,000 residents together with their surrounding suburbs. The concept reflects the fact that many people who live ouside the boundaries of large incorporated cities are linked socially and economically to the city. The suburbs sprouted after World War II to house families who needed room to raise their children. The suburbs have grown to include nearly half of all Americans, versus less than a third in the central cities. At the time of the 1980 census, there were 318 metropolitan areas, plus 5 in Puerto Rico.

Metropolitan areas reflect links; the terms *urban* and *rural* reflect population density, the number of people per square mile. Any incorporated place, a small city or town, for example, is urban if it has a population of at least 2,500. Metropolitan areas include both urban and rural territory. *Rural* and *urban* are used to define different life-styles for the residents; *metropolitan* and *nonmetropolitan* are opposites by definition. But these distinctions are becoming less meaningful.

America's history has been one of continual urbanization. In the 1970s, however, as rural areas grew faster than urban areas, that trend reversed. The population in urban areas grew more slowly than ever before in the country's history. Many rural areas grew enough in the past decade to be redefined as urban. Although the country is about as urban today as a decade ago—some 74 percent of Americans live in urban areas—the percentage of urbanites increased much more slowly than a decade ago—just 0.1 percentage point in the 1970s, compared to 3.6 percentage points in the 1960s. About 14 percent of metropolitan residents are now rural, up from 12 percent a decade ago.

Metropolitan areas are expanding into less densely settled territory. In many metropolitan areas only the outer suburbs grew in the 1970s, while the inner suburbs began to decay like the central cities. Areas beyond the borders of the suburbs, but close enough to benefit from suburban services, are growing rapidly too. The center city was once the beacon for the modern way of life, but now its light is fading. Americans favor smaller places that offer many of the amenities of cities but do not have big city problems. Particularly popular with movers are those once sparsely settled places that have such natural attractions as mountains, rivers, or lakes or that combine small-town living with cultural opportunities. University towns are popular. State capitals have grown along with state government.

But more than mountains and lakes, the changing economy is

responsible for new settlement patterns. In an era of heavy industry, efficiency meant concentrating manufacturing and distribution in port cities or at railheads. Areas of growth radiated out from these centers. Today, businesses find it efficient to locate outside metropolitan centers, relying on telephone services, air travel, Express Mail, and computer networks to provide the links that used to require people to work in great commercial clusters and to live near their work. The spread of people reflects the spread of new kinds of jobs. The energy crises of the 1970s gave many nonmetropolitan areas a boost. Mineral extraction brought ghost towns to life, particularly in the West and South. Fully one third of nonmetropolitan counties that lost population in the 1960s gained population in the 1970s.

The nation's most densely settled cities are in the industrial Northeast and Midwest. Cities have long grown by annexing suburbs. Highrise buildings go up when room to expand horizontally is too costly or does not exist. The suburbs of the older cities of the North are already fully developed, and there is little room to accommodate further population growth, even vertically. Jersey City, New Jersey, America's most densely settled metropolitan area, has 12,000 people per square mile. Casper, Wyoming, the nation's least densely settled metropolitan area, has 13. The Jersey City metropolitan area lost 8 percent of its residents between 1970 and 1980; Casper's population grew 40 percent.

All but one of the ten most densely settled cities among the nation's twenty largest cities are in the East or Midwest, where there is no room to expand—New York City, Chicago, Philadelphia, Boston, Washington, D.C., Baltimore, Detroit, Cleveland, and Milwaukee. San Francisco, the thirteenth largest city, is second in population density because of its setting: it is virtually surrounded by water. Significantly, it is the only western city on the high-density list, and its population dropped 5 percent in the 1970s.

High-density cities have become the country's population losers. That is why the Northeast and Midwest as a whole are growing more slowly than the South and West. Among the country's twenty largest cities, the ten most densely settled all declined in population in the 1970s, while all but one of the ten least densely settled cities gained population. Early in this century, more than 40 percent of urban Americans lived in cities with populations over 250,000. Today, although the number of cities this large has doubled, their share has dropped to only one quarter of the country's urban population.

If one were to divide the fifty states into four groups based on population density, the least densely settled one quarter would show an average annual net gain from migration of 15 people per 1,000 during the 1970s; the most densely settled one quarter would show an annual net loss of about 4 people per 1,000. The number of people per square mile for the nation as a whole is 64. But the Northeast, which is the most densely settled region, has 302 people per square mile, whereas the West, which is least densely settled, has only 25.

GAINERS AND LOSERS

Among cities with 100,000 people or more, all but one of the top-ten cities in growth rate during the 1970s were in the South or West. Sterling Heights, Michigan, ranking number five, was the only northern city to make the top ten. Not one of the Northeast's large cities gained population, and only eight gained in the North-Central States. In contrast, only fourteen cities of over 100,000 in the South lost population, and just eight in the West did so. Among the nation's fifty largest cities, twenty-nine lost population, and four of the six with populations over 1 million lost population—New York, Chicago, Philadelphia, and Detroit. Such cities as St. Louis, Seattle, Pittsburgh, Denver, and Kansas City fell below the half-million mark in the 1970s.

Three large cities more than doubled their population, led by Anchorage, Alaska's, gain of 260 percent—due partly to its annexation of its suburbs. The city now ranks seventy-ninth in size. Mesa, Arizona, grew 142 percent and Aurora, Colorado, 112 percent. The seven other fastest-growing cities were Lexington-Fayette, Kentucky, up 89 percent; Sterling Heights, Michigan, and Arlington, Texas, each up 78 percent; Modesto, California, up 72 percent; Garland, Texas, up 71 percent; Tempe, Arizona, up 68 percent; and Colorado Springs, Colorado, up 59 percent.

St. Louis's population drop of 27 percent made it the decade's leading loser, followed by Cleveland, down 24 percent, and Buffalo, down 23 percent. Pittsburgh lost 18 percent of its residents; Rochester, New York, and Youngstown, Ohio, each dropped 18 percent.

Detroit lost over 300,000 residents, Houston gained over 360,000, and the two cities changed places among the ten largest cities, with Houston moving up to fifth. Baltimore dropped from seventh to tenth largest, while San Diego moved up from fourteenth to eighth, and Phoenix rose from twentieth position to take ninth. Annexations helped the rapid growers, whereas the leading losers were already hemmed in by places they could not annex.

The Census Bureau's city population estimates for 1982 show more shifts among cities in the North and East than those in the South and West. Chicago, long the nation's "second" city, dropped to third place as Los Angeles rose to number two. Houston replaced Philadelphia in fourth place. San Antonio and Honolulu pushed Baltimore to twelfth place as they took over the ranks of tenth and eleventh among the nation's largest cities. In a rebound of sorts, however, New York City grew by 14,000 people during the early 1980s. Could this be the start of something big for the Big Apple?

St. Louis is a telling example of what is happening to industrial cities. The St. Louis metropolitan area as a whole, including the city and its suburbs, lost 2 percent of its population during the 1970s, after gaining over 12 percent during the 1960s. The suburbs of St. Louis as whole gained 6 percent in population, but those suburbs that touch on the central city dropped by about 15 percent in the past decade, an acceleration over their slight decline of the 1960s. The outer suburbs continued to gain residents, however, at a rate of about 17 percent for the decade—above the national growth rate, but well below their 55 percent growth rate of the 1960s. The problems of the big city are spreading.

The pattern is similar for other older large metropolitan areas of the Northeast and Midwest and even for older areas of the South and West. For example, Pittsburgh's suburbs as a whole are now losing population, after gaining in the 1960s. In Baltimore, Minneapolis, and Seattle, where central-city populations declined in both the 1960s and 1970s, suburban growth was only about half of what it was in the 1960s. In Atlanta, the suburbs grew 61 percent in the 1960s, but only 46 percent in the 1970s.

Even though its cities were sagging, the Northeast's rural areas were reviving. They grew 7 percent between 1970 and 1980, but only half as much as the rural population in the South, which grew 13 percent. In the West, the rural population grew 18 percent. In the North-Central Region, the number of rural residents rose 8 percent from 1970 to 1980. As once-remote areas become more accessible, they attract more people, and soon more services, giving them suburban characteristics; then, they attract even more people. In this way, the American people are spreading themselves more evenly across the land.

The new growth of rural areas does not signal a revival of the rustic farmer in American life. The farm population has been declining for nearly a century. In 1920, when the census first separately identified statistics for people who live on farms, nearly one third of Americans lived on farms. By 1950, that percentage had been cut in half. By 1970, only 5 percent of Americans lived on farms. Today, the percentage has been cut in half again; only one American in forty-two lives on a farm. The share is likely to continue dropping as agriculture requires even fewer workers.

It has become harder to earn a living from farming. The median income of farm families in 1981 was $17,082, compared to $22,554 for nonfarm families. Almost two thirds of the total income of farm families comes from nonfarm sources. Rare is the young person who becomes a farmer today without being born into a farm family.

As a result, the farm population has become much older than the general population. Half of Americans who live on farms are at least thirty-five years old; and fully 44 percent of farm residents have reached the age of forty, compared to only 36 percent of Americans who do not live on farms. In the early years of this century, almost three quarters of the people who lived on farms were under age thirty-five, but young people have been leaving the farms. Left behind are older farm families, most of them without children living at home. Nearly one farm family in four contains a person aged sixty-five or older, compared to less than one in five for nonfarm families.

The spread of jobs and people to rural areas may breathe new life into the farm population, even as the number of people employed as farmers continues to drop. As population growth spreads to the rural areas that were once dependent on farming, other kinds of jobs become available for those Americans who live on farms, enabling them to supplement their farm income, and thus to survive. Those who live on farms increasingly commute to nonfarm jobs. And, in a reversal from 1970, only a minority of farmers live on the farm—just 46 percent. The growth of nonmetropolitan America is not simply a spillover from brimming metropolitan areas, but rather a blossoming of new growth centers. Fewer than 20 percent of people who move from metropolitan areas to nonmetropolitan areas continue working in metropolitan areas.

THE REALIGNMENT

Migration is changing the face of America. One third of all nonmetropolitan counties that lost population in the 1960s gained it in the 1970s. These counties were largely rural. Their population trends reversed direction in large part because the flight out of such areas finally slowed, or stopped completely.

By the same token, metropolitan areas with at least 1 million residents grew only 7 percent in the 1970s—less than half their 18 percent growth in the 1960s. The country had thirty-eight such areas in 1980, with a combined population of over 90 million, home to 41 percent of all Americans.

Ten of the metropolitan areas with at least 1 million residents lost population during the 1970s. All were in the Northeast or Midwest. But the large metropolitan areas with the greatest gains were all in the South and West, led by Phoenix, Arizona.

Grouping the 1 million club by region, those in the Northeast lost 5 percent of their residents, while the rest of the Northeast's population as a whole grew 7 percent. The large metropolitan areas of the North-Central Region grew less than 1 percent, while the rest of that region grew over 6 percent. But in the South, even the metropolitan areas of 1 million or more grew more than 20 percent—faster than the rest of the South. In the West, metropolitan areas of 1 million or more grew 18 percent, compared to over 30 percent for the balance of the West.

All of the fastest-growing metropolitan areas, of any size, are in the South and West. Five of the top ten are in Florida. Fort Myers–Cape Coral, Florida, grew the fastest of any metropolitan area between 1970 and 1980, increasing its population by 95 percent. Ocala, Florida, grew 77 percent. Of the twenty-nine metropolitan areas that lost population, all but two are in the Northeast or North-Central regions. Great Falls, Montana, which is in the West, lost 1 percent of its population, and Steubenville-Weirton, which is in both West Virginia and Ohio, lost 2 percent.

Had the number of households not been growing more than twice as fast as the population as the size of the average household shrank in response to demographic trends, the decline of metropolitan areas in the North would have been even more dramatic. These areas would then have been losing households as well as population, with an even more serious economic impact.

Households in the country's largest metropolitan areas grew more slowly than for the nation as a whole in the 1970s because metropolitan population growth was below the national average. Even so, the fifty most populous metropolitan areas contain nearly half of all households and people in the country. Households in Fort Lauderdale–Hollywood, Florida, grew 88 percent in the decade, the most rapid household gain of any large metropolitan area. Houston gained the most new households, 413,000, followed by Dallas and Chicago.

The major metropolitan area that grew most slowly in the number of households was New York, up less than 1 percent. This performance may sound sluggish, but it is in fact a remarkable feat because New York lost so many people. It was saved by the shrinking household. New York is still the number-one metropolitan area in the number of households, with 3.5 million. Second is Los Angeles, followed by Chicago, Philadelphia, and Detroit.

Had the nation's birthrate not declined so precipitously during the 1970s, suburban population growth probably would have been even greater. The suburbs have long been the choice location for families with children. Household size within metropolitan areas in 1980 averaged 2.73 persons per household; outside metropolitan areas it was higher, 2.79. The number of married-couple households grew just 7 percent inside metropolitan areas during the decade. Outside these areas they grew three times as much, 21 percent.

The cities grew poorer in a decade when the suburbs grew richer. American cities have more than their share of poor, who lack the mobility of middle-class Americans, and a higher share of their population is black. The median income for households in central cities was about $15,000, as measured by the 1980 census; in the suburbs, it was over $20,000. Although the city median income dropped, after adjusting for inflation, it rose in the suburbs.

Demographic data for cities and suburbs reveal other important differences: Over 70 percent of housing units in the suburbs in 1980 were owned by their occupants, compared to less than 50 percent in central cities. More than one in three suburban households contained a married couple with children, compared to less than one in four in central cities. Almost 9 percent of central-city households are headed by a woman living with her children but no husband; only about 5 percent of suburban households fit this description.

It is misleading, however, to speak of the suburbs as if they were all alike. There are broad differences based primarily on their size and when they were settled. In the suburbs settled longest ago, the average age of residents is rising. The families who settled in the suburbs in the 1950s are likely to remain in their homes because older people move less fequently than younger ones, whereas their children are moving to the newer cities and suburbs elsewhere, or to the countryside.

Some older, decaying cities pinned their hopes on a return of young people, who would set about restoring old homes and pioneering the urban frontier. The *gentrification* trend, which appeared in almost every city of over 200,000 in population, owes its origins to the baby-boom generation. Gentrification typically is portrayed as a a "back to the city" trend, but this description is inaccurate. Although selected neighborhoods in certain cities have been gentrified—the Capitol Hill area of Washington, D.C., for example, changing the broken windows and peeling paint of urban blight for the louvered shutters and potted plants of the modern metropolis—the trend has not overcome such powerful demographic trends as a lower birthrate and the flow of jobs and people to nonmetropolitan areas.

Ironically, the gentrification has even contributed to a decline in the number of city residents, because gentrified households are smaller, less likely to contain families, and more likely to contain singles than the type of households that have been moving out of the cities, which typically contain families with children. Gentrification may have displaced black residents from some decaying neighborhoods, but it has not contributed to a net return of whites to the central cities.

Neither is gentrification likely to revitalize cities in the future. Much of the force behind the trend has come from the fact that the baby-boom generation, in reaching adulthood, has vastly increased the number of young people who are most likely to move to cities and renovate. But these people will not stay young forever. In the 1970s, while the population of Washington, D.C., declined 16 percent, the number of people aged thirty to thirty-four, the "gentry's" heart, grew 18 percent in the District, enough to patch up aging row houses and send housing prices soaring. However, this was no movement back to the city. Nationally, the same age group grew 54 percent—three times the rate in Washington, D.C. If cities are becoming gentrified, so is the countryside.

Later in the 1980s, as the baby-boom generation ages and its children reach school age, they will be as likely as previous generations to favor suburbs and small towns. As members of the baby-bust generation replace the baby-boomers in the young adult years, central cities may be hard pressed to match even their dismal population performance of the 1970s, when the combination of a record number of young adults and a surge in the number of immigrants, the two traditional sources of urban residents, failed to spur central-city growth.

PERIPHERAL COMMUTERS

When cities were the hub of economic activity, and residents lived around the rim, city planners built streetcars and subways to handle the growing horde of commuters. Now, as the working-age population moves farther out and jobs spring up in suburbia, commuting between suburbs is growing faster than commuting from the suburbs to the center city. Commuting is the chief measure the government uses to determine the boundaries of metropolitan areas. As commuting links weaken, so does the concept of the traditional metropolitan area. This development also causes grave problems for public transportation planners and, particularly, for advocates of fixed-rail transit systems.

The number of people who travel to work on public transportation declined by almost half a million in the 1970s. Public transportation was intended to move the masses, wooing them from the automobile. Transit systems do not work well when jobs and workers are dispersed. Today, it takes the average worker longer to get to work on public transportation than by any other means of transportation. The average public transportation user travels thirteen miles in forty-two minutes to get to work, an average speed of about eighteen miles per hour, whereas a person who drives to work alone travels only an average ten miles in twenty minutes, at about thirty miles per hour.

Such statistics help explain why a mere 6 percent of American commuters use public transportation. A full 64 percent of workers drive to work alone, and another 20 percent car-pool. Average commuting time also varies according to whether a person lives in a city, suburb, or nonmetropolitan area. Those who work in the suburbs have the longest average trip, but they make good time. They travel about thirteen miles in twenty-four minutes, averaging thirty-one miles per hour. Central-city commuters go just nine miles, on average, but it takes them twenty-three minutes. They average only twenty-three miles per hour.

In the suburbs, people use public transit far less than in the central cities. About 67 percent of workers who use public transportation live in the central cities; some 30 percent live in the suburbs, and just 3 percent live in nonmetropolitan areas. Public transportation is most available in the densely settled Northeast, so its use is greatest there. In fact, nearly half of all commuters who travel to work by public transportation live in the Northeast—twice the number in either the Midwest or the South, and three times the number of public transit users in the West.

The shift of jobs to the suburbs and beyond is a transportation planner's nightmare. It means that autombiles may play even more of a role in the future in getting people to and from their jobs. For rapidly growing metropolitan areas, where the periphery is growing faster than the core, new public transit systems will have to extend farther and be more flexible than planners imagine and, probably, than citizens will pay for. For the large metropolitan areas of the North, yesterday's systems—built to accommodate a different residential and employment pattern—will become even more outmoded.

Public transportation was not designed to move people from one suburb to another, or to the suburbs from areas even farther out. But now that the largest group of commuters both live and work in the suburbs, mass transit will have to be redesigned. Planners will have to sell the current systems not as the efficient means of moving large numbers of workers that they were designed to be, but rather as a service to those who cannot afford to drive. Congested cities and densely settled inner suburbs need public transportation systems to keep from getting even more congested, but the constituency for them is diminishing. Such areas host a smaller share of the nation's workers and residents, and so there will be a smaller share of concerned congressmen to speed mass transit bills through the corridors of Congress.

METROPOLITAN MOODS

Metropolitan areas have a difficult time finding common cause. Some are spread across thousands of square miles and more than ten counties. Others are only a single county. Some are completely urban; others include stretches of wilderness. Some are populous and densely packed. Others barely exceed the 50,000 person definition and are sparsely settled. They differ in age structure, household characteristics, racial composition, and income distribution.

In 1980, the nation's 318 metropolitan areas contained a total of 169 million Americans. Of these, the 7 areas that were home to at least 3 million residents apiece contained 39 million people, or nearly one quarter of the metropolitan total. Combined, these 7 lost population between 1970 and 1980.

The 31 metropolitan areas with between 1 million and 3 million residents grew 14 percent in the 1970s. At the time of the 1980 census, they contained 54 million people, or nearly one third of all metropolitan residents.

The country has 41 metropolitan areas containing between one-half and 1 million population. Together, they are home to 28 million Americans, or 17 percent of all metropolitan residents. There are 71 areas with between one-quarter and one-half million inhabitants, about 15 percent of the total metropolitan population; 140 areas with between 100,000 and 250,000 residents, containing 13 percent of all metropolitanites; and 28 areas, with fewer than 100,000 residents, who constitute a mere 1 percent of metropolitan dwellers. Each of the three smaller classifications added people at a faster rate than did the larger metropolitan areas.

In 1970, the 178 metropolitan areas each with fewer than one-half million residents contained 26 percent of all metropolitan Americans. In 1980, there were 239 areas of this size and their share of metropolitanites had risen to 29 percent. Were it not for the losses in the country's large metropolitan centers of over 3 million people, the nation's metropolitan areas as a whole would have grown 14 percent instead of just 10 percent. The growth of these smaller metropolitan areas has meant a drop in the average size of a metropolitan area—from 4.2 million residents in 1970 to 4 million in 1980.

Even though they may no longer be growing at a rapid rate, the large metropolitan areas still contain most of the country's population. In 1980, for example, the 168 metropolitan areas with under 250,000 people contained only 10 percent of the country's total population, whereas the 150 areas of 250,000 people or more were home to about two thirds of all Americans.

In nonmetropolitan America, even the remote areas have been growing rapidly. Nonmetropolitan counties that were not adjacent to metropolitan areas, and in which the largest settlement was fewer than 2,500 people, grew 14.6 percent in the 1970s compared to a 4 percent loss in the 1960s. Employment in such counties increased by 25 percent between 1975 and 1979, more than the employment increase in metropolitan areas as a whole. The spread of jobs is allowing Americans to live where they prefer to live, outside of congested urban centers.

In a majority of states, the percentage of residents who live in metropolitan areas declined during the past decade. In twenty-three states, however, the metropolitan portion grew, reflecting the fact that metropolitan areas in the South and West, and in the Farm Belt states, are still growing more rapidly than nonmetropolitan areas. The only two states in the Northeast in which the metropolitan population grew faster than the nonmetropolitan population were Vermont and Rhode Island. Rhode Island is already virtually entirely metropolitan, whereas Vermont gained its first metropolitan area in 1980 as a result of the growth of the Burlington area—formerly an area classified as nonmetropolitan.

Every state of the industrial Midwest saw its metropolitan share decline, but among the Farm Belt states, only Missouri had a relative drop in its metropolitan population because of the population loss in St. Louis. In nine of the sixteen southern states, the proportion of residents who live in metropolitan areas increased; the same was true in five of the eight Rocky Mountain States. California became somewhat less metropolitan, along with Washington, Oregon, and Hawaii in the Pacific States, whereas Alaska became more metropolitan.

In one sense, the country will always be predominantly metropolitan, because as undeveloped areas around metropolitan areas, or cities approaching eligibility for metropolitan status, are developed and grow in population, they are reclassified as metropolitan by becoming attached to an existing metropolis or becoming one in their own right. Since 1950, 149 new metropolitan areas have come into being, the metropolitan population has nearly doubled, and the land area considered metropolitan increased by 173 percent. After the 1980 census, the government designated 35 new metropolitan areas. There is now a metropolitan area in every state.

At the turn of this century, northern metropolitan areas were growing as rapidly as areas in the South and West are growing now. Detroit's population more than doubled between 1910 and 1920, Cleveland was up almost 50 percent—more than Houston in the 1970s. Among the nation's largest metropolitan areas, only Los Angeles has grown faster than Detroit grew during the boom decades for the automobile. Then, as now, Americans were propelled by the search for opportunity. But there is no precedent for the kind of population losses that are beginning to be seen in the country's former centers of progress. Today, as yesterday, they may be establishing trends that will eventually appear in metropolitan areas of the South and West.

Save for uninhabitable desert and remote places, will the country one day be entirely metropolitan? There is still plenty of room for spreading out. Population density in the central cities averages 3,000 people per square mile. In the suburbs it averages 187 people per square mile; for metropolitan areas as a whole, the average is 299 persons per square mile. But in nonmetropolitan areas, the average is just 19 people per square mile.

As population grows more evenly across the country, only Rhode Island and New York are less densely settled today than they were a decade ago. But as people move outward from crowded city centers, the average American lives in a less densely settled place than a decade ago. Nationally, population density ranges from New Jersey's 986 people per square mile to Alaska's less than 1. The Census Bureau projects that by the year 2000 average national population density will be 76 people per square mile, 12 more than today, and people are likely to be distributed more evenly.

The nation will always have remote areas: northern Maine, for example, mountainous areas, the Alaskan arctic, or the vast Great Plains. But the dispersal of Americans is a powerful trend. Behind it are the decisions millions of people are making about where to live and work—in the cities, suburbs, or beyond.

TRENDS TO WATCH

– America's past has been one of steady centralization; its future is likely to be one of steady population deconcentration. Over three-quarters of Americans still live in metropolitan areas—major cities and their suburbs—but changes in the economy are reducing the pull of central cities and creating jobs in less densely settled areas.

– Because young, educated, affluent people with families are most likely to move out of cities, the large cities and their inner suburbs are becoming older, and poorer and have a higher share of racial minorities, despite the renovation of selected urban neighborhoods by young, childless professional couples.

The Ethnic Mosaic

"America's immigrants . . . are not what they used to be. The farmers and laborers from Ireland and Italy who flocked to these shores early in the century have grown old. In their wake are physicians from the Philippines, economists from India, and entrepreneurs from Korea."

Americans have always been of two minds about immigrants. Even while they welcome the new arrivals, they are wary of immigration's impact. The country's assimilation of new groups is surprising, given the successive waves of immigrants it has absorbed. But the cultural differences between native-born Americans and today's new immigrants from Asia and Latin America are wider than was once the case when immigration was primarily from Europe.

These differences, and the fact that the government seems to have little control over illegal immigration from Latin America, have raised fears that the character of the American people may be changing and that future generations will be unlike today's Americans. Behind these fears are some statistics.

More immigrants came to America during the past decade than in any decade since before 1920. America is still a land of opportunity— but less so for Europeans. Their standard of living now nearly matches our own. As late as the 1950s, more than 50 percent of all immigrants came from Europe. During the 1970s, however, less than 20 percent came from Europe. Instead, more than 33 percent came from Asia; only 6 percent were from Asia in the 1950s.

European birthrates have dropped even more than American. Germans coming to the United States are unlikely ever again to sow the seeds of new growth on the farms of Minnesota or in the factories of Milwaukee. The average German woman will give birth to only 1.4 children during her lifetime, the lowest fertility of any women in the world, well below the number necessary to prevent the German population from eventually disappearing unless that country attracts immigrants of its own.

But the population is still growing rapidly in Asia and the standard of living is not as high. In 1965, Congress lifted restrictions against Asian immigration that had been in place since the 1920s, and Asians were quick to respond. An average of 160,000 per year came to America during the 1970s. Nearly two thirds come from four countries: the Philippines, Korea, China, and India. The Philippines alone sent 313,-000 people to America, the most for any Asian country.

The sudden rise in the number of immigrants and the shift in their place of origin is changing the ethnic composition of some cities, such as New York City, Los Angeles, and San Francisco. As these are centers of media and commerce, the new pieces of America's ethnic mosaic are receiving even more attention than their numbers alone might warrant. If immigration continues at its present pace and from its current sources, the ethnic character of the entire country will eventually change.

America has always received its character and its vitality from successive waves of immigrants, but the circumstances today are unlike any seen before. The first decade of the twentieth century saw the heaviest wave of immigration in American history. In those ten years, almost 9 million foreigners came to the United States. Immigration contributed more than 50 percent of the nation's total population growth in that decade, and over 40 percent in the following decade.

The country welcomed these new arrivals to people its vast expanses and to serve its growing economy. In the 1930s, however, immigration fell sharply, as the economy faltered; only 528,000 immigrants entered the United States. But following the Depression and World War II, immigration rose again.

In the 1950s, even when the number of immigrants rose above 2 million, immigration contributed only 9 percent of the country's total population growth. In the middle of a baby boom, during a decade that saw 40 million births to American women, a mere 2.5 million immigrants had little impact. But the 1970s were different. The birthrate had dropped below its Depression lows, and so the decade's 4.5 million immigrants were a startling 19 percent of total population growth. The last thing the stagnant economy of the 1970s—already struggling to accommodate a surge of young workers and the rising aspirations of women—needed was a new wave of immigrants. But they came anyway.

The new immigrants are all the more noticeable, not only because their ethnic characteristics are different from the majority of Americans but they also have come in waves. Since 1953, special acts of Congress have brought almost 1 million political refugees to the United States who could not have been admitted under normal immigration quotas. Over 50 percent of this total arrived between 1971 and 1980, according to the Immigration and Naturalization Service, and 133,000 in 1978 alone—66 percent from Vietnam.

According to the Department of State, which may define refugees differently from the Immigration Service, the number peaked at 207,-000 in 1980, and by 1983 it had fallen to about 62,000. In 1980, the Department of State reported, 28 percent of all legal aliens accepted for permanent residence in the United States were refugees.

The new wave of immigrants is changing the stock of America's foreign born. The 1980 census counted 14 million Americans who had been born abroad, 6 percent of the total population. In contrast, the 10 million foreign-born Americans counted by the 1970 census made up only 5 percent of all Americans.

But the share of the population who came to this country as immigrants is far below its levels in the early part of this century, when the total population was much smaller and immigration from Europe was at its peak. The size of the foreign-born population in 1910 was as large as it is today, but then it equaled an incredible 15 percent of the total American population.

America's immigrants, however, are not what they used to be. The farmers and laborers from Ireland and Italy who flocked to these shores early in the century have grown old. In their wake are physicians from the Philippines, economists from India, and entrepreneurs from Korea.

Recent waves of this new kind of immigrant—the educated professional—have done much to raise the status of America's foreign-born population as a whole. For example, Korean immigrants are more than twice as likely as native-born Americans to be college graduates. A higher share of Korean-born Americans work as professionals, and their median household income is higher than that for native-born Americans.

Over half of all Americans who were born in Korea came to America between 1975 and 1980. Over one third of all immigrants from the Philippines came between 1975 and 1980, as did 44 percent of Indian immigrants, and 55 percent of immigrants from Taiwan. In contrast, just 6 percent of immigrants born in Germany arrived between 1975 and 1980, and only 4 percent of Italians and Irish.

About 16 percent of native-born residents of the United States aged twenty-five or older have a college degree, but European immigrants fall below this average: just 5 percent of Italians, 9 percent of Irish, and 15 percent of Germans counted in the 1980 census have completed four years of college. Asian immigrants, however, are far ahead of the U.S. average: 66 percent of immigrants from India have completed college, as have 60 percent of Taiwanese, 42 percent of Filipinos, 34 percent of Koreans, and 30 percent of mainland Chinese immigrants counted in the 1980 census.

Were it not for the fact that the size of these groups is smaller than the group of Americans who were born in Europe—and that among Mexican immigrants, by far the largest group of immigrants to the United States, only 3 percent have completed college—America's foreign-born residents would have a higher educational profile than native-born Americans. Even so, as a group, 15.8 percent of immigrants aged twenty-five or older have completed college, just behind the 16.3 percent for native-born Americans.

The new immigrants' professional credentials are as impressive as their educational achievements. Among Asian immigrants, only the Vietnamese and Laotians have a smaller share working in the professional occupations than do native-born Americans. Virtually all Southeast Asians in the United States have come as refugees, but large proportions of other Asian groups have come as professionals. While 12 percent of native-born Americans work as professionals, 15 percent of Koreans do, 20 percent of Filipinos, and a staggering 43 percent of the 200,000 Americans born in India.

European immigrants generally are close to the U.S. average in the percentage who are professionals: for example, 13 percent of Germans, 17 percent of English, and 14.5 percent of Irish (but only 6 percent of Italians, 8 percent of Greeks, and 2 percent of Portuguese). As in education, Mexican immigrants bring down the average of all foreign-born Americans who work in professional occupations. Only 2.5 percent of employed Mexican Americans work as professionals; as a group, 12 percent of all foreign-born workers are professionals.

The foreign-born lag behind the native-born in income, but as with education and occupation, there are wide variations among nationalities. Overall, the median household income of Americans born in this country was $17,010 in 1979, according to statistics from the 1980 census. For Americans born elsewhere it was only $14,588.

However, with exceptions, European immigrants had lower household incomes than those from Asia. Among the three largest groups of each, Europeans were all below the average for the native-born population, while Asians were all above average. Median household income in 1979 for Americans born in Germany was $15,790; Italians, $13,736; and English, $16,006. For those born in the Philippines the median was $22,787; Koreans, $18,085; and Chinese, $18,544.

With their impressive educational and professional qualifications, Americans born in India had the highest median household income of any group: $25,644. At the other extreme, the 2.2 million Americans born in Mexico were among the lowest in household income, with a median of just $12,747.

The foreign-born, in general, have a higher than average proportion of elderly than do native-born Americans, 21 percent versus 11 percent. The share under age fifteen is much lower: 9 percent versus 24 percent. But, again, there are vast differences by nationality.

As many as four out of ten Laotians counted in the 1980 census had not yet reached the age of fifteen on Census Day—the highest share of any of the more than one hundred nationalities tabulated by the Census Bureau. And only 1 percent of Laotian Americans had reached the age of sixty-five. On the other hand, a record 60.5 percent of Lithuanian Americans were at least sixty-five years old on Census Day, while a mere 0.3 percent were under fifteen.

Among large groups of immigrants, 28 percent of Americans born in Germany have reached the age of sixty-five, while fewer than 5 percent are under age fifteen. Fewer than 8 percent of Mexican immigrants have reached the age of sixty-five, however, while nearly 15 percent are under fifteen. Filipinos have an even balance: 10 percent aged sixty-five and older, 11 percent under fifteen, and the pattern is the same for the Japanese. But fewer than 3 percent of Korean immigrants are sixty-five or older, while nearly one in four is under age fifteen.

Differences in demographic characteristics reflect different circumstances for immigrant groups. For example, nearly half the Nigerians counted by the 1980 census are college graduates, and nearly two thirds arrived in the five years preceding the census. But their median household income is just $7,000, because many are students.

There are 279 male Nigerian immigrants per 100 Nigerian women in America, overseas education being mainly for male Nigerians. In contrast, among European immigrants there are only 78 men per 100 women, because the European immigrant population is aging and women live longer than men. Immigrants from Finland have a male-to-female ratio of only 56 per 100, the lowest of any immigrant group. Ireland has just 59 per 100, and Iceland 60 per 100. Japan, too, is an aging society, and among the Japanese immigrants in America there are only 56 men per 100 women.

At the other extreme, Arabs and Africans tend to leave their women behind when they come to the United States. Among the 534 U.S. residents who were born in the United Arab Emirates, the ratio of males to females is over five to one, the highest of any foreign-born group. Among Americans born in Kuwait, Qatar, and Saudi Arabia, the male-to-female ratio is over two to one, as it is for those born in Ghana, Mozambique, Somalia, and Libya.

About half of all foreign-born Americans have become naturalized U.S. citizens, ranging from a low of just 5.3 percent of immigrants from Laos and 6.4 percent from Cambodia (now Kampuchea) to a high of 87 percent of those from Austria and Czechoslovakia. In general, Europeans have high rates of naturalization, while immigrants from South America and Africa are well below the average. Asian immigrants are near the average naturalization rate for all immigrants.

Almost one quarter of all immigrants to the United States counted by the 1980 census arrived here between 1975 and 1980, and another 16 percent arrived between 1970 and 1974—a total of 40 percent for the 1970s. In contrast, only 22 percent of all immigrants came to America in the 1960s.

The Census Bureau reports that 3.3 million of the 14 million Americans born in other nations came to the United States between 1975 and 1980. Of these, 1.3 million came from Latin America, and half of these from Mexico alone. Another 1.2 million came from Asia. Only 384,000 came from Europe. Among the 5.4 million foreign-born who came to America before 1960, however, a full 57 percent came from Europe.

America's immigrants differ according to when they arrived in this country and the circumstances that brought them here. Mexicans are moving across the Rio Grande in search of work. Southeast Asian refugees are fleeing political upheaval. These new immigrants fit the traditional image of the poor, unskilled worker making a fresh start in America—the image that fit so many European immigrants early in the century.

Other immigrant groups have a different story. America does not yet know what to make of the new flows of students, tourists, and professionals from Asia, but these new arrivals are rapidly changing the face of immigrants to this country.

CITIES WITH A FOREIGN FLAVOR

Those who live in New York, California, and Florida notice America's immigrants most, and immigrants have had the most impact in these three states. Half of all Americans who were born in another country now reside in these three states in which 22 percent of all Americans live. Immigrants are concentrated in three of the nation's most populous states, drawing more attention than if they were dispersed. New arrivals tend to cluster together, whereas their children and grandchildren disperse.

Table 10 THE FOREIGN-BORN

U. S. Average, 6.2 percent			
States		Cities	
1 California	15.1%	1 Hialeah, FL	61.9%
2 Hawaii	14.2	2 Miami, FL	53.7
3 New York	13.6	3 Union City, NJ	48.7
4 Florida	10.9	4 Miami Beach, FL	48.7
5 New Jersey	10.3	5 East Los Angeles, CA	45.2
6 Rhode Island	8.9	6 South Gate, CA	33.5
7 Massachusetts	8.7	7 Daly City, CA	32.6
8 Connecticut	8.6	8 El Monte, CA	31.4
9 Illinois	7.2	9 Monterey Park, CA	31.2
10 Nevada	6.7	10 Santa Ana, CA	30.5
11 Texas	6.0	11 Montebello, CA	30.1
12 Arizona	6.0	12 Elizabeth, NJ	29.9
13 Washington	5.8	13 San Francisco, CA	28.3
14 Maryland	4.6	14 Alhambra, CA	27.8
15 Michigan	4.5	15 Los Angeles, CA	27.1
16 New Hampshire	4.4	16 Glendale, CA	26.4
17 Vermont	4.1	17 Brownsville, TX	25.3
18 Oregon	4.1	18 Baldwin Park, CA	25.0
19 Alaska	4.0	19 Passaic, NJ	24.5

States		Cities	
20 New Mexico	4.0	20 New Bedford, MA	23.8
21 Colorado	4.0	21 New York, NY	23.6
22 Maine	3.9	22 Oxnard, CA	23.1
23 Utah	3.5	23 McAllen, TX	22.7
24 Pennsylvania	3.4	24 Cerritos, CA	22.1
25 Virginia	3.3	25 Fall River, MA	22.0
26 Delaware	3.2	26 Hawthorne, CA	22.0
27 Ohio	2.8	27 Salinas, CA	22.0
28 Wisconsin	2.7	28 Santa Monica, CA	21.9
29 Minnesota	2.6	29 Laredo, TX	21.8
30 Idaho	2.5	30 Pico Rivera, CA	21.7
31 Montana	2.3	31 El Paso, TX	21.4
32 North Dakota	2.3	32 Pasadena, CA	20.9
33 Wyoming	2.1	33 Skokie, IL	19.8
34 Kansas	2.0	34 Honolulu, HI	18.6
35 Louisiana	2.0	35 Paterson, NJ	18.5
36 Nebraska	2.0	36 Cambridge, MA	18.4
37 Oklahoma	1.9	37 Kendall, FL	17.9
38 Indiana	1.9	38 Hartford, CT	17.5
39 Missouri	1.7	39 Silver Spring, MD	17.5
40 Georgia	1.7	40 Somerville, MA	17.4
41 Iowa	1.6	41 Burbank, CA	17.4
42 South Carolina	1.5	42 Mountain View, CA	17.3
43 South Dakota	1.4	43 Inglewood, CA	17.2
44 North Carolina	1.3	44 Norwalk, CA	17.2
45 West Virginia	1.1	45 New Rochelle, NY	17.2
46 Tennessee	1.1	46 San Mateo, CA	17.1
47 Alabama	1.0	47 Irvington, NJ	17.1
48 Arkansas	1.0	48 Mount Vernon, NY	17.1
49 Kentucky	0.9	49 Bethesda, MD	17.0
50 Mississippi	0.9	50 Brookline, MA	17.0

Source: 1980 census

In five states, all ports of entry, Americans born abroad make up more than 10 percent of the state's residents. California, which attracts Hispanics and Asians, leads with 15 percent. Hawaii, America's Asian way station, is next with 14 percent. New York, through which most European immigrants passed, is close behind with over 13 percent. Immigrants are 11 percent of Florida's population in 1980, because of that state's proximity to Cuba, and 10 percent of New Jersey's, because of its proximity to New York.

States in the South, Florida excepted, have the smallest proportions of foreign-born. Arkansas, Kentucky, Mississippi, and Tennessee are the only states in the country in which less than 1 percent of the residents are immigrants. In thirteen other states, fewer than 2 percent are immigrants—Alabama, Georgia, North Carolina, South Carolina, and West Virginia in the South, as well as Indiana, Iowa, Kansas, Missouri, Nebraska, Oklahoma, South Dakota, and Wyoming.

California's 3.6 million foreign-born residents are more than the population totals of about half of all the other states. They far surpass New York's 2.4 million immigrants. Florida is the only other state that is home to at least 1 million immigrants. South Dakota has the fewest; the 1980 census reported only 9,599. Nor have the foreign-born flocked to Wyoming; that state has just 9,607.

Immigrants are much more likely than other Americans to live in the central cities, and some cities have a strong foreign flavor. Of all Americans, fewer than one in three live in central cities, but nearly half of the nation's immigrants live in central cities. Among large cities, 24 percent of New York City's residents were born abroad, 27 percent of Los Angeles's, and 28 percent of San Francisco's. Fifteen percent of Boston's residents are immigrants, and 14 percent of Chicago's, but only 3 percent of Baltimore's, St. Louis's, and Kansas City's.

Only 7 percent of immigrants live outside metropolitan areas (large cities and their suburbs), compared to 25 percent of Americans as a whole. With its large Cuban population, Miami has the highest share of foreign-born of any large metropolitan area. Thirty-six percent of Miami residents were born in another country. Next comes the Los Angeles–Long Beach metropolitan area, with 22 percent, and the New York area, with 21 percent. In eleven major metropolitan areas, each containing a port city, immigrants are over 10 percent of the total population. Together, they are home to over 6 million immigrants, nearly half of America's total foreign-born population.

The New York metropolitan area is home to more immigrants than any other: almost 2 million. New York is the only large metropolitan area in the country in which more residents were born in another country than in another state. Four other metropolitan areas each have more than half a million immigrants: Los Angeles–Long Beach, Chicago, Miami, and San Francisco.

In the big cities, therefore, it is hard not to notice that the origins of America's immigrants have changed dramatically. A native New Yorker, who grew up in the shadow of Ellis Island and its memories of European immigrants seeking a better life in America, notices that the service jobs traditionally held by new European arrivals are now filled by Puerto Ricans and Asian Americans.

Until World War II, Germany had been the largest contributor of immigrants to America. But in 1940, Italy replaced Germany as the leading country of origin for the foreign-born. Now, Mexico has become the leading country of birth for people who came to the United States as immigrants. In the 1970s, Italy sent just 130,000 of its sons and daughters to the United States, still the most of any European country. But Mexico sent 637,000 of its citizens to the United States, officially, and several million more illegally.

No one knows how many new residents of the United States are here illegally. Census statistics understate the number of Mexican immigrants because people who are in this country without legal documents are not inclined to fill out government questionnaires, even though the Census Bureau stresses the confidentiality of its survey and encourages all Americans to answer the census.

Even if the census asked people whether they were legal residents of the United States, illegal residents would not tell the truth, and they would be more likely than ever to dodge the census enumerator. It is impossible to measure the number of illegal residents, but a study that appeared in the journal *Demography* estimated the number of illegal residents from Mexico at between 1.5 million and 4 million in 1980.

With so many people wanting to get into America, the U.S. government has paid little attention to those native-born Americans who want to leave. Only after young people began to leave the country in large numbers in the 1960s to avoid being sent to war in Vietnam did it come to light that official estimates of emigration were low. Recent studies have shown that some 1.5 million more Americans than the Census Bureau estimated left the country permanently during the 1960s and 1970s.

THE RACIAL TAPESTRY

America's racial tapestry is becoming more complex than ever before. Although whites are 87 percent of the total population, their number grew only 6 percent during the past decade, about half the rate for the population as a whole. The number of blacks rose 17 percent. But the number of American Indians grew an impressive 71 percent; the number of Asians and Pacific Islanders grew an even more impressive 127 percent; the number of people whose race was listed as "other" grew an astounding 1,208 percent. What strange forces were at work?

The impressive performance of "other" was related to the laggard growth of whites, each being opposite sides of a change in census coding procedure that will confound future anthropologists who try to use census statistics to untangle the racial roots of twentieth-century America.

In 1970, when a person checked "other" in answer to the census race question and wrote in "Mexican," "Puerto Rican," or "Cuban," the Census Bureau changed this answer to "white." The bureau does not consider Hispanics to be a race, and a separate census question inquires about Spanish origin. Following complaints from Hispanic leaders, however—because it appeared to be a statistical form of discrimination that discouraged Hispanic ethnic identification—the bureau changed its coding practice. In the 1980 census, when a person checked "other" in response to the race question and wrote in a Hispanic origin, the bureau left such answers alone and tabulated them as "other."

The result, of course was a dramatic increase in the "other" races category—from about 500,000 people in 1970 to 6.8 million in 1980. The white category, then, was stripped of several million people considered to be white one decade, but considered "other" the next.

The social climate shapes the census questionnaire and influences Americans' responses to it. Self-identification can be an important indicator of race or ethnicity, but what goes up one decade may go down the next. The Asian and Pacific Islander population grew from 1.5 million people in 1970 to 3.5 million in 1980 partly because of an influx of Vietnamese, but also because of the addition to the census questionnaire of four new Asian and Pacific Islander categories. Asking "Are you a Samoan?" is going to turn up more Samoans than merely asking "What are you?" Perhaps you are Samoan, but had never thought about it.

Before 1980 no previous census had listed Samoan, Vietnamese, Asian Indian, or Guamanian among the races. The 1970 census question about race asked for "color or race," listing as choices white, negro or black, Indian, Japanese, Filipino, Hawaiian, Korean, and other. In 1980, the words *color or race* disappeared completely—such were the sensitivities of the decade—and instead the Census Bureau inquired, "Is this person?" one of the following 15 categories: white, black or negro, Japanese, Chinese, Filipino, Korean, Vietnamese, American Indian, Asian Indian, Hawaiian, Guamanian, Samoan, Eskimo, Aleut, and other.

People who were "negro or black" in 1970 became "black or negro" by 1980. In the 1960 census, the word *black* did not appear. The only choice was *negro.* In 1910, census enumerators were instructed to observe the skin color of respondents and write down *black* if the person appeared full-blooded, but *mulatto* for anyone who had some observable trace of black heritage. The 1890 census asked whether a person with negro blood was black, mulatto, quadroon, or octoroon. In 1850, when slavery was still practiced, the census race question asked whether slaves were black or mulatto. "The color of slaves should be noted," read the enumerators' instructions.

The country has come a long way in its views toward blacks, and it is still on the move. One of these decades *black or negro* may become simply *black,* but the census is unlikely to return to simpler days when it assumed that all Americans were either white or some shade of black.

As woven by the 1980 census, the American racial tapestry is a complex work of art. The census counted 188 million whites, nearly 27 million blacks, and 7 million "other" races, virtually all of whom are Hispanics who used to consider themselves whites. The census counted 1.4 million American Indians; 806,000 Chinese; 775,000 Filipinos; 701,000 Japanese Americans; 362,000 Asian Indians; 355,000 Koreans; 262,000 Vietnamese; 167,000 Hawaiians (of whom 115,500 resided in Hawaii); 42,000 Eskimos; 42,000 Samoans; 32,000 Guamanians; and 14,000 Aleuts.

No state is without at least a handful of each of the fifteen racial groups. No state has fewer than 13 Guamanians. Vermont has 8 each of Eskimos, Aleuts, and Samoans. Delaware has 8 Aleuts and 13 Eskimos. Florida has 199 Eskimos. Even Hawaii has 68 Eskimos, and Alaska has 402 Hawaiians. Fewer Asian Indians reside in Montana than in any other state, only 162, but Montana is home to 458 Filipinos, 754 Japanese, 301 Koreans, 275 Vietnamese, and 24 Samoans. Arkansas and Delaware have the fewest Samoans—only 6 apiece.

ESKIMOS AND INDIANS

Immigration is in the eye of the beholder. Some Americans were here long before others. In 1900, less than half of Alaska's total population was white—59 percent of the men but only 18 percent of the women. Today, over 75 percent of Alaskans are white, with a close balance between the sexes. The 1900 census found only 3 Chinese women in Alaska, but 3,113 Chinese men. By 1980, the number of Chinese women in Alaska had risen to 284, and the number of men had dropped to 238.

Eskimos and Aleuts today are only 11 percent of Alaska's population, although Alaska is home to 81 percent of the nation's Eskimos and to 57 percent of Aleuts. White Americans have been immigrating to Alaska for decades. The original Alaskans have different demographics from the newcomers; a higher share of Eskimos and Aleuts are under age fifteen or aged sixty-five and older, because the youth have been moving to other states. Their average family size is larger.

Native Americans are far less metropolitan than other Alaskans. Over 43 percent of all Alaskans live in Anchorage, but only 19 percent of Aleuts and 11 percent of Eskimos. Almost two thirds of Alaska's Aleuts, Eskimos, or American Indians live in one of 209 native villages, designated by the Census Bureau. The largest Alaskan native village is home to 3,576 people, whereas the smallest, Paimut, on the Bering Sea, has a total of only 1 person, as located by the 1980 census. Life can be lonely in the Arctic. Uyak, on Kodiak Island, has 2 people—who presumably are acquainted.

When the 1980 census found 1.4 million American Indians, it was the first time their count exceeded 1 million since the census began asking about American Indians in 1860. In 1970, census takers had found only 764,000 Indians, or 79 percent fewer than in 1980. An improved census count and a rise in the number of people who decided they were Indian were as much responsible for this huge increase as was a surge in Indian births, even though 21 percent of American Indians are under the age of ten.

Indians have always had their ups and downs. Until 1860, the census did not even report on this country's native Americans. Since then, changing methods of counting Indians and shifts in government policy toward who should be considered Indian have affected the number of Indians as much as have Indian births and deaths. Until 1960, the census takers decided who was an Indian and who was not. In the 1960 census, when respondents could make their own decision, the Indian population leaped 48 percent.

Half of all American Indians live in the American West; only 6 percent live in the Northeast, and 18 percent in the North-Central Region. Five states—California, Oklahoma, Arizona, New Mexico, and North Carolina—are home to more than half of all American Indians. California's share of the total Indian population rose from 12 percent to nearly 15 percent between 1970 and 1980. Today, California is home to relatively more Indians than any state. It displaced Oklahoma, which was in first place a decade ago with 13 percent of all American Indians.

Every state contains Indians. In New Mexico, Indians are as much as 8 percent of the total state population, the highest ratio of any state. But in only four other states—South Dakota, Oklahoma, Arizona, and Alaska—are American Indians more than 5 percent of the state's total population.

THE WHITE ETHNICS

If America's original inhabitants and its new immigrants are still relatively concentrated in a few states, the descendants of Europeans are everywhere. Ethnic clusters of Europeans still exist, however, and past settlement patterns have created differences in the ethnic texture of the individual states.

The census questionnaire asked respondents an open-ended question about their ancestry. Respondents wrote in a rich variety of answers, including single ancestries, "English" for example, dual ancestries, such as "German-English," or triple ancestries such as "German-Irish-Swedish." The Census Bureau coded for its computers all single and dual ancestries, plus the seventeen triple ancestries the bureau expected to be most frequently reported. Such triple ancestries include "Dutch-German-Irish," "English-French-German," "English-Irish-Scottish," and "German-Irish-Swedish."

The Census Bureau's ancestry question was intended to examine, for the first time, the ethnic characteristics of all Americans. The ethnic background of America's European whites, for example, is not revealed in other census questions that ask about race, country of birth, parentage, or language spoken, although these questions tell a lot about racial minorities, immigrants, and non-English speakers.

Of the people who responded to the census ancestry question, 52 percent said they were of a single ancestry; another 31 percent reported dual ancestry, or more; whereas 17 percent failed to specify an ancestry, probably because they did not know the roots of their family tree. Ethnic groups most likely to report a single ancestry include Greek, Israeli, Nigerian, and Saudi Arabian. Those most likely to report multiple ancestry are Scottish, Dutch, French, Irish, and Welsh. Americans reporting a single ancestry are older, on average, than those reporting multiple ancestry, and they are more likely to have been born in another country.

Such statistics reveal the difference between first-generation immigrants and later generations who have spread out, intermarried, and no longer identify with a single country of origin. Instead, they view themselves more as melting-pot, homogeneous Americans.

America has always digested ethnic groups as it digests their foods. The ice cream cone was the creation of an immigrant from Damascus, so goes the tale, who rolled a circular Persian pastry into the shape of a cone and placed a scoop of ice cream in the top. German immigrants brought the hamburger to America about a century ago, and it was placed on its first bun in 1904, according to the *Ethnic Almanac*—about fifty years after the frankfurter had immigrated to America. A question for the future is whether the country will digest its Hispanic and Asian immigrants as readily. Already, tacos are everywhere. In a few cities, Japanese sushi bars are taking hold.

European-Americans have been intermarrying for generations. The Irish have married the English, Germans have married Swedes, the Poles have married Italians, and so forth. Almost a third of all Americans say they are of mixed ancestry. The state with the highest share of such residents is Minnesota, the original destination of so many German, Norwegian, and Swedish immigrants. Clearly, they found each other likable. In five other states, at least 40 percent of residents report multiple ancestry—Colorado, Iowa, Oregon, Washington, and Wisconsin.

It is a measure of the extraordinary intermarriage among immigrants from Europe and their descendants that the most common ancestry, English, is reported as a single ancestry by fewer than 11 percent of all Americans—a smaller minority group than black Americans, if the government were to consider white ancestral groups as minorities. But 50 million Americans reported that they are at least partly of English descent.

Americans who have some German blood in them are the second most numerous ancestry group, cited by 49 million people, but only 8 percent of Americans say they are solely of German heritage. Irish is the third most commonly reported ancestry—40 million Americans claim to have some Irish in them (the number rises on Saint Patrick's Day), but only 10 million, or fewer than 5 percent, say they are all Irish.

English or German is the largest single ancestry reported in all but six states. German holds sway across the Midwest, from Pennsylvania to Montana; English sweeps around the edges, from the Pacific Northwest through the South, and in Maine, New Hampshire, and Vermont. Italian is the largest single ancestry reported in New York, New Jersey, Connecticut, and Rhode Island. The Irish lead in Massachusetts, and the French in Louisiana. These findings fit America's regional ethnic stereotypes—from the beer-drinking blue-collar German Americans of

Ohio, Indiana, and Illinois to the English Southern gentry and Western frontiersmen in the mold of Lewis and Clark.

But a closer look changes these familiar images. German is the second-largest single ancestry group in the West. In Oregon, 10 percent of residents said they are of pure English ancestry, but almost as many, 9 percent, said their ancestry is purely German. In most midwestern states, English is a close second to German. Only in Iowa do Germans hold a solid edge—21 percent versus 7 percent for the English. French is the second-largest single ancestry in Maine, New Hampshire, Vermont, and Rhode Island. Irish is second in seven states of the South. Norwegian is the second-largest ancestry in Minnesota and the Dakotas. Polish pops up second in Wisconsin.

Looking at the third-largest single-ancestry group that Americans claim may explain why there seems to be a little Irish in almost everybody. From Maine to California and from Florida to Washington, Irish appears as the third-largest single ancestry all over the map. In as many as thirty-three states, Irish is the third-largest ancestry.

But Ukrainian, Russian, Swedish, Dutch, and other ancestry groups also turn up in every state. The 1980 census found 146 Americans of pure Portuguese ancestry in North Dakota; 559 Hungarians in Mississippi; 792 Russians in Arkansas; and 659 Greeks in Alaska. Vermont may have only 8 Samoans; it is, however, home to 1,807 Dutch ethnics, 2,534 Swedes, 5,485 Poles, 528 Greeks, 771 Hungarians, 340 Portuguese, 384 Ukrainians, and 1,824 Russians.

Amid this diversity, the dominant ancestries are still English, German, Irish, French, and Italian. In only five states does any single-ancestry group besides this big five make up even 5 percent of the population: Poles are 5 percent of Connecticut's population; Norwegians are 5 percent of Montana's, 7 percent of Minnesota's and South Dakota's, and 15 percent of North Dakota's. This hardy bunch has staked out territory where others fear to tread.

Not all these groups have been welcomed with open arms by those who got here first. This is one reason that there are still clusters of European ethnic groups, just as there are clusters of Asians and Mexicans. People fear the unfamiliar, and it can take generations before the unfamiliar becomes familiar.

ENGLISH SPOKEN HERE?

More than one American in ten does not speak English at home. Almost 23 million Americans told the 1980 census takers that they speak a language other than English in the home, and almost half of these people—some 11 million—speak Spanish. New Mexico leads the nation in the proportion of state residents who speak a language other than English at home. There, nearly one third of all state residents speak Spanish. Following New Mexico among states with high proportions of residents who use a language other than English at home are Hawaii, California, Texas, Arizona, New York, Rhode Island, New Jersey, Connecticut, and Florida. These states have been among the most popular destinations for immigrants, past or present. Over 25 percent of all the residents of Hawaii do not speak English in the home, but only 1 percent speak Spanish. Much more popular are Japanese, Chinese, Hawaiian, or a Philippine language.

Because Latin America supplies so many new immigrants, high proportions of the residents of some states speak Spanish at home: 19 percent of Texans, 14 percent of Californians, and 13 percent of Arizona's residents. But in the Northeast, Spanish speakers are a minority of those who speak a foreign language at home. Almost 17 percent of Rhode Island residents do not speak English in the home, but fewer than 2 percent speak Spanish. In New Jersey, 16 percent speak a language other than English, but only 6 percent speak Spanish. In Connecticut, 14 percent speak a foreign language, but only 3.5 percent speak Spanish.

Even in New York, with its large Puerto Rican population, Spanish speakers are less than 9 percent of all residents, although 19 percent of New Yorkers told the 1980 census they speak a language other than English. These non-English speakers include the European immigrants who came to America earlier in the century. Some, it appears, have retired to Florida. In that state, home to more than 850,000 Hispanics, 13 percent of the population speaks a language other than English at home, but only 8.6 percent are Spanish-speakers.

Among major metropolitan areas, Miami contains the highest proportion of residents who speak a foreign language at home—43 percent. Over 33 percent of Miami's people speak Spanish. In San Antonio, where slightly less than 43 percent of residents speak a language other than English, nine out of ten of these people speak Spanish. In Los Angeles, 22 percent of all residents speak Spanish at home, and an additional 9 percent speak a language other than English. In the New York metropolitan area, 31 percent of all residents speak a language other than English at home, and nearly 50 percent of these speak Spanish.

A decade ago, more Americans spoke German in childhood than any other language except English. But today, Spanish has become by far the most popular second language in the United States. The mother tongue that grew the most in the United States in the 1970s was not Spanish, however, but Korean. The number of Korean speakers rose over 300 percent. Both of these statistics are witness to the changing American ethnic mosaic.

The number of Americans reporting German as their mother tongue declined 15 percent during the past decade. Slovakian was down 30 percent, Lithuanian 27 percent, Russian 26 percent, and Yiddish 25 percent. However, the number of Americans reporting a Philippine language as a mother tongue rose more than 120 percent, Chinese almost 70 percent, and Arabic 40 percent. The number of first-generation European ethnics is ebbing, as death reduces their number, while first-generation Asians are still flowing in.

Children are somewhat more likely than their parents to speak English in the home, according to the 1980 census. Among Americans aged eighteen and older, 11 percent speak a language other than English. But for children between the ages of five and seventeen, the share who speak a language other than English was 10 percent. Only 16 percent of the children are not able to speak English as well as their native language, whereas 28 percent of the adults who use another language in the home cannot speak English well, or do not speak it at all.

Immigrants have made America a land of many tongues, but the children of immigrants have learned English in the schools and joined the mainstream of American life. Their own children grew up speaking English, not German, Italian, or Serbo-Croatian. Although more than 3 million Americans have a mother tongue other than English, only slightly more than half still use their mother tongue.

Not all immigrants assimilate into mainstream American culture, however, and in the 1970s it became easier not to assimilate. In that decade, Congress amended the Voting Rights Act of 1965 to offer foreign-language voting material in areas with high concentrations of Americans whose first language is not English. The rationale was that some American citizens were being denied their constitutional right to vote because of language discrimination. The 1980 census questionnaire was printed in Spanish and other languages for areas in which many people do not speak English.

The Bilingual Education Act of 1976 called for school instruction in other languages in areas where children could not speak English. In Los Angeles, the 1980 census found more than 450,000 children who speak Spanish at home, and almost one in four could not speak English. In the New York metropolitan area, more than half a million speak a language other than either English or Spanish at home, and more than

64,000 of them report that they speak no English. Is it any wonder that English-speaking residents of New York City ponder the passing scene and wonder where all this is heading? The New York City schools now offer instruction not only in Spanish, but also in such languages as Chinese, Italian, Russian, French, Greek, Yiddish, Hebrew, Korean, Vietnamese, and Arabic—and English.

More than 1.5 million Americans still speak Italian, German, or French. More than 600,000 speak Chinese; 265,000, Japanese; 191,000, Korean; and 157,000, Vietnamese. It is not necessary to speak English to make it in America, but it still helps. Citizens who do not speak English are as American as those who do, with as many inalienable rights, and the preservation of their own culture may be high among these rights. But it will be much harder for their children to participate in the mainstream of American life if it becomes possible to grow up in America without having to use English in the neighborhood, in local stores, in school systems, in voting booths, and on census questionnaires.

SOCIETY AT THE CROSSROADS

Few things are more central to a nation than its cultural heritage; few boundaries are more important than national borders. Today, some say America has lost control of its borders and its cultural heritage, and fear for the future. The influx of Asians and Latin Americans is a profound change from past patterns of immigration, and the pattern is unlikely to reverse.

If America is to remain a land of immigrants, its future culture will inevitably be much more Asian and Hispanic than that of today. Demographer Leon Bouvier of the Population Reference Bureau has calculated that if the immigration rates, birthrates, and death rates that are predicted for various racial and ethnic groups come to pass, non-Hispanic whites will become an ever-shrinking majority of the American people.

If immigration averages about half a million new arrivals per year, Bouvier calculates, for example, non-Hispanic whites would decline from eight of every ten Americans in 1980 to seven of every ten in 2020. The proportion of Hispanics would rise from 6 percent of all Americans to 11 percent. Because they have higher fertility than whites, America's blacks would increase their share from 12 percent to 14 percent, and Asians and other races would increase their share from 2 percent to 5 percent.

These may not be startling numbers in themselves—seven out of ten still makes a majority—but the direction of change means the cultural heritage of America could change dramatically in the future. "If current demographic behavior continues," Bouvier has written, "40 percent of America's 2080 population will be post-1980 immigrants and their descendants. Perhaps 80 percent of these will be Hispanic, Caribbean, or Asian in origin."

Bouvier has written that this nation must decide whether to become a "status quo" society that maintains the dominance of the Anglo culture or a "multicultural" society that favors greater cultural pluralism and diversity. The first kind of society would accept only as many immigrants as it could assimilate. The second would not be concerned with assimilation, and the culture would change as the origin of immigrants changed. This is not the kind of choice Americans like to make.

Society is likely to continue to change ethnically, subject to the political and economic forces that create pressures for immigration and shape public opinion about its desirability. Today, developing countries are not creating enough jobs to match their population growth. If their birthrates fall, pressures for immigration should lift. In recent years, as the American birthrate has dropped to record lows, immigration has once again become a significant share of our population growth. Because unemployment has been high in the United States, political pressure for immigration reform has risen. But these circumstances could change.

America has always obtained its vitality from immigrants, and it continues to do so today. The new immigrants are not like those of the past, but hasn't that always been the case?

TRENDS TO WATCH

– Immigration has become a larger share of America's total population growth than it used to be, because the number of immigrants has risen, while the domestic birthrate has fallen.

– The origin of the majority of immigrants has shifted from Europe to Asia and Latin America.

– These trends account for the growing attention to national immigration policy and for the rise of new ethnic markets. Recent immigrants are still highly concentrated, geographically and culturally, but in time they may assimilate, as previous immigrant waves have done.

Chapter

 8 | *From South of the Border*

"America's notions about assimilation are built on the experience of groups that crossed oceans to come here. Mexicans need only walk and cross a river, and they become Americans in the census."

A rising tide; a river of aliens flowing through a leaky border. America's Hispanic immigrants are being welcomed with watery metaphors. But the migratory currents, so far, have flooded only certain American cities and states. Elsewhere Hispanics constitute still just a trickle.

The 1980 census found 14.6 million Hispanics. But their number starts at 3,300 in Vermont and rises to more than 4.5 million in California. That state is home to over 30 percent of all Americans of Spanish origin. Texas has almost 3 million Hispanics, or 20 percent of the Hispanic population; New York has 1.7 million, or 11 percent of the total. Together, these three states contain well over 60 percent of America's Hispanics.

Add six more states—Florida, Illinois, New Jersey, New Mexico, Arizona, and Colorado—in which the census counted at least 300,000 Hispanics, and more than 85 percent of Hispanics in this country have been accounted for. In all, over 90 percent of America's Hispanics live in the fifteen states in which the census counted at least 100,000 Hispanics. Hispanics are a majority of the population in thirty-seven counties: Santa Cruz in Arizona; Imperial in California; Conejos and Costilla in Colorado; and in eight counties of New Mexico and twenty-five of Texas. Starr County, Texas, which lies on the border between the United States and Mexico, is 97 percent Hispanic.

More than the American people in general, Hispanics congregate in the nation's cities. Whereas some 75 percent of all Americans are metropolitan, 81 percent of blacks and 88 percent of Hispanics are metropolitan. Over 60 percent of all Hispanics counted in the 1980 census live in one of the nation's fifty largest metropolitan areas. The Los Angeles and New York metropolitan areas combined are home to 3.6 million Hispanics—almost 25 percent of the U.S. total. Ten other metropolitan areas contain 250,000 or more Hispanics. Chicago and Miami each have about 580,000. San Antonio has over 480,000, and Houston about 425,000. The San Francisco–Oakland metropolitan area has more than 350,000 Hispanics. The other five areas are all in California and Texas.

Table 11 PERCENT HISPANIC IN 1980 CENSUS

U.S. Average, 6.4 percent

States		Cities	
1 New Mexico	36.6%	1 East Los Angeles, CA	94.1%
2 Texas	21.0	2 Laredo, TX	93.0
3 California	19.2	3 Brownsville, TX	83.8
4 Arizona	16.2	4 Pico Rivera, CA	76.1
5 Colorado	11.8	5 Hialeah, FL	74.3
6 New York	9.5	6 McAllen, TX	71.5
7 Florida	8.8	7 Union City, NJ	64.0
8 Hawaii	7.4	8 El Paso, TX	62.5
9 Nevada	6.7	9 El Monte, CA	61.3
10 New Jersey	6.7	10 Montebello, CA	59.1
11 Illinois	5.6	11 South Gate, CA	58.3
12 Wyoming	5.2	12 Baldwin Park, CA	58.0
13 Utah	4.1	13 Miami, FL	56.0
14 Connecticut	4.0	14 San Antonio, TX	53.7
15 Idaho	3.9	15 Corpus Christi, TX	46.7
16 Washington	2.9	16 Santa Ana, CA	44.5
17 Kansas	2.7	17 Oxnard, CA	44.3
18 Oregon	2.5	18 Norwalk, CA	40.1
19 Massachusetts	2.5	19 Monterey Park, CA	38.6
20 Alaska	2.4	20 Salinas, CA	38.0
21 Louisiana	2.4	21 Alhambra, CA	37.6
22 Rhode Island	2.1	22 Pueblo, CO	35.5

States		Cities	
23 Oklahoma	1.9	23 Passaic, NJ	33.9
24 Nebraska	1.8	24 Albuquerque, NM	33.8
25 Michigan	1.8	25 Victoria, TX	33.7
26 Delaware	1.6	26 Pomona, CA	30.5
27 Indiana	1.6	27 Paterson, NJ	28.7
28 Maryland	1.5	28 Los Angeles, CA	27.5
29 Virginia	1.5	29 Ontario, CA	27.1
30 Wisconsin	1.3	30 Elizabeth, NJ	26.4
31 Pennsylvania	1.3	31 San Bernardino, CA	25.4
32 Montana	1.3	32 Tucson, AZ	24.8
33 Georgia	1.1	33 Fresno, CA	23.5
34 Ohio	1.1	34 Carson, CA	23.4
35 South Carolina	1.1	35 Whittier, CA	23.3
36 Missouri	1.1	36 Chula Vista, CA	23.3
37 Mississippi	1.0	37 Odessa, TX	23.2
38 North Carolina	1.0	38 San Angelo, TX	23.0
39 Iowa	0.9	39 San Jose, CA	22.3
40 Alabama	0.9	40 Santa Barbara, CA	22.2
41 Minnesota	0.8	41 Miami Beach, FL	22.1
42 Arkansas	0.8	42 Stockton, CA	22.1
43 Kentucky	0.7	43 West Covina, CA	21.1
44 Tennessee	0.7	44 Compton, CA	21.1
45 West Virginia	0.7	45 Hawthorne, CA	20.9
46 Vermont	0.6	46 Hayward, CA	20.3
47 New Hampshire	0.6	47 Hartford, CT	20.3
48 North Dakota	0.6	48 New York, NY	19.9
49 South Dakota	0.6	49 Camden, NJ	19.5
50 Maine	0.4	50 Daly City, CA	19.3

Source: 1980 census

Hispanics are a majority of the population in five metropolitan areas, four of them Mexican border towns. In eleven other metropolitan areas, they make up more than 25 percent of the total population. Among the nation's central cities of metropolitan areas and cities of 50,000 and over, eighteen have Hispanic majorities, including San Antonio, Texas, and Miami, Florida. All but one are located in Texas, California, or Florida. Union City, New Jersey, also has a 64 percent Hispanic majority.

Because America's Hispanics concentrate in the big cities, they command the attention of the national media, which also concentrate in the big cities. Corporations find it convenient to market to Hispanics because the Hispanic market is concentrated in major cities in a handful of states.

Elsewhere, Americans wonder what all the furor over Hispanics is about. They scarcely ever encounter someone of Spanish origin. Hispanics are 1 percent or below of the residents in fourteen states from Maine to Mississippi. In fourteen others, from Ohio to Oklahoma, they are less than 2 percent. Hispanics number at least 10 percent of the population in only five states and 47 metropolitan areas. In only about 250 of the country's more than 3,000 counties are Hispanics more than 10 percent of all residents. In only 41 of the nation's 318 metropolitan areas are there more than 50,000 Hispanics.

THREE DISTINCT GROUPS

Hispanics are not a monolithic minority group, but rather three culturally distinct groups spread about as far apart geographically as it is possible to get within the United States. Mexicans, Puerto Ricans, and Cubans are nearly as different from each other as they are from other Americans. They differ in their ability to speak English, in their family life, in their economic status, and in their demographic characteristics.

Hispanics cluster by their country of origin. Three out of four of the 8.7 million Hispanics of Mexican origin live in either California or Texas. Fifty percent of the nation's Puerto Ricans live in New York, with 43 percent in New York City. Nearly two out of three Cubans live in Florida, more than half in the Miami metropolitan area. Nearly 20 percent of Mexican-Americans live in the Los Angeles–Long Beach metropolitan area.

In Laredo, Texas, which is 92 percent Hispanic, 95 percent of all Hispanics are of Mexican origin. In California, Los Angeles–Long Beach is 28 percent Hispanic, and 80 percent of the Hispanics there are Mexican. Of Miami's 581,000 Hispanics, 70 percent are Cuban. Of the residents of Albuquerque, New Mexico, 36 percent are Hispanic—and of these Hispanics 56 percent belong to a group the Census Bureau terms *other Spanish*. The category includes all Hispanics who are not of Mexican, Cuban, or Puerto Rican origin.

Of all New Mexicans, in fact, one resident in five is of *other Spanish* origin. Nine other states also contain concentrations of more than 50,000 other Spanish—California, Colorado, Florida, Illinois, Louisiana, Massachusetts, New Jersey, New York, and Texas. Although in other parts of the country some of these others are from Spain and various Caribbean and Latin American countries, in New Mexico most are Hispanos. *Hispanos* are people native to the United States whose ancestors lived in the Southwest before Europeans arrived in the Northeast, a rising tide of European immigrants flowing westward.

Hispanos must wonder at the historic trends that have made this country English speaking. Given a few different twists of fate, it could have been otherwise, had more Spanish speakers joined Hispanos to populate the land before the English moved westward. But this is an English-speaking country. According to the 1980 census, 89 percent of Americans speak only English at home; just 5 percent speak Spanish at home, and of these 75 percent also know English. However, the share of Spanish-speaking adults who cannot speak English is more than twice as high as the share of adults who speak some other language at home and who cannot speak English. Spanish has become the nation's second most widely used language.

Sharp differences exist between Hispanic groups. Hispanics of Mexican origin are most likely to know English, because, as a group, they have been in the United States the longest. Cubans, who are the most recent arrivals, are less likely than either Mexican Americans or Puerto Rican Americans to be bilingual.

The median age of America's Hispanics is twenty-three, but Mexican Americans are even younger. The median age of Mexican-origin Hispanics is only 21.9. More than one third of Mexican Americans are under age fifteen, whereas fewer than one quarter of all Americans are in that age group. Only 4 percent of Mexican-origin Americans have reached the age of sixty-five, compared to 11 percent of Americans in general.

In contrast, the median age of Cuban Americans is thirty-eight, eight years higher than that for Americans as a whole. Only 16 percent of Cubans are under age fifteen, whereas 12 percent are sixty-five or older. The older age profile of Cubans reflects the exodus from Cuba following the revolution in 1959, whereas the young age profile of Mexican Americans reflects the continuing flow of Mexicans northward.

The family structure of Puerto Ricans is strikingly different from that of either Cubans or Mexicans. One reason is an unusual difference in the sex ratio. Mexican-American men outnumber women, but Puerto Rican women outnumber men. Different migration patterns provide the explanation: Among Mexicans, men have been more likely to migrate to the United States looking for work, whereas Puerto Rican women have been better able than the men to find jobs in the states.

Thirty-five percent of all Puerto Rican families are maintained by a woman without a husband. Fully 28 percent of all Puerto Rican households are families headed by a woman—nearly three times the proportion for all U.S. households. In contrast, only 15 percent of Cuban families and 16 percent of Mexican families have a woman at their head. One third of Puerto Ricans are younger than age fifteen. Twenty-three percent of Puerto Rican women who gave birth in 1980 were teen-agers. Such statistics help explain why Puerto Rican families have such low incomes.

Nationwide, the proportion of Hispanics in poverty was 30 percent in 1982, double the 15 percent for all Americans. Hispanic incomes are lower because America's Hispanics have fewer two-earner households; they are younger; and they are less well educated. Hispanics as a whole had a median family income of $16,200 in 1982, well below the $23,400 for all U.S. families. "Other" Spanish are the most affluent of Hispanics. Their 1982 median family income was $19,100. Cubans were second, with a median family income of $18,900, followed by Mexican Americans, $16,400, and Puerto Ricans, $11,100.

Cubans share with other Hispanic groups a strong family orientation, but because the average age of Cubans is older than that of the other groups, Cuban households are much less likely to contain children. Cuban fertility in 1980 was even lower than the national average. The number of Cuban married couples without children at home is greater than the number who have children living at home. Only 49 percent of Cuban households contain children, for example, compared to 70 percent of Mexican-American households.

Because Cubans are such a small share of all U.S. Hispanics, however, their characteristics have little effect on the average characteristics of Hispanics. The fertility of Mexican Americans is still as high as American fertility was during the years of the baby boom, and because they are by far the largest Hispanic group, fertility for Hispanics overall is much higher than the U.S. average. Thus, family size is larger for Hispanics than for Americans in general.

Only 46 percent of Hispanics who have reached the age of twenty-five are high school graduates, compared to 71 percent of all American adults. But younger Hispanics are more educated than their elders. Among Hispanics aged twenty-five to thirty-four, 58 percent have completed high school, and 24 percent had had at least one year of college in 1982. Because they are less well educated, Hispanics are less likely than Americans in general to work in professional and technical jobs. Whereas over 50 percent of the American work force held white-collar jobs in 1982, only 37 percent of Hispanics did. Hispanics are more likely than other Americans to wear blue collars. In 1982, only 9 percent of Hispanic workers were in professional or technical jobs, compared to 17 percent of all employed Americans. But 23 percent of Hispanics operated machinery, 7 percent were laborers, and 15 percent were in such service occupations as food workers and janitors, all higher proportions than for Americans in general. As with the other measures of status, Cubans' labor force characteristics are more likely to resemble those of Americans in general, whereas Mexicans and Puerto Ricans pull down the socioeconomic averages.

Although Hispanics, like Asian immigrants, remain clustered in a few geographic areas, there are a few signs that this may be changing. The 1980 census found that Hispanics are beginning to become less concentrated. In 1970, 87 percent of Mexican-origin Hispanics lived in the Southwest; by 1980 the share had dropped to 83 percent. In 1970, 64 percent of all U.S. Hispanics of Puerto Rican origin lived in New York State. By 1980, the share had declined to 49 percent.

In 1970, Illinois and Michigan were the only states outside the Southwest to contain more than 50,000 Mexican Americans. By 1980, Indiana, Ohio, Washington, and Florida had joined them. Chicago now has 581,000 Hispanic residents, 64 percent of them Mexican; Detroit has 72,000, 62 percent Mexican. Puerto Ricans have spread from New York City to Newark, New Jersey, where the census found 132,000 Hispanics, of whom 47 percent are Puerto Rican. In Philadelphia there are 116,000 Hispanics, 68 percent Puerto Rican. Even Boston has 66,000 Hispanics, 44 percent Puerto Rican. However tentative, these are signs that, like other immigrants before them, Hispanics are being woven into the fabric of American life.

WHO IS HISPANIC?

The number of Hispanics in the United States grew by 5.5 million in the 1970s, a 61 percent increase that grabbed the headlines. But the Census Bureau's procedures for counting Hispanics affects who is considered Hispanic, and the methods of counting changed between 1970 and 1980. The 1980 census was the first one to ask every person whether or not they were of Spanish origin and, if so, to specify that origin. In 1970, by contrast, no Spanish-origin question was asked of all Americans, the government's Hispanic consciousness not yet having been raised.

Instead, the Census Bureau used four different methods, and, of course, they produced different results. Among these, the bureau considered residents of Arizona, California, Colorado, New Mexico, and Texas Hispanic if their surnames matched those on an official list of some 8,000 Hispanic surnames. If your name was "Lopez" in 1970, you became Hispanic whether or not you considered yourself Hispanic.

The total count of Hispanics from 1970 most commonly used as the basis for comparison with the 14.6 million Hispanics counted in 1980 was 9.1 million. This count was the result of a 5 percent national sample. Asking only 5 percent of the population to declare whether or not they consider themselves Hispanic is certain to produce a different number than asking the same question of everyone. Moreover, the rise in ethnic awareness that prompted the Census Bureau to pay more attention to Hispanic origin in 1980 also made it likely that more Americans would consider themselves Hispanic.

Nevertheless, the Census Bureau has declared that comparisons of Hispanics between 1970 and 1980 are valid for those states that contain many Hispanics, because the large numbers compensate for the differences caused by the switch in methods. Thus, it is safe to say that Hispanics nearly doubled their number in California—from 2.4 million in 1970 to the 4.5 million 1980 total. The share of U.S. Hispanics who live in California rose from 26 percent of the total to 31 percent of the total between 1970 and 1980. In Texas, second only to California in the size of its Hispanic population, the number of Hispanics rose 62 percent between the two censuses—from 1.8 million to 3 million.

The state with the third-largest concentration of Hispanics, New York, gained 300,000 Hispanic residents during the 1970s—a decade in which the state's total population did not grow at all. Almost all New York Hispanics live in the New York City area. Although New York State's Hispanic population grew 23 percent, that did not match their growth rates in California, Texas, and Florida. Florida's Hispanic population more than doubled, and its 1980 census count of 858,000 Hispanics does not include the wave of more than 100,000 Cubans that came ashore just after the 1980 census was taken.

Because a larger share is young, with higher birthrates, Hispanics should increase as a share of the total American population in the years ahead. The 1983 Current Population Survey counted 15.9 million Hispanics, up 9 percent since the census, and now representing 6.8 percent of Americans, but Hispanics will not soon outnumber blacks. Some newspaper stories have suggested that they will, but that prediction rests on exaggerated estimates of illegal Hispanic immigration that the

Census Bureau's own estimates show to be too high. Still, as Hispanic Americans approach 10 percent of the total population—they are already much more than that in some areas—they will become an increasingly important group, and the most important of all will be Mexican.

Already, 60 percent of all Hispanics in the United States are of Mexican origin, but that share will probably rise to as much as 66 percent by the turn of the century. The number of Mexican Americans will nearly double by the year 2000 because of their high fertility and continued immigration. Cubans are now just 5 percent of all Hispanics in the United States, and the Cuban population will grow the slowest of any Hispanic group. Migration from Cuba is lower than migration from Mexico, and Cubans have the lowest number of births per woman of any Hispanic group.

One common assumption about Hispanics is that their birthrates will fall to the level of Americans in general the longer they remain in the United States. This has been the pattern of other immigrant groups. A smaller proportion of tomorrow's Hispanic Americans, therefore, will be children, pushing up the median age of Hispanics. Nevertheless, because Mexican Americans have the lowest median age of all Hispanics and form such a large share of all Hispanics, the average Hispanic is likely to remain younger than the average American for decades to come.

Americans still tend to speak of Hispanics as a single group, but differences among Hispanics make it difficult for them to think or act as one. It is even more difficult for national Hispanic leaders to speak for all American Hispanics than it is for black leaders to speak for the nation's blacks. The three major Hispanic groups are so separated geographically, and have such different demographic characteristics, that they are unlikely to resemble each other more closely unless each group gradually becomes more like other Americans in education, language, household characteristics, income, and occupation. But in following the assimilation of other immigrant groups, their Hispanic identity may diminish.

America's notions about assimilation are built on the experience of groups that crossed oceans to come here. Mexicans need only walk and cross a river, and they become Americans in the census. Cubans and Puerto Ricans cannot walk into this country, but they do not have far to float or fly. This proximity works against assimilation. So close is Mexico, and so easy is the trip, that immigrants from Mexico may choose to remain Mexican in their language and culture, and impart these views to their children, even if they live and work across the border in the United States.

TRENDS TO WATCH

– Hispanics are becoming a larger share of Americans. Because they cluster in several of the nation's big cities, including Los Angeles, Miami, and New York, and in the Southwest, Hispanics have a strong cultural influence there.

– Hispanic groups—Mexicans, Puerto Ricans, and Cubans—differ widely in their demographics. They are more likely to assimilate into the dominant American culture than to become more like each other.

The Asians

"America's 3.5 million Asians as a group do not fit the image of a minority group—poor, downtrodden, or excluded."

For years, the U.S. government prevented Asians from joining the streams of European immigrants flowing to America. Then, in 1965, Congress opened the floodgates.

In 1965, the country admitted just 17,000 Asians, versus 114,000 Europeans. In 1981, 244,000 Asians immigrated to the United States, versus 67,000 Europeans.

After Mexico, the next four countries sending the largest number of immigrants to America in 1981 were all Asian—Vietnam, the Philippines, Korea, and China. India and Laos were also in the top-ten sending countries in 1981. The only European country in the top ten was the United Kingdom, in tenth place.

In contrast, in 1960, no Asian country was in the top ten; seven out of ten were European. Mexico, Canada, and Cuba were the only three non-European countries in the top ten in 1960, with Mexico number one, then as now. In 1981, Jamaica, the Dominican Republic, Mexico, and the United Kingdom were the only non-Asian countries.

Asian immigration may be just beginning. Asians comprise nearly

60 percent of the world's people—India and China together contain eight times as many people as live in the United States. As more Asians come to America, family and business ties with Asia will increase, encouraging even further migration.

Leon Bouvier of the Population Reference Bureau has projected that, if current trends continue, there will be over 8 million Asians and Pacific Islanders in the United States by the year 2000, up from the 3.5 million counted by the 1980 census. By the turn of the century, unless immigration slows, America will be far more Asian than it is today, with profound implications for American society, its tastes, culture, schools, and communities.

Since 1960, more immigrants have come to the United States from the Philippines than from any other country except Mexico. Immigrants from the countries of Indochina have increased over eightyfold, mostly as a result of the refugee programs put in place after the Vietnam war. Today, five Asian countries account for nearly 75 percent of all Asian immigration to the United States: Vietnam, the Philippines, Korea, China (including Hong Kong and Taiwan), and India.

So recent is the wave of Asians to the United States that only a decade ago it could not have been imagined that this country would become increasingly Asian in the future. In 1965, when Congress amended the immigration law, Representative Emanuel Celler (D., N.Y.) announced, "There will not be, comparatively, many Asians or Africans entering this country," as reported in *The New York Times*. He had no way of knowing how wrong he would be. An astonishing 92 percent of all Vietnamese in this country immigrated after 1970. Among Korean Americans, 68 percent are post-1970 immigrants; and 41 percent of Asian Indians in the United States arrived here after 1970, as have 42 percent of Filipinos.

One effect of this change in the countries of origin of America's Asians has been to change radically the ethnic characteristics of Asians in America. Just 14 percent of all Japanese Americans came to this country after 1970 and 17 percent of Chinese. In 1960, nine of ten Asians in America were Japanese, Chinese, and Filipino. Now, the figure is only two of three; the Japanese share has dropped by more than half.

In 1965, before Congress amended the immigration laws, China sent just 4,000 immigrants; in 1981, 25,800. Immigration from Japan increased scarcely at all, from 3,200 in 1965 to 3,900 in 1981. India, however, jumped from 582 to 21,500; Korea from 2,200 to 32,700; and the Philippines from 3,100 in 1965 to 43,800 in 1981. The other countries of Asia, primarily those of Indochina, supplied fewer than 4,000 immigrants to the United States in 1965; by 1981, the total had risen to 116,400. Vietnam alone supplied 23 percent of all Asian immigrants to the United States in 1981, versus less than 1 percent from 1960 to 1964, whereas Japan dropped from 24 percent of all Asian immigrants to less than 2 percent.

Asians come as students, tourists, or refugees and, increasingly, they send for their families. Unlike the image of the typical European immigrant arriving at Ellis Island to seek a new life, over half of all Asian immigrants in 1981 were already in the United States as refugees, visitors, or students and then adjusted their status to permanent resident.

America's 3.5 million Asians as a group do not fit the image of a minority group—poor, downtrodden, or excluded. On average, Asians have higher incomes and more education than the white majority. Compared to white Americans, proportionately more Asians are managers and professionals, a higher share of women are in the labor force, and relatively more live in families. These facts are remarkable, given that Asians are the newest immigrants of all and that many have come to the United States as refugees, unable to speak English. Still, a higher share of Asian families than of American families in general live in poverty, and more Asian family members contribute to their family's income.

Of the 14 million foreign-born Americans counted by the 1980 census, 18 percent were born in Asia. The 1980 census counted 806,000 Chinese; 775,000 Filipinos; 701,000 Japanese; 362,000 Asian Indians; 355,000 Koreans; 262,000 Vietnamese; 167,000 Hawaiians; 42,000 Samoans; and 32,000 Guamanians.

The Chinese are 23 percent of all Asians and Pacific Islanders in the United States; the Filipinos 22 percent; and the Japanese 20 percent. No other group is more than 10 percent.

Whereas 95 percent of white Americans were born in the United States, only 41 percent of U.S. Asians were born here. But there are important differences by race. Over 70 percent of Japanese Americans were born in the United States, but only 37 percent of the Chinese; 35 percent of the Filipinos, and fewer than 10 percent of the Vietnamese. The Japanese are the oldest wave of Asian immigrants, the Vietnamese the newest.

WHERE ASIANS LIVE

To an incredible degree, Asians concentrate in just a few states. California is home to 35 percent of the country's Asians and Pacific Islanders, Hawaii to 16 percent, and New York to 9 percent. Hawaii is the only state in which whites are a minority; Asians outnumber whites there by nearly two to one. California and Hawaii contain nearly three of every four Japanese Americans and two of every three Filipinos.

California and New York together contain a majority of Chinese Americans. A majority of the Vietnamese living in America are in just four states: California, Texas, Virginia, and Louisiana. One in three lives in California.

Less than one American in five lives in the West, but three of five Asians live in that region. In contrast, one American in three lives in the South, but just 13 percent of Asians. About 25 percent of Americans live in the Midwest, but just 11 percent of Asians. And 22 percent of all Americans live in the Northeast, compared with 16 percent of Asians and Pacific Islanders.

Asian Americans represent 60 percent of the total population of Honolulu; the Japanese are 25 percent of all Honolulu residents. In San Francisco, Asians and Pacific Islanders are 10 percent of the total metropolitan population, with the Chinese the largest group, at 4 percent. Los Angeles is 6 percent Asian, and Japanese Americans are the largest group. New York is the other metropolitan area in which Asians concentrate. There, 3 percent of the total are Asians, about 50 percent of them Chinese.

Asians are far more metropolitan than the American people as a whole—more than 90 percent live in metropolitan areas, equally divided between central cities and suburbs. Only 9 percent live outside the cities and their suburbs. However, only four American cities have concentrations of more than 50,000 Asians of any one ethnicity. More than 50,000 Japanese live in Honolulu and Los Angeles; more than 50,000 Chinese live in San Francisco, Honolulu, New York, and Los Angeles; more than 50,000 Filipinos live in Los Angeles, San Francisco, and Honolulu; and more than 50,000 Koreans live in Los Angeles.

Americans of an Asian or a Pacific race made up 1.5 percent of all Americans counted in the 1980 census. Excluding Hawaii, they made up just 1.3 percent. And if California were also excluded, they would have been a mere 0.7 percent. Still, some people may find it surprising that even Vermont, the state with the fewest Asian residents, had 1,355 in the 1980 census count. There are 14,000 Koreans in Texas and

19,000 Japanese in Illinois. No state has fewer than 13 Guamanians. Even Montana has 24 Samoans, and the census found 6 each in Arkansas and Delaware.

ASIANS' STATUS

The status of America's Asians varies depending on whether they are native born or were born abroad; how long they have lived in the United States; and their nationality. The median age for Asians and Pacific Islanders as a group in 1980 was twenty-nine years, a bit younger than the thirty years for Americans as a whole. But the median age for Japanese Americans was nearly thirty-four years, whereas for Samoans it was under twenty.

Nearly 50 percent of Asian Indians are managers or professionals, versus less than 25 percent of whites. But only 13 percent of Vietnamese are managers or professionals. Over 68 percent of Filipino women are in the labor force, but less than 47 percent of Samoan women.

The median family income for all Asians and Pacific Islanders was $22,700, as reported by the 1980 census, versus $19,900 for American families in general, and above the $20,800 for white families. Japanese median family income was about $27,000, for Koreans about $20,000; both far above the Vietnamese median of under $13,000. Over 30 percent of Vietnamese are below the poverty level, versus 13 percent of Koreans and just 4 percent of Japanese.

Although Asian immigrants have higher family income than whites, they also have more workers per family. The Asian immigrants who have come to this country since 1970 are more likely than whites to have three or more workers per family. Even for Asians born in the United States, more workers per family is one reason for their high family incomes. If Asian families had the same number of workers as white families, Asians would have lower incomes.

According to the 1980 census, 55 percent of families headed by a white person contain two earners or more, and 12 percent have at least three. For Asians, the comparable shares are 63 percent and 17 percent.

A higher share of America's Asians live in families than do whites, and a greater proportion of their families are married couples with children, but the differences are not great. Whereas 73 percent of whites live in families, 77 percent of Asian households are families. Thirty-one percent of white families are married couples with children, versus 42 percent for Asians.

Family characteristics differ by Asian ethnicity. The Japanese are the only Asian group in which the share of households containing married couples with children (29 percent) is less than among whites (36 percent), whereas half of Filipino and Vietnamese households are married couples with children. The average Vietnamese household contains 4.4 people, versus the 2.7 people for the average Japanese household in the United States.

It is in education that Asians stand out. Whereas 17 percent of white Americans aged twenty-five or older are college graduates, 33 percent of Asians and Pacific Islanders are college graduates. An incredible 52 percent of adult Asian Indians in the United States are college graduates, and more than 33 percent of Chinese and Filipinos.

INDOCHINESE AMERICANS

In 1960, a total of only 59 immigrants were admitted to the United States from Vietnam, Cambodia, and Laos combined, and all but 3 of these people came from Vietnam. Even by 1974, only about 18,000 Vietnamese refugees had been admitted to the United States, despite the war raging in Vietnam.

That is all history. In 1975, the United States admitted some 130,-000 Vietnamese and Cambodians following the fall of Saigon. The totals dropped for the next two years before rising to 167,000 in 1979, and 133,000 in 1980. When Congress passed the Refugee Act of 1980, a year in which over 100,000 Cubans and Haitians also arrived on these shores, the total number of Southeast Asians admitted to the United States rose by nearly two thirds in a single year.

But these new arrivals went uncounted by the 1980 census, which was taken on April 1, the same day the refugee act was passed. Census statistics understate the number of Vietnamese, Cambodians, and Laotians living in America. By the middle of 1984, according to the Office of Refugee Resettlement in Washington, a total of some 700,000 Southeast Asian refugees had arrived in the United States. They now constitute more than one Asian American in five.

About 90 percent of this country's more than 100,000 Cambodians have arrived since 1980, and 66 percent of its nearly 150,000 Laotians. The biggest single year for Vietnamese refugees to arrive in the United States was 1975. Still, since 1980, more than 250,000 Vietnamese, or over half the total Vietnamese population of this country, arrived in the United States. These new arrivals are markedly different from other Americans, and even other Asians.

The U.S. government tried to spread these newer refugees through-out the country—in contrast to other Asian groups who have clustered together—and Southeast Asian refugees were at first more dispersed than other Asian immigrants. No state has fewer than 100, except Alaska. Even so, California now contains more than one Southeast Asian refugee in three because refugees have moved there from other parts of the country to join relatives and friends. The Vietnamese also cluster in Texas, Washington, Pennsylvania, New York, Louisiana, and the District of Columbia. Concentrations of Laotians can be found in places as far flung as Minnesota, Rhode Island, and Oregon.

America is still digesting its Indochinese refugees, and they, in turn, are still having difficulty adapting to life in a strange land. However, these new arrivals are likely to learn English, find jobs, and rise in education and economic status as other immigrant groups have done before them. One study by the Office of Refugee Resettlement found that whereas refugees as a whole had unemployment rates below those of the total population, the first waves who arrived from 1975 to 1978 are now more likely to be employed than the average American. Although their income is still below the U.S. average, it is rising as family members find jobs, aided by government efforts to educate and settle America's newest immigrants.

There are still well over 100,000 refugees in resettlement camps in Southeast Asia. About 40,000 per year have entered the United States in recent years, and the U.S. government plans to admit some 50,000 more to the United States in 1985. But soon these refugee waves may diminish. In addition, about 12,000 Vietnamese are eligible to enter the United States each year under the Orderly Departure Program that was agreed to by the United States and Vietnam.

Most refugees apply for permanent immigrant status as they become eligible to do so. Once they obtain citizenship, they are able to bring in family members under the quotas established by immigration law. Thus, America is likely to continue gaining new immigrants from Vietnam, Cambodia, and Laos, although each new wave is unlikely to equal the flood of refugees of the past few years.

PACIFIC ISLANDERS

Pacific Islanders are swallowed up in the larger pool of Asian Americans. The 1980 census counted just under 260,000 Pacific Islanders, a mere 7 percent of the total Asian and Pacific Islander population. Two thirds of them are Hawaiian. Adding to Hawaii the other islands of Polynesia, principally Samoa and Tonga, Polynesian Americans are 85 percent of all Pacific Islanders in the United States.

Micronesians are 14 percent, and almost all of them are Guamanian. Melanesians are a mere 1.3 percent, and almost all of them are Fijian.

The 1980 census was the first in history to collect statistics separately for any of these island races except Hawaiians. We now know something about how the nation's 2,800 Fijians, 6,200 Tongans, 30,700 Guamanians, and 40,000 Samoans are faring.

More than 50 percent of all Pacific Islander Americans live in Hawaii. California and Hawaii together contain more than 75 percent of Pacific Islanders in the United States. In all, the West is home to 86 percent of this country's Pacific Islanders.

Twenty-nine percent of Tongans live in Utah. Mormon missionaries have been active in Tonga. If you have never been to California, Utah, or Hawaii (or Tonga), your odds of having ever met a Tongan are low. These three states are home to 91 percent of America's Tongans; only 579 Tongan Americans live outside these states. Your odds are also low within these states as well, however, because a total of only 5,647 Tongans live there.

Guamanians favor California over Hawaii; over 55 percent (17,000) live in California, and just 5 percent (1,600) in Hawaii. Seventy-three percent of Fijians live in California and just 9 percent in Hawaii. Samoans are spread more evenly between California and Hawaii. Hawaiians, it is no surprise, concentrate in Hawaii, where 69 percent (118,000) live. Another 14 percent live in California. Pacific Islanders are more urban than other Americans; virtually all Samoans, Tongans, and Guamanians cluster in urban areas, chiefly San Francisco, Los Angeles, and Honolulu.

Pacific Islander Americans are much younger than other Americans. Twice as high a share of Tongans and Samoans than of Americans in general are under five years old, for example. More than six Samoans in ten are under the age of twenty-five, versus just over four of every ten Americans as a whole. About 11 percent of all Americans had reached the age of sixty-five at the time of the census, but just 6 percent of Hawaiians and 2 percent of Samoans and Guamanians.

A disproportionate share of U.S. residents from the islands of Micronesia other than Guam (the census counted only about 5,000 such people) are in their twenties; 23 percent are aged twenty to twenty-four, compared to only 9 percent of all Americans. The reason is that most of them have come to the United States for schooling, taking advantage of the financial assistance offered them as residents of U.S. trust territories. A high 58 percent of these Micronesians are enrolled in college, the census reports, versus 20 percent of all Americans. Twenty-three percent of Guamanians are in college, but only 14 percent of Samoans or Hawaiians.

One reason for the younger age profile is that a high share of Pacific Islander Americans are immigrants, who tend to be young adults. Also, Pacific Islanders have higher fertility than the U.S. average, and a relatively small share of older Pacific Islanders have moved to America.

Because they are younger than the average American and have more children, Pacific Islander families are larger than the typical American family. For Samoans and Tongans, average household size is over four people, compared to fewer than three for American households in general. Another reason household size is larger is that extended families are more common. In fact, among Tongans and Samoans, some six out of ten household residents were relatives and not part of the nuclear family, the Census Bureau has reported.

Even so small a group as Pacific Islanders differ from each other demographically, according to their origins. Samoans have the lowest incomes—a median family income of just $14,200 in the 1980 census, for example. Three times as high a share of Samoan families lived in poverty in 1979 as the general population. Poverty is a problem for other Pacific Islanders as well: Twice as high a share of Tongans as all Americans lived in poverty. The poverty rates for Hawaiians and Guamanians were also above the U.S. average.

Pacific Islanders have yet to assimilate. Forty percent of Samoans speak their native language at home, 25 percent of Micronesians, and even 20 percent of Hawaiians. Whereas 89 percent of Americans speak only English, just 50 percent of Guamanians know only English, 23 percent of Samoans, and 12 percent of Tongans. Excluding Guamanians, who are U.S. citizens, and Hawaiians, who were born in the United States, a total of 46,000 Pacific Islanders counted in the 1980 census were born on a Pacific Island including twenty-seven on Pitcairn Island, twenty on Wallis and Futuna, twenty-seven on Nauru, and thirty on Vanuatu.

Although America's Pacific Islanders are a long way from home, in the age of jet travel many return home after receiving schooling in the United States or after working at temporary jobs. In this they differ from Asians, who like the Europeans before them, are more likely to come to America to start a new life. Many Pacific Islanders may be only temporary residents of the United States. Most Pacific Islander immigrants are from U.S. territories, or the former Trust Territory of the Pacific Islands, and movement from these places to American shores is less restricted than from foreign countries. If residents of Hawaii can send their children to Boston for college, so can the residents of Guam.

THE ASIAN FUTURE

Not only the number but also the characteristics of America's Asians will continue to change in the future, shaped by new patterns of migration. More Americans will have an Asian heritage, and proportionately fewer Asian Americans will be Japanese. But to pinpoint the future characteristics of immigrant Asians is impossible. Not only could Congress change legislation and lower total immigration, including Asian, but also current immigration patterns may change.

In demographer Leon Bouvier's population projections, which are based on current trends, not only will the number of Asian Americans more than double by the turn of the century but their ethnic composition will also shift radically. In a decade or two, the number of Filipinos in the United States will outnumber Japanese by nearly two to one, and Filipinos will outnumber Chinese to become the largest Asian racial group in the United States. Koreans will also pass the Japanese, rising from just over 350,000 in 1980 to a projected 1.8 million in 2000. Given the current regional distribution of Asian Americans, California will have an increasingly Asian appearance, with some 2.7 million Asians and Pacific Islanders by the turn of the century.

America has never been a completely homogeneous society, but over the years the differences that Americans perceived between European immigrants—the Irish, the Italians, the Germans—have been reduced by assimilation. Today, the sharp differences are between white mainstream Americans—the Anglo or European—and the new Asian immigrants. Will assimilation work for these groups as it has for others? Is Hawaii representative of America's racial future? There, interracial couples are so common as to be unremarkable, and children are of every hue.

Although birthrates are dropping in Asia, the region's population is huge—and growing more rapidly than the population of the Western world. America may not continue to absorb immigrants at the pace it has absorbed them in the recent past, but those it does welcome will increasingly cross the Pacific instead of the Atlantic. And that will continue to change the face of America.

TRENDS TO WATCH

– Asians will grow in numbers; in share of the total American people; and in educational, occupational, and income status.

– A diminishing share of Asian Americans will be Japanese, the oldest wave of Asians. The origins of most of today's immigrants from Asia are the Philippines, Korea, China, and India.

Chapter 10

Black and White Gaps

"The overriding difference between black and white households today is that black households are more than three times as likely to have a woman at their head. . . .

"The poverty of black families headed by women is so pervasive that it masks the economic progress made by black families that contain married couples."

America's blacks may be better off today than before the civil rights movement of the 1960s, but little on the horizon suggests that they will soon catch up to whites. Although there is now a black middle class, and some blacks have made striking progress, others lag even further behind.

It has been two decades since the federal government passed laws to end discrimination in education, housing, and the labor force. Blacks have advanced in education, but the black family structure—so different from that of whites—contributes to lower income and more poverty for a much higher share of blacks than of whites.

For half a century, America's black minority has steadily become a larger part of the total population. Before 1930, however, blacks were shrinking as a share of the total population. Then almost all immigrants were white, and immigration was an important part of population growth.

Two hundred years ago, according to the first census, blacks comprised 19 percent of all Americans, and 92 percent of blacks were slaves. By 1930, the proportion of blacks in the population had fallen by nearly half, to 9.7 percent. By 1950, however, the black share had risen again, to 9.9 percent, and then to 10.5 percent in 1960.

The proportion of black Americans has continued to rise, from 11.1 percent in 1970 to 11.7 percent in 1980. The 1980 census counted 26.5 million blacks in a total population of 226.5 million Americans. In 1983, there were an estimated 28.2 million blacks, or 12 percent of the American population. By the year 2000, the number of blacks should grow to 36 million in a total population of 268 million, or 13 percent of Americans. By the middle of the next century, blacks probably will be about 17 percent of all Americans—some 52 million in a total population of 309 million.

The number of blacks is growing faster than the number of whites, not only because a smaller share of today's immigrants are white but also because blacks have proportionately more children than whites. The average black woman has 2.2 children in her lifetime, whereas the average white woman has 1.7. As a result, blacks are a larger share of young Americans than their share of the total population, and relatively more blacks than whites are in their childbearing years.

Black Americans had a baby boom just as whites did, and it was even larger, relatively, than for whites. Blacks born between 1955 and 1964, the peak years of the baby boom, represented 22 percent of all blacks counted by the 1980 census. Whites born during the same period were only 18 percent of all whites. The ensuing decline in fertility in the late 1960s and the 1970s that created a baby bust was much less steep for blacks than whites. Blacks under age fifteen represent 29 percent of all blacks counted in the 1980 census, but whites under age fifteen are just 21 percent of all whites.

In life expectancy, all Americans are not created equal. On average, blacks do not live as long as whites. At birth, a white girl can expect to live to age seventy-eight, a black girl to age seventy-two. A newborn white boy's odds are to live until age seventy-one, a black's to age sixty-four. The life-expectancy gap between the races has narrowed, however, because infant mortality has declined rapidly for blacks. Whites in 1900 lived an average of sixteen years longer than blacks. Still, black infant mortality is twice that of white infant mortality, and death rates for black youths are much higher than those for white youths.

Differences in fertility and in life expectancy by race and sex combine to have a powerful impact on the relative sizes of the black and white elderly populations. Whereas 12 percent of whites are aged sixty-five or older, only 8 percent of blacks have reached age sixty-five. The ratio of women to men is higher for blacks than for whites. Women are a majority of whites, 51 percent, but an even greater majority—53 percent—of blacks.

For those who reach age sixty-five, however, the gap in life expectancy between the races has shrunk to only one year for men and two for women. The sex balance in old age is more favorable for blacks than for whites. Only 43 white men are left alive per 100 white women by age eighty-five, but 50 black men per 100 black women.

The proportion of blacks who live to be 100 is greater than that of whites. But research has discovered that older people tend to exaggerate their age—particularly as they approach the triple digits—and those who are less well educated and poorer than others are more likely to overstate their age. The 1980 census found that states with the highest proportion of blacks among the general population also reported the highest proportion of centenarians. Mississippi had the highest of all—twenty-four centenarians for every 100,000 residents; next was Washington, D.C., with twenty-two and Arkansas with twenty.

In contrast, states with the smallest proportion of centenarians tend to have a small share of blacks among the total number of residents. The states that had the smallest share of reported centenarians were the almost all-white states of Nevada and Utah, where the 1980 census could find only six centenarians per 100,000 population. As with centenarians in general, the exact number of black centenarians remains a mystery.

If there are fewer blacks in their hundreds in fact than in census statistics, there are also more black men who are young in fact than in the statistics. According to the 1980 census, there are 277,000 more black women than men between the ages of twenty and twenty-nine, a 12 percent difference. Among whites, the gap is much smaller—and it is in the opposite direction. The census counted almost 104,000 more white men than women aged twenty to twenty-nine. Among black teens aged fifteen to nineteen, there are almost 7,000 more women than men, whereas among whites in this age group men outnumber women by more than 306,000.

Part of the explanation is higher mortality for young black men, but another important part is the census undercount. Historically, young black men are the most likely of all Americans to be missed by the census. Census takers have difficulty reaching low-income people, those frequently on the move, and those who are harder to persuade that the national interest impels them to answer the census.

After the 1980 census, a follow-up survey and a match of the census returns with other records estimated that the census failed to count 1.3 million blacks, or nearly 5 percent of all blacks. Although the census missed only 2 percent of black women, it missed almost four times as many black men, or some 7.5 percent. Among black men aged thirty-five to forty-four, the undercount was as much as 16 percent.

FRAGMENTING FAMILIES

The black male is harder for the census to pin down because the black family is in fragments. The overriding difference between black and white households today is that black households are more than three times as likely to have a woman at their head. Among blacks, 38 percent of families are headed by a woman, versus only 11 percent of white families. In 1981, over 50 percent of black births were to unmarried women, compared with only 19 percent of births to Americans in general.

Nearly 50 percent of all never-married black women have had a child, compared with only 7 percent of never-married white women. In 1982, only 44 percent of black women were married, compared with 60 percent of white women in America. More black children now live with their mother only than with both parents. Whereas 81 percent of white children live with two parents, just 42 percent of black children do. And 8 percent of black children live with neither parent—four times the share of white children.

In 1982, more than one black family in four was headed by a woman with children under the age of eighteen, but without a husband, versus about one in twelve for whites. In 1960, there was only an 8 percentage point difference between blacks and whites in the share of single-parent families headed by women. By 1982, the difference had grown to 21 percentage points.

A smaller share of black households and white households alike contain married couples than in the past, but here too the gap between the races is widening. Only 39 percent of households headed by blacks contain a husband and wife, versus 62 percent of white households.

Two decades ago, 60 percent of black households contained married couples, and 76 percent of white households. The black family is far more likely to be headed by a woman today than in 1970.

Blacks are far more likely than whites to divorce. As of 1981, for every 1,000 married blacks, 233 got divorced, an enormous increase from the 92 per 1,000 a decade earlier. In contrast, 100 of every 1,000 married whites divorced in 1981, up from 48 in 1971. The doubling of the divorce rate among whites has been the subject of endless debate about America's changing life-styles. Less noticed has been the fact that the black divorce rate increased half again as much as the rate for whites.

One can debate the reasons for these differences between the black and white family. Blacks carry the legacy of slavery in America; the black family structure has never been as nuclear as the white. Black women have long had to assume responsibilities that white women have been spared. Black kinship networks, rather than the nuclear family, may be a way that blacks survive better in a society in which they have always been the underclass, hardest hit by recessions and inflation. Whatever the reasons for the fragmenting black family structure, changes in the family during the 1970s pushed an estimated 2 million people into poverty, and a large share of them were black.

If changes in family composition had not affected blacks more than whites, the average income of black families would have risen more rapidly during the 1970s than the average income of white families rose. In per capita income, a measure unaffected by changes in family structure, blacks have moved closer to whites. But in family income, they have moved further behind, because of family fragmentation.

The median income of white families rose to $21,904 in 1980, up slightly from an inflation-adjusted $21,722 in 1970. But black families, overall, had a median income of $12,674 in 1980, below their $13,325 income in 1970, after adjusting for inflation.

The poverty of black families headed by women is so pervasive that it masks the economic progress made by black families that contain married couples. Black husband-wife families narrowed the income gap with white married couples during the past decade. In 1970, their incomes were only 73 percent as much, but in 1980 they moved closer to 79 percent as much. Among those husband-wife families in which the wife was in the labor force, black family income was 84 percent of white family income in 1980.

In the past, as black women went to work to supplement their husband's wages, black families were even more likely than white families to have a working wife. But black families now are less likely than white families to have a working wife; the two trend lines crossed in 1972. Today, 42 percent of white families have a working wife, but only 32 percent of black families, because so many black families today are single-parent families headed by women, instead of married couples.

Some blacks have made great progress in occupational prestige, but blacks as a group are more likely to be unemployed today than a generation ago. Black youths, who form a higher share of all blacks than white youths do of whites, have a particular unemployment problem. Young whites and blacks once were equally likely to hold a job, but in 1983, the unemployment gap was more than 20 percentage points. Whereas 19 percent of whites between the ages of sixteen and nineteen were unemployed, nearly 50 percent of black youths were out of a job. Considering all age groups, one black in five was unemployed in 1983, versus one white in twelve.

Black Americans are much more likely to live in poverty than whites. Among black families, 33 percent were living in poverty in 1982, compared to only 10 percent of white families. Over half the black female-headed households live in poverty, compared to just over one quarter of such households headed by whites. A black underclass remains untouched by opportunity, unable to find jobs, no longer even counted as looking for work, because they have given up.

The poorest blacks are further behind the wealthiest blacks than ever before. A minority of blacks have advanced their status following changes in laws and attitudes that reduced racial discrimination. They have joined the middle class, live as married couples, work as professionals, and have incomes closer to those of similar whites than was true a decade ago. But the blacks who remain at the bottom of the economic order are still so numerous, and their number grew so much during the 1970s, that they dominate the racial statistics, obscuring the gains of other black Americans.

WHERE BLACKS LIVE

For most of this century, blacks were moving out of the South in growing numbers. But during the 1970s, they started moving back. This trend reflects the South's change of heart about blacks and the change of heart blacks have had about the South. In the 1960s, as the civil rights movement took hold, the South lost a net of 1.4 million blacks.

But in the late 1970s, the South gained a net of over 195,000 blacks—
a striking turnaround. Before the 1970s, blacks had always moved out
of the South in greater numbers than they had moved (voluntarily) to
the South. For the first decade ever, the Northeast and North-Central
regions lost more black residents than they gained, a net loss of 226,000
between 1975 and 1980.

Up to the turn of the century, more than 90 percent of all black
Americans lived in the South, compared to less than 25 percent of all
white Americans. By 1980, following years of black flight, the percentage of blacks who lived in the South had dropped to 53 percent, while
the share of whites had risen to 31 percent. According to the 1980
census, 18 percent of blacks live in the Northeast, compared to 22
percent of whites; 20 percent of blacks live in the North-Central Region, compared to 28 percent of whites. Less than 9 percent of blacks
live in the West, compared to 19 percent of whites.

Blacks were not the only Americans heading South and West in the
1970s, so their share of the total population in each of the nation's four
regions changed little during the decade. Blacks are now 19 percent of
the South's population, 5 percent of the West's, 10 percent of the
Northeast's, and 9 percent of the North-Central Region's total population.

Table 12 BLACK POPULATION, 1980 CENSUS

United States, 26,495,025

States		Cities	
1 New York	2,402,006	1 New York, NY	1,788,377
2 California	1,819,281	2 Chicago, IL	1,197,174
3 Texas	1,710,175	3 Detroit, MI	758,468
4 Illinois	1,675,398	4 Philadelphia, PA	638,788
5 Georgia	1,465,181	5 Los Angeles, CA	504,301
6 Florida	1,342,688	6 Washington, DC	448,370
7 North Carolina	1,318,857	7 Houston, TX	439,604
8 Louisiana	1,238,241	8 Baltimore, MD	430,934
9 Michigan	1,199,023	9 New Orleans, LA	308,039
10 Ohio	1,076,748	10 Memphis, TN	307,573
11 Pennsylvania	1,046,810	11 Atlanta, GA	283,158
12 Virginia	1,008,668	12 Dallas, TX	265,105
13 Alabama	996,335	13 Cleveland, OH	251,084
14 Maryland	958,150	14 St. Louis, MO	206,170
15 South Carolina	948,623	15 Newark, NJ	191,968
16 New Jersey	925,066	16 Oakland, CA	159,351
17 Mississippi	887,206	17 Birmingham, AL	158,200

States		Cities	
18 Tennessee	725,942	18 Indianapolis, IN	152,590
19 Missouri	514,276	19 Milwaukee, WI	147,055
20 Indiana	414,785	20 Jacksonville, FL	137,150
21 Arkansas	373,768	21 Cincinnati, OH	130,490
22 Kentucky	259,477	22 Boston, MA	126,438
23 Massachusetts	221,279	23 Columbus, OH	124,689
24 Connecticut	217,433	24 Kansas City, MO	122,336
25 Oklahoma	204,674	25 Richmond, VA	112,426
26 Wisconsin	182,592	26 Gary, IN	107,539
27 Kansas	126,127	27 Nashville–Davidson, TN	105,869
28 Washington	105,574	28 Pittsburgh, PA	101,549
29 Colorado	101,703	29 Charlotte, NC	97,896
30 Delaware	95,845	30 Buffalo, NY	95,622
31 Arizona	74,977	31 Jackson, MS	95,218
32 West Virginia	65,051	32 Norfolk, VA	93,977
33 Minnesota	53,344	33 Fort Worth, TX	87,635
34 Nevada	50,999	34 Miami, FL	87,018
35 Nebraska	48,390	35 San Francisco, CA	86,190
36 Iowa	41,700	36 Shreveport, LA	84,691
37 Oregon	37,060	37 Louisville, KY	84,254
38 Rhode Island	27,584	38 Baton Rouge, LA	79,848
39 New Mexico	24,020	39 San Diego, CA	77,508
40 Hawaii	17,364	40 Dayton, OH	75,136
41 Alaska	13,643	41 Mobile, AL	72,697
42 Utah	9,225	42 Montgomery, AL	69,821
43 New Hampshire	3,990	43 Savannah, GA	69,265
44 Wyoming	3,364	44 Flint, MI	66,060
45 Maine	3,128	45 East Orange, NJ	64,650
46 Idaho	2,716	46 Tampa, FL	63,578
47 North Dakota	2,568	47 Rochester, NY	62,256
48 South Dakota	2,144	48 Jersey City, NJ	61,957
49 Montana	1,786	49 Toledo, OH	61,855
50 Vermont	1,135	50 Compton, CA	60,874

Source: 1980 census

The 1980 census counted 2.3 million blacks in the West, 4.8 million in the Northeast, 5.3 million in the North-Central States, and 14 million in the South. Until 1930, no census ever found more than 100,000 blacks in the entire West. Blacks began moving to California in large numbers after 1940. Between that year and 1960, California's black population rose from 124,000 to 884,000; today, it is approaching 2 million. Eighty percent of all blacks who live in the West make their home in California, as do 50 percent of western whites. But New York has the largest black population of any state, with 2.4 million.

After New York and California, the states that are home to the most blacks are Texas, Illinois, Georgia, Florida, North Carolina, Louisiana, Michigan, Ohio, Pennsylvania, and Virginia. Each of these states has more than 1 million blacks, and together they are home to more than 17 million blacks. Sixty-five percent of America's black population live in these twelve states, versus 55 percent of all whites.

Vermont has the fewest blacks of any state—just 1,135, according to the census. Montana is home to only 1,786 blacks; South Dakota, 2,144; North Dakota, 2,568; Idaho, 2,716; Maine, 3,128; Wyoming, 3,364; and New Hampshire, 3,990. Utah has 9,225 blacks. These nine states, the only states with fewer than 10,000 blacks, together have less than 1 percent of the nation's total black population. For that matter, they have only 4 percent of its total white population.

Blacks are a majority in 90 of the nation's counties, concentrated in the South. More than half of the residents in 22 of Mississippi's 82 counties are black. Blacks are a majority in 19 Georgia counties, 12 in South Carolina, and 10 in Alabama. Macon County, Alabama, has the highest percentage black population of any county, 84 percent. The 1980 census located not a single black person in 170 counties. Of these, 28 counties were in Nebraska, 22 in Montana, and 21 in South Dakota. In some of these sparse rural counties, the census could not find many whites either.

Table 13 PERCENT BLACK IN 1980 CENSUS

U.S. Average, 11.7 Percent

States		Cities	
1 Mississippi	35.2%	1 East St. Louis, IL	95.6%
2 South Carolina	30.4	2 East Orange, NJ	83.2
3 Louisiana	29.4	3 Compton, CA	74.9
4 Georgia	26.8	4 Gary, IN	70.8
5 Alabama	25.6	5 Washington, DC	70.2
6 Maryland	22.7	6 Atlanta, GA	66.6
7 North Carolina	22.4	7 Detroit, MI	63.0
8 Virginia	18.9	8 Newark, NJ	58.3
9 Arkansas	16.3	9 Inglewood, CA	57.3
10 Delaware	16.1	10 Birmingham, AL	55.6
11 Tennessee	15.8	11 New Orleans, LA	55.3
12 Illinois	14.7	12 Baltimore, MD	54.8
13 Florida	13.8	13 Camden, NJ	53.0
14 New York	13.7	14 Richmond, VA	51.3
15 Michigan	12.9	15 Wilmington, DE	51.2
16 New Jersey	12.6	16 Pine Bluff, AR	49.1

States		Cities	
17 Texas	12.0	17 Savannah, GA	49.0
18 Missouri	10.5	18 Monroe, LA	48.6
19 Ohio	10.0	19 Mount Vernon, NY	48.4
20 Pennsylvania	8.8	20 Richmond, CA	47.9
21 California	7.7	21 Alexandria, LA	47.8
22 Indiana	7.6	22 Memphis, TN	47.6
23 Kentucky	7.1	23 Albany, GA	47.5
24 Connecticut	7.0	24 Durham, NC	47.1
25 Oklahoma	6.8	25 Oakland, CA	47.0
26 Nevada	6.4	26 Jackson, MS	46.9
27 Kansas	5.3	27 Charleston, SC	46.6
28 Wisconsin	3.9	28 St. Louis, MO	45.5
29 Massachusetts	3.9	29 Trenton, NJ	45.4
30 Colorado	3.5	30 Portsmouth, VA	45.1
31 Alaska	3.4	31 Macon, GA	44.5
32 West Virginia	3.3	32 Cleveland, OH	43.8
33 Nebraska	3.1	33 Harrisburg, PA	43.6
34 Rhode Island	2.9	34 Flint, MI	41.4
35 Arizona	2.8	35 Shreveport, LA	41.2
36 Washington	2.6	36 Fayetteville, NC	40.9
37 New Mexico	1.8	37 Port Arthur, TX	40.6
38 Hawaii	1.8	38 Columbia, SC	40.3
39 Iowa	1.4	39 Winston-Salem, NC	40.2
40 Oregon	1.4	40 Chicago, IL	39.8
41 Minnesota	1.3	41 Montgomery, AL	39.3
42 Wyoming	0.7	42 Irvington, NJ	38.1
43 Utah	0.6	43 Lake Charles, LA	38.0
44 New Hampshire	0.4	44 Philadelphia, PA	37.8
45 North Dakota	0.4	45 Pontiac, MI	37.1
46 South Dakota	0.3	46 Dayton, OH	36.9
47 Idaho	0.3	47 Beaumont, TX	36.6
48 Maine	0.3	48 Baton Rouge, LA	36.4
49 Montana	0.2	49 Mobile, AL	36.3
50 Vermont	0.2	50 Greenville, SC	35.6

Source: 1980 census

Mississippi has the largest concentration of blacks of any state, 35 percent; 30 percent of South Carolina residents are black. In five other states more than one resident in five is black: 29 percent in Louisiana; 27 percent in Georgia; 26 percent in Alabama; 23 percent in Maryland; and 22 percent in North Carolina. The District of Columbia, which the Census Bureau counts as a state, is 70 percent black.

A few southern states lost blacks during the 1960s, but gained in the 1970s. South Carolina lost 40,000 blacks in the 1960s, but gained 160,000 in the 1970s. Alabama lost 77,000 in the 1960s, but gained

93,000 in the 1970s. Mississippi, which lost 100,000 of its black residents during the 1960s, gained 71,000 during the 1970s. Arkansas lost 37,000 blacks between 1960 and 1970, but gained 22,000 between 1970 and 1980. West Virginia and Montana were the only states that lost blacks in the 1970s. Every other state, North or South, saw an increase in the number of blacks since 1970—even New York and Rhode Island, both states in which the total population dropped during the 1970s. This is one consequence of higher black fertility.

Reversing the historic trend, blacks have been moving to the suburbs. The percentage of blacks who live in central cities declined between 1970 and 1980, mirroring the general migration trend. The 1980 census found 58 percent of all blacks in central cities, a drop from the 60 percent a decade earlier. However, blacks were a greater share of all central-city residents in 1980 than in 1970. In 1970, blacks were 20 percent of all central-city residents; but by 1980, they had risen to over 22 percent. Whites were fleeing the central cities even faster than were blacks.

Whereas blacks leaving central cities settled in the suburbs (not necessarily in the suburbs of the city they left), whites settled in the small cities, towns, and villages beyond metropolitan America. The number of whites who live in nonmetropolitan areas grew 14 percent in the 1970s; the number of blacks in nonmetropolitan areas grew less than 7 percent. Only 19 percent of blacks now live in nonmetropolitan areas, versus 27 percent of whites. Even more significant, the share of all blacks who live in nonmetropolitan areas has dropped from its level in 1970, when 21 percent of blacks lived beyond cities and suburbs.

The number of blacks who live in the suburbs grew 43 percent in the 1970s, while the number of whites living in the suburbs grew just 13 percent. The suburbs are now home to 23 percent of all blacks, up from only 19 percent in 1970. As a result of these trends, blacks today form a greater share not only of central-city residents but also of all metropolitan residents than in 1970. Blacks were 12.7 pecent of all metropolitan Americans in 1980, up from 11.6 percent in 1970.

If it were not for the large share of blacks who live in the rural South, blacks would be even more metropolitan than these statistics show. Blacks are still much less metropolitan in the South than elsewhere. Outside the South, virtually all of America's blacks live in the central cities and their suburbs. The blacks who are moving to the South from other regions also are settling in metropolitan areas, not returning to the small farms.

The term *suburbs* may suggest green lawns, barbecues, and middle-class families, but there are distinctions. Some blacks are moving to the stereotypical surburbs and integrating white neighborhoods, but about twice as many blacks as whites move to the low-income inner suburbs closest to the central city, a Rand Corporation study has reported. Black suburbanites have higher incomes and more education than blacks who live in central cities, but they have a much lower economic status than whites. The inner suburbs of large central cities could become the urban ghettos of the future.

More than 25 percent of all blacks lived in seven of the nation's largest metropolitan areas in 1980—New York, Chicago, Detroit, Philadelphia, Washington, D.C., Los Angeles, and Baltimore. The great majority of these residents live within the central city. In New York City, blacks are 25 percent of all residents, up from 21 percent a decade earlier. Forty percent of Chicago residents are black, compared to 33 percent in 1970. In Philadelphia, blacks have risen from 34 percent of all residents in 1970 to 38 percent in 1980.

Blacks increasingly dominate the nation's central cities. In 1960, only two central cities had a black majority: Charleston, South Carolina, and Washington, D.C. Today the list also includes Atlanta, Detroit, Baltimore, Newark, New Orleans, Richmond, Gary, and Birmingham. According to projections by the Joint Center for Political Studies, a Washington, D.C., nonprofit research organization, more than fifty cities will have a black majority by the year 2000—up from only ten in 1980. Of these, thirty-six will be in the South.

As the big cities gain black residents and a larger proportion of city residents are black, more big cities will elect black mayors. Blacks will increasingly dominate America's urban politics. Black mayors now represent more than 13 million big-city residents, the Joint Center reported. Black mayors in 1983 headed twenty-seven cities with 50,000 or more residents. Eleven of these cities have black majorities, and another five are at least 40 percent black. America has about 250 black mayors, according to the Joint Center. As large city after large city elects black mayors, black voices will speak louder on the national scene.

But though their voices may be louder, a smaller share of all Americans, black or white, live in the big cities that elect black mayors. Blacks are gaining in urban power because whites are moving out of central cities faster than blacks. Migration trends are contributing to a growing imbalance between the political visibility of blacks as spokespeople for the problems of the cities and the influence city leaders have over the rest of the nation.

Black voters could become a potentially important force in states that have high proportions of black residents. However, because of their younger average age, blacks are not as large a share of the voting-age population as they are of the total population. Nevertheless nearly 33 percent of Mississippi's voting-age population is black; 27 percent of South Carolina's and Louisiana's; 24 percent of Georgia's; and 23 percent of Alabama's. Because black fertility is not dropping as fast as white fertility in states that now contain large numbers of black residents, a growing share of potential voters in the future will be black, unless migration patterns alter the balance.

In the past, few blacks have registered to vote. Only 51 percent of blacks in North Carolina, and 50 percent in Georgia, for example, registered to vote in the 1982 elections. Nationally, 66 percent of whites, but just 59 percent of blacks, registered to vote in those elections. In the 1980 presidential election, 61 percent of voting-age whites cast a ballot, but only 51 percent of blacks. Among white registered voters, 89 percent cast a ballot, versus 84 percent of blacks.

White voter participation has been declining, but black voter participation has been increasing. In the 1984 Democratic presidential primaries, Jesse Jackson's candidacy reflected the new optimism of black voters and encouraged more blacks to register as voters and to participate in politics. In the 1980 elections, blacks increased their voter-participation rate, but whites and Hispanics did not. Is this trend a sign of things to come?

TRENDS TO WATCH

– By some measures blacks, overall, are further behind whites in economic well-being than they were in 1970, though a portion of the black population has moved closer to whites in status.

– The economic gaps between blacks themselves are growing, and differences in family structure are the major reason.

– Blacks are more concentrated in the cities, where their political power has risen. But the impact of this concentration on national politics is weakened by the decline in the share of Americans who live in big cities.

Chapter
11

What Color Is Your Collar?

"The surge of women into the labor force is a milestone, not only for women but also for the American economy. Had the economy not moved rapidly from manufacturing and agricultural industries to service industries, finance, public administration, and communications, the women's revolution might still be on the drawing boards."

Getting to know the American worker used to be easy. You could find him in a factory, on a farm, or at the office. The color of his collar was blue or white. And he was a he. But things are no longer so simple.

Americans still work in factories, on farms, and at offices, but a growing share work in hospitals, banks, restaurants, and computer centers. Professional and technical jobs have grown almost two and a half times as fast as all jobs have grown in the past twenty years. Half of all job growth in the 1970s occurred in just two occupational categories—professional and technical workers, and clerical workers. The number of Americans who work in agriculture has continued to decline. And for every two people employed in manufacturing today, three are employed in the service industries.

Today's worker is almost as likely to be a woman as a man. The surge of women into the labor force is a milestone, not only for women but also for the American economy. Had the economy not moved rapidly from manufacturing and agricultural industries to service industries, finance, public administration, and communications, the women's revolution might still be on the drawing boards.

More than one worker in five still works in manufacturing, but the economy has become more complex as it has matured. Today, workers provide an incredible array of goods and services to increasingly diverse groups of consumers. The mass market of a generation ago has splintered, and new markets are emerging. Consumers' characteristics and economic circumstances have changed.

As consumers change, so do the industries that serve them and the occupations that employ them. So dramatically have occupations changed that the government has abolished altogether the job classification system that divided workers into blue-collar and white-collar categories. These two familiar occupational categories used to sum up almost everything about an American's job, educational background, and social status. The term *pink collar* was coined, although it was never part of the official government occupational classification system, to describe the growing number of women working as secretaries and clerks and in other occupations dominated by women. Now, following the 1980 census, collars are out, no matter what their color.

The decision to do away with collar classifications, probably the government's most familiar demographic indicator, is significant. The government's classifiers made the decision in recognition that in today's economy, what matters is what you do, not what social class your job falls into. The new classifications reflect this important change. Dividing workers principally by a symbolic job uniform, rather than by their work, could impede the social mobility of blue-collar workers or impart a false sense of prestige to white-collar workers. Precision production work, for example, can pay more, require more education, and carry higher prestige than clerical work. Yet, despite the low pay, modest educational requirements, and minimal prestige some clerical jobs carry, they were all classified as white collar—the same color as nuclear physicists—whereas precision workers were lumped with laborers among the blue-collar classes. The new system recognizes that today's occupations demand a more complicated mixture of education and skills and are more varied than yesterday's occupations.

Before the classification system was revamped, American workers fell into one of four categories: (1) white-collar workers included professional and technical workers, managers and administrators, sales personnel, and clerical staff; (2) blue-collar workers included craft and kindred workers, operatives, transportation workers, and laborers; (3)

service workers belonged to one of two subgroups, private household workers and service workers not working in private households; and (4) farm workers were the fourth occupational category. In all, under the old system, these four major groups contained ten subgroups. The new system recognizes, instead, six major groups, with thirteen subgroups.

It is impossible directly to compare the employment of America's workers according to the new system's occupations with those according to the old, so radical are the shifts. The following table shows how each system divides the labor force by occupation. Each column reports the percentage of workers in different occupational subgroups as of the fourth quarter of 1982. Each column adds up to 100 percent:

Table 14 OCCUPATIONAL CLASSIFICATIONS

System	Workers (in percent)
Old Occupational Group	
Managers and administrators,	11.7
Professional and technical workers	17.4
Sales workers	6.8
Clerical workers	18.6
Craft and kindred workers	12.1
Operatives, except transport	9.1
Transport equipment operatives	3.4
Nonfarm laborers	4.4
Service workers	13.8
Farm workers	2.7
New Occupational Group	
Executive, administrative, and managerial	10.7
Professional specialty	13.0
Technicians and related support	3.1
Sales occupations	11.7
Administrative support, including clerical	16.5
Private household workers	1.1
Protective service	1.6
Service, except private household and protective	10.9
Precision production, craft, and repair	11.6
Machine operators, assemblers, and inspectors	7.5
Transportation and material moving	4.2
Handlers, equipment cleaners, helpers, and laborers	4.5
Farming, forestry, and fishing	3.6

Source: Bureau of Labor Statistics

The word *occupation* describes what people do at work; the word *industry* describes the sector of the economy in which people work. To some extent, occupations and industries are two sides of the same coin, and some occupations closely fit their industry. For example, the agriculture industry employs 3.4 million people, of whom 2.7 million are farm workers. However, the agriculture industry also employs 88,000 professional and technical workers, 38,000 managers and administrators, and 330,000 nonfarm laborers.

Other industries employ workers from a wide variety of occupations. The service industries, which include such diverse tasks as advertising, computer programming, and legal services, employ 30 million Americans, but only 7.7 million service workers, such as janitors and security guards, work in the service industries. The service industries employ almost 2 million craft workers, and over 500,000 nonfarm laborers.

Although occupations are spread relatively evenly across the country, industries are more concentrated. Manufacturing dominates northern industries, whereas construction industries are stronger in the South and West, regions in which the economy and population have been growing more rapidly than the North. Finance, insurance, and real estate are most important in the Northeast and the West, largely reflecting the influence of financial centers in New York and California.

Some states have concentrations of particular occupations and industries. South Dakota employs five and a half times the national share of farmers, fishers, and foresters, the occupational group with the most variation among the states. In Washington, D.C., the share of people employed in the farming, fishing, and forestry occupation is 83 percent below the national average. Still, it is surprising that the 1980 census found as many as 1,588 people in the nation's capital working as farmers, fishermen, or foresters. Or perhaps they were farming on paper in the Department of Agriculture.

In just two states, Alaska and Maryland, plus the District of Columbia, managers, professionals, and administrators are at least 20 percent above the national average. But only in Arkansas, the nation's poorest state, is the proportion at least 20 percent below average. Service occupations are in greatest relative abundance in states where tourism is a major industry—Hawaii and Nevada, plus Washington, D.C.

In contrast, the share of people working in craft, operative, or production occupations is greatest in Alabama, Arkansas, Indiana, Kentucky, Mississippi, North Carolina, South Carolina, Tennessee, and West Virginia.

Industries vary far more than do occupations in their concentration by state. The statistics support state stereotypes. Washington, D.C., has four and a half times the national average of workers in public administration. The finance, insurance, and real estate industries are particularly high in Connecticut and New York. Manufacturing is most heavily represented in Connecticut, Indiana, Michigan, New Hampshire, Ohio, Rhode Island, and the Carolinas. Construction is at least 30 percent higher than nationally in such growth states as Arizona, Florida, Nevada, Texas, and Wyoming.

THE SERVICE ECONOMY

Services are spreading everywhere. The rise of service industries has been the most important industrial shift of recent time. This sector, which now employs some 30 million Americans, includes over forty different industries that have little to do with each other, except that each represents a kind of service—business and repair services; personal services; entertainment and recreation services; and, particularly, professional services, by far the largest of the four service subgroups, employing over two thirds of all service-industry workers.

Professional services include hospitals, the public schools, law, medicine, and colleges and universities. The second-largest category within the service industries includes business and repair services, which employ 4.5 million workers in fields as different from each other as advertising and automobile repair. Personal services, an industry that employs about 4 million Americans, ranges from dressmaking shops to motels, and also includes the 1.3 million people who work in private homes. Entertainment and recreation services employ just over 1 million Americans in bowling alleys, theaters, gambling casinos, and whatever the 692,000 people who work as "miscellaneous" do for a living.

The country is moving from an economy in which manufacturing commands center stage to one in which services play the leading role. But still, 20 million people work in manufacturing. The manufacturing industry has two parts: durables and nondurables. Durables include wood and metal products, machinery, equipment, and scientific instruments (the manufacturing industry, too, can be hi-tech); nondurables include food, textiles, tobacco, paper, drugs, leather, and printing (even in the information society, the informative trade of publishing falls into the manufacturing sector).

Employment in manufacturing grew only 2 percent between 1972 and 1982, but employment in the service industries grew 39 percent. Within the service sector, private household service employment dropped by 25 percent, while other services rose 45 percent. People who once worked as maids or cooks in private homes now have found new jobs in business services, professional services, and entertainment and recreation services. Private household service was one of only two industries to have fewer employees in 1982 than a decade earlier.

The only other industry to lose employment in the 1970s—a decade in which total employment rose 22 percent—was agriculture. In 1972, the agriculture, forestry, and fishery industry provided only 4.4 percent of all employment; but by 1982, the figure had dropped even farther, to just 3.4 percent. Agriculture requires fewer workers every year because agricultural production becomes continually more efficient.

As energy crises and inflation stimulated demand for oil, gold, and metals during the 1970s, the mining industry expanded more rapidly than any other—even than the service industry. Employment in the mining industry rose 72 percent between 1972 and 1982, causing the economies of Texas, Colorado, Wyoming and other mineral-rich states to boom. The mining industry is accustomed to cycles of boom and bust, and the boom of the 1970s has already subsided, forcing some of the 1 million Americans who were mining for coal, oil, and metals in 1982 to find jobs in other industries. By 1990, the industry could be booming again.

Employment in public administration—a term synonymous with *government*—rose just 19 percent during the 1970s, less than the 22 percent growth for the work force as a whole. By reputation, the federal government is growing out of control, but in fact it may have been getting a bad rap: Employment in the federal government rose only 7 percent between 1972 and 1982, only about a third as much as the average rise in employment.

Employment in state government, however, rose 42 percent. Local government workers increased their ranks by 30 percent. Local and state government probably will not shrink again (it is easier to gain weight than to lose it), but the federal government could start growing again (so great are the temptations). The rapid growth of state and local government has been partly a consequence of federal pressures to shift responsibilities, and the tax burden, from Washington to the states. In turn, the states have tried to shift responsibilities to local governments, who have no one except the taxpayers to whom they can pass the buck (or, rather, from whom they can get the bucks).

Fleeing the wrath of taxpayers, local officials could start trying to pass the buck for government programs back to the states, and the states to the federal government, where the buck stops. This is how the federal government got so big in the first place and how state and local governments grew in the second and third places. It comes as a surprise that those who spend our tax money were a smaller share of all workers, just over 5 percent, in 1982 than they were in 1972. The number of people employed in postal services actually declined. There's a statistic to write home about.

The retail and wholesale trade industry employs more workers than any other industry in America except services. Some 17 million workers engaged in retail trade in 1982. Employment in this sector rose 24 percent; the wholesale trade part rose an even higher 35 percent and now employs over 4 million people.

For a quick view of the changing American economy, count the people who produce goods versus those who provide services of one kind or another, public or private. The manufacturing, construction, and mining industries employed 24 million Americans in 1983. The services-producing sector, including transportation, trade, finance, services proper, and public administration, employed 66 million. In other words, nearly three times as many people today are employed in industries that include such activities as teaching, health care, government, sales, banking, and insurance, as in those industries that manufacture products.

JOB GAINERS AND LOSERS

The ten occupations that gained the most workers in the 1970s were, in order of the magnitude of their gain, secretaries, cashiers, registered nurses, cooks, truckdrivers, accountants, engineers, computer operators, bookkeepers, and computer specialists. The biggest losers were delivery workers, cleaners and servants in private households, farm workers, gas station attendants, stitchers and sewers, and child-care workers in private homes.

That says a lot about the 1970s. In the glum faces of the losers see the energy crisis, the decline in births, the vanishing family farm, the spread of automation, and the loss of household help. In the smiling faces of the gainers see job opportunities for women, rising education and affluence, population decentralization, the growth of services and finances, and the fast-food craze.

By 1982, 110 million men and women were holding jobs (and over

4 million held at least two jobs). Of the 110 million, 53 million were employed in white-collar jobs and 30 million in blue-collar jobs. Services employed another 14 million, but agriculture fewer than 3 million. In 1982, both the number of employed Americans and the number of unemployed rose to record levels—at the same time—quite an accomplishment for the economy.

Between 1972 and 1982, the total number of jobs rose 22 percent. But white-collar jobs grew 37 percent. White-collar jobs have been growing nine times as fast as blue-collar jobs. In 1976, for the first time, white-collar jobs became a majority of all American jobs. That is probably when the labor force experts in the federal government began to consider revamping the job classification system. Secretaries, who have a white-collar occupation, had grown to become the most numerous of all.

Among the white-collar occupations, professional and technical jobs grew the fastest between 1972 and 1982, rising 48 percent. These jobs include accountants, computer specialists, engineers, registered nurses, doctors, and lawyers, among others. Such jobs now employ 17 million people, or 17 percent of the labor force, up from 11 million people in 1972.

Among the professional and technical specialties, computer systems analysts were the fastest growing of any occupation during the 1970s, nearly tripling in number. But the demand for analysis is also being met by a variety of other occupations. Jobs for authors grew over 130 percent; the number of psychologists and research workers more than doubled; the number of therapists increased over 85 percent.

Among the service occupations, employment in people's homes dropped 27 percent between 1972 and 1982, faster even than the decline of farming. But other service occupations—notably welfare and health services—were among the fastest growing of all. Private household service workers are now just 1 percent of all workers. In the 1970s, America lost nearly 250,000 cleaners and servants, and over 100,000 child-care workers. But some million new jobs for cooks, waiters, and janitors opened in this decade.

Blue-collar occupations as a group have grown much more slowly than other occupations, making them a diminishing share of all jobs. The economy added nearly 18 million jobs between 1972 and 1982, an average of nearly 2 million per year, but added only 1 million blue-collar jobs, an annual average of only about 100,000. One blue-collar occupation, operatives—folks who assemble, manufacture, fabricate, operate equipment, run gas pumps, and work sewing machines—fell 9 percent from 1972 to 1982. The nation lost about 250,000 textile jobs to foreign competition and automation in the 1970s alone.

Another blue-collar occupation, craft and kindred workers—carpenters, machinists, mechanics—grew 14 percent between 1972 and 1982, a rate of growth slower than that of any of the white-collar or service occupations except the laggard household workers. The third major blue-collar occupation, laborers, grew 7 percent, from about 4.2 million laborers in 1972 to some 4.5 million in 1982, less than 5 percent of the total labor force. Laborers include construction laborers, freight and material handlers, stockhandlers, and gardeners and groundskeepers, but not farm workers.

In the past decade, over 300,000 farming jobs disappeared. Farming is a tough row to hoe; few occupations are more strenuous and less rewarding. Most of the decline in farm workers in the 1970s took place among farm owners, tenant farmers, and unpaid family workers, but hardly any among those working for wages. The corporate farm is replacing the family farm, and most farm workers now live off the farm. This is a reversal from a decade ago, when as many as 63 percent of farm workers lived on farms.

Modern agriculture requires ever fewer workers, so the family farmer will become even scarcer. In his place will be a new breed of agricultural technician, crop specialist, and the like. In the future, more Americans may be planting tomatoes or radishes on weekends, but they will not be planting new seeds of life for the occupation of farming. When farmers earn more money from the government for not planting corn or producing milk than they can from the sweat of their brow (or from the sweat of their cow's brow), there are still too many farmers in America.

AMERICA'S WORKERS

As occupations have changed, so has the American worker. The work force has been growing younger as the baby-boom generation has grown older and reached the age when most people go to work. In 1970, as many American workers were over the age of thirty-nine as were younger. By 1982, half of all workers were younger than thirty-five.

The baby-boom generation has had an enormous impact on the labor force. In 1970, only 17 million workers were between the ages of twenty-five and thirty-four. By 1982, over 30 million workers were in this age group. Baby-boomers have flooded the labor market, and the economy has had trouble absorbing them all. The deluge of new workers helps explain why unemployment and employment alike could reach record levels. As the baby-boom group continues to age, the labor force as a whole should grow older and gain in experience. Entry-level workers will begin to dry up, as the small baby-bust generation born during the 1960s and 1970s reaches working age. The soggy economy of the 1970s may find firmer ground in the 1980s. As the labor force grows in experience, its *productivity*—the amount each worker contributes in goods or services—will rise.

The average worker is becoming more educated. As recently as 1970, only one worker in eight was a college graduate. In 1983, however, one worker in five was a college graduate. The share of workers without a high school diploma dropped from more than one in three in 1970 to just one in five in 1983. Earlier, America moved from an economy that depended on muscles to one that valued technical abilities. Now it is moving to an economy that requires brains—for leading, organizing, planning, and motivating. Although a college degree by itself is no guarantee that its holder has more brains or will be a better worker than the next person, employers will look for workers who can solve problems and adjust to change, skills that a liberal arts education, not technical training, teaches best.

As the economy has shifted from heavy industry to services and the professions, the work force has become more female. Many of the fastest-growing jobs of the past decade went to women. For every ten new jobs created since 1970, six went to women. But far more women have entered some occupations than others. Some jobs still are almost completely male, while other remain completely female. One occupation still employs only women. Women may be only 15 percent of physicians, but in 1982 almost every medical secretary in the country was a woman. Before the lawyers start suing the doctors for job discrimination, they should consider that although 15 percent of lawyers are women, 99 percent of legal secretaries are women.

Women have made particular gains in employment as accountants —one of the fastest-growing occupations in the 1970s. In 1972, for example, only about one accountant in five was a woman; now over one in three accountants is a woman. Women went from filling 17 percent of jobs for computer specialists, one of the country's fastest-growing occupations of the 1970s, to filling 29 percent in 1982. Women rose from just 2 percent of industrial engineers to 14 percent.

Women's share of the clergy rose from only 1.6 percent to 5 percent. Even so, there are over 260,000 clergymen in America, but just

15,000 clergywomen. Women rose from 12 percent to 28 percent of economists, and from 19 percent to 37 percent of bank officials— probably as tellers were promoted. Women are 92 percent of all bank tellers, up from 88 percent in 1972. The share of women guards tripled to nearly 13 percent of all guards.

These are among the most notable of women's job gains during the past decade. But the most notable achievement of all may be that, in many occupations, women's share of total employment has declined since 1972. Most of these occupations are traditionally female jobs or low-status jobs or both. A few are burly men's work, such as carpet installers and derrick operators, which employ few women to start with and to which women have not been gravitating, nor men either.

Women declined as a proportion of registered nurses and elementary-school teachers. They declined as a share of stenographers, and telephone operators—all occupations in which women still hold the great majority of jobs. They dropped as a share of cooks, dishwashers, waiters, cosmetologists, and unpaid farm workers. For some reason, they dropped from being 31 percent of musicians and composers to only 29 percent.

As women increasingly find acceptance in fields previously considered the preserve of men, men are finding openings in occupations once reserved for women. The labor force may not yet have become unisex, but it has taken a few steps in that direction. Women are now over 50 percent of editors and reporters and 50 percent of bartenders. A woman is likely to sell you a house, but not to build one for you. Women are fully 50 percent of real estate agents, but only 1.7 percent of carpenters. Women outnumber men as computer equipment operators, but men outnumber women two to one as computer programmers. The share of women athletes rose from 31 percent to 51 percent in the 1970s. Men still far outnumber women as professional athletes, but women outnumber men as physical therapists.

The women's revolution still has a way to go. Of the 514 job categories in the 1980 census, women outnumbered men in 125. The census counted almost 4 million women secretaries, but only 250 women hunters and trappers. Fully 27,000 men are chief executives in government, but only 8,000 women. Still, signs of progress abound: The census found 3,557 women legislators and 3,510 women funeral directors (about the same number for death as for taxes). Over 27,000 women work as construction laborers, and another 27,000 as garage or gas station workers. Over 45,000 women work as police officers or detectives. And almost 14,000 women work as postmasters and postal supervisers (still a mail, but no longer a male, occupation).

For several decades, women have been achieving growing occupational equality with men. In a single generation, women have increased their representation in virtually every occupation. In 1972, women were less than 48 percent of white-collar workers; in 1982, they were 54 percent (becoming a majority just in time for the white-collar category to disappear). Women rose to 19 percent of blue-collar workers in 1982, up 2 percentage points from 1972. Among the male-dominated crafts, they have doubled their participation, if only to 7 percent. They have also doubled their share among laborers.

In their move into the labor force, women have been the beneficiaries of economic trends. The fastest-growing large occupations of the past decade were those that traditionally employed a high proportion of women. The decade's recessions hit the male-dominated industries harder than the industries that employed primarily women. And as women make further gains in employment, the economy should benefit. Consumer spending should rise, pressure on wages ought to become more moderate, and unemployment will not hold the terror it once did for a family when most families depended only on the male breadwinner. Women are expected to fill more than two of every three new jobs in the 1980s and 1990s, and so their share of all workers will continue to increase. By 1995, over 80 percent of women in their twenties and thirties will be in the work force.

Black Americans also made job gains in the past decade, but they are still disproportionately represented in lower paying, less prestigious jobs. The share of blacks in white-collar occupations has almost tripled since 1960, from 13 percent to 38 percent. But blacks remain underrepresented in white-collar jobs and overrepresented in blue-collar and service jobs (or were until the categories vanished). Whereas 35 percent of employed blacks work in blue-collar occupations, only 29 percent of whites do. Blacks are about twice as likely as whites to be working in the service occupations. Only 4 percent of stockbrokers are black, but nearly 50 percent of servants and cleaners.

In 1982, blacks were 9 percent of all employed Americans, but only 6.6 percent of white-collar workers. Among the white-collar jobs, blacks exceeded 9 percent only among some of the medical professions and among social and recreation workers. Blacks' 16 percent representation among social and recreation workers was their highest representation in any white-collar occupation. Among managers and administrators, however, blacks were represented at less than half their overall average. Blacks filled just 3.9 percent of such jobs, ranging from 11.3

percent of school administrators to only 2.6 percent of buyers in wholesale and retail trade.

Blacks were 11 percent of blue-collar workers, and their greatest representation was in the low-paying end of blue-collar work; their least among the high-paying trades. Blacks ranged from being just 4 percent of carpenters to 29 percent of orderlies and almost 50 percent of garbage collectors. Blacks were also represented disproportionately in such blue-collar occupations as taxidrivers and chauffeurs, textile workers, laundry and dry cleaning operators, and bus drivers. They were less than half their share of the population among mechanics, typesetters, and mine operatives.

Blacks and other racial minorities were 20 percent of all service workers, but ranged from just 5 percent of bartenders to 49 percent of cleaners and servants. Nonwhites were over 25 percent of janitors, but only 8 percent of waiters, 5 percent of dental assistants, and 9 percent of hairdressers.

JOBS OF THE EIGHTIES

More Americans now work in jobs that prepare and serve food than in those that raise the livestock, grow the crops, and catch the fish for others to prepare and serve. Managers and professionals now outnumber production workers, craftsmen, and people who make repairs. The country knows how to grow and produce things more efficiently than it can manage and market them.

Human problems require more workers than do technical ones. The 1980 census found 530,000 lawyers and judges, but only 121,000 production helpers. It found 218,000 social scientists and urban planners, but only 47,000 people who maintained machines. The country, it appears, now requires more people to straighten out people's problems than to keep things running. Why, however, does the economy support 189,000 taxicab drivers and chauffeurs but only 16,000 social scientists? Do Americans prefer help in reaching their destinations to help in understanding why they are going there?

Some little-known occupations have surprisingly large numbers of workers—the 8,800 termite treaters and helpers counted in 1980, for example. Such offbeat occupations as fish cleaner and pin chaser each employ about 9,000 workers. Despite the computer age, the nineteenth century lives on in American capitalism. A handful of people work as scouts, escorts, greasemakers, buttermakers, and pullers-over. Somewhere out there are yeast pushers, tube winders, toe lasters, pot liners, and mold cleaners—but fewer than 1,000 each. Even in the world of high technology, a few people have to clean the molds and line the pots.

The Bureau of Labor Statistics has ranked occupations on a scale of one to ten in order to advise young people of the occupations that hold promise. The bureau ranked each occupation according to four criteria: 1980 employment size, projected growth in employment during the 1980s, average weekly earnings, and average unemployment rate. The size of the occupation and its growth potential indicate the prospects for employment. The unemployment level indicates job security, and earnings indicate how much money you can expect to make. The top score possible was 40, the lowest was 4.

Doctors, lawyers, systems analysts, and electrical engineers scored at the top of the list, with near-perfect ratings of 37. Messengers, school monitors, duplicating machine operators, and ushers ranked at the bottom, each with a score of 11 or less. Barbers and firefighters—both occupations whose services no sane person would forgo—scored perfect ratings for job security. College teachers scored well overall, but flunked in projected employment growth, in which they got only a 1 because the baby-bust generation is now of college age.

A few jobs ranked 10 in growth but only 1 in earnings, including the predominantly women's occupations of nurses' aides and dental assistants. Those who don't care about making money can also find work as elevator operators, vehicle cleaners, and cooks. All three should have many job openings for the rest of the 1980s, but they offer low wages.

In the years ahead, the economy will require more than 20 million new workers. By 1995, more than 131 million Americans will be in the labor force. The fastest-growing jobs will be related to computers. As more Americans own computers, and as businesses increasingly come to rely on them, someone will have to keep them running. Jobs for computer service technicians should nearly double by 1995. Systems analysts, programmers, and operators will also grow rapidly in the age of the computer. As the country gains more lawyers—there will be over 150,000 more by 1995—someone will have to keep them running too. The nation's second fastest-growing occupation throughout this decade and into the next will be legal assistants, up over 90 percent. Engineers will also grow rapidly.

But high-technology fields will supply only 6 percent of all new jobs created in the next decade. The occupations projected to gain the most new workers are decidedly low-tech. Building custodians top the list, up almost 800,000 by 1995. Next come cashiers, secretaries, and clerks, up around 700,000 each. The country will also need many more nurses, waiters, nursing aides, and truckdrivers. Nursing jobs should grow by 640,000; truckdriving by 425,000. Many of the occupations projected to gain the most new jobs require little education. The Bureau of Labor Statistics says people with a high-school diploma or less can fill the following occupations, all expected to grow by at least 33 percent during the 1980s: nursing aides, jailers, dental assistants, and child-care attendants. Opportunities for the less educated may be even better in the fast-food business, as food preparation and service workers are expected to grow over 50 percent. It may not be bioengineering, but someone has to make the burgers.

For people with some college education, the most available jobs will be computer operators, tax preparers, travel agents, nurses, or brick masons. For those with a college degree, the best opportunities lie in such occupations as computer programmer, economist, physical therapist, dietitian, architect, law clerk, and psychologist. Among the fifteen fastest-growing occupations for college graduates, two are computer related, five are in health care, and three are in engineering.

The work force will be growing more slowly this decade than in the past decade because by now the baby-boom generation has been almost completely absorbed. In 1995, the baby-boom generation will be between the ages of thirty-one and forty-eight, squarely in the middle of workers' most productive years. The smaller generation that follows the baby boom will mean a drop in the share of entry-level workers. Fewer entry-level workers should alleviate unemployment, and make it easier for women to find better jobs.

Changing technology and the shift away from heavy industry toward professions and services will continue to affect the jobs Americans hold. Professional and technical workers will continue to grow faster than average. So will service workers, except for those who work in people's homes, an occupational category expected to decline further. Jobs for laborers and operatives will continue to grow more slowly than average. Salespeople, management, and craftworkers should grow at about the average, as in recent years.

Farming will continue to decrease, but probably at a slower rate. Clerical workers will continue to increase, but probably not so fast as in recent years because office automation will limit their growth. As the number of small children rises again in the 1980s, and day care grows, some clerical workers may find themselves trading their typewriters not for computers, but rather for crayons and construction paper.

Fourteen occupations are projected to lose at least 10 percent of their employment between 1982 and 1995. Down more than 30 percent will be railroad conductors and shoemaking machine operators. Aircraft structure assemblers, central telephone office operators, taxidrivers, postal clerks, private household workers, farm laborers, and college and university faculty members will all decline 15 percent or more. No more jokes about unemployed college teachers driving cabs, please.

Opportunities will thin for roustabouts, postmasters, rotary drill operator helpers, graduate assistants, and data entry operators, each expected to decline between 10 and 15 percent. But in decline is growth. Data entry operators can retool to become computer operators, one of twenty occupations that should grow at least 50 percent between 1982 and 1995. Graduate assistants can instead become physical therapy assistants, slated to grow by two thirds—a case of matter over mind.

Computers create jobs and take jobs. The nation's largest occupation, secretaries, will become more productive in the coming decade because of advances in office equipment, but growing productivity should reduce the explosive growth in this occupation. However, receptionists will be among the fastest growing of the clerical occupations. Not even IBM has figured out how to perform this human job with a machine. But among production occupations, welders and people who load machines, spray paint, and perform other low-skill operations may face competition from robots.

As the forces reshaping the economy continue to work their changes on occupations, they should contribute to a growing split between Americans. Professionals and executives rank at the top in family income. Service workers rank at the bottom. Both are among the fastest-growing occupations. The one requires a college education. The other may not even require a high school education. Americans may no longer live for their job, but the kind of job they hold determines largely how they live.

TRENDS TO WATCH

– The American economy is moving from one based on manufacturing to one based on services. Professional jobs and clerical jobs are both growing rapidly, while blue-collar jobs are declining in share.

– Jobs traditionally filled by women have been growing fastest.

– The labor force is splitting into two parts—high-status, high-paying professional and technical work and low-status, low-paying clerical and service work.

Degrees of Difference

"Differences in educational attainment may be the single greatest reason that young people today have a perspective on life that is different from their elders. The generation gap is an education gap."

A country that reveres equality offers education as a leveler. A country that rewards individual enterprise offers education as a leavener. America offers both. Education in America is both a bond that unites and a barrier that separates.

Education is not only a chance for individuals to excel, for the cream to rise to the top, it is also an investment, and those with more to invest may enjoy greater returns. The relationship between education and income is important. Median income rises directly and dramatically with years of schooling. Households headed by college graduates make $24,000 per year more than households headed by a person with less than an eighth-grade education. Among households headed by a college graduate, as many had incomes over $33,500 in 1982 as had incomes under that figure. Among households headed by a high school dropout, the dividing line was just $14,000.

Overall, the country has made an enormous investment in education, and it has paid off. A century ago, one American in six could neither read nor write. Today, the illiteracy rate has fallen to only one American in 200. A greater share of Americans today finish high school, attend college, and graduate from college than ever before. In 1950, only half of all adults had gone beyond the ninth grade. By 1967, the median had risen to 12 years—the first year in which the average American was a high school graduate. In 1982, the average American aged twenty-five or older had completed 12.6 years of school.

Table 15 RELATIONSHIP BETWEEN EDUCATION AND INCOME

Years of schooling	Median income, 1982 ($)
16 or more	33,500
13 to 15	24,600
12	21,100
9 to 11	14,000
8	11,300
7 or less	9,400

Source: Census Bureau

The 1980 census was the first in history to report that a majority of adults in every state had completed high school. Nearly 90 percent of people aged twenty-five to thirty-four are high school graduates, remarkable testimony to America's educational upgrading. Twenty-four million Americans are college graduates, and 21 million more have had at least one year of college. In 1982, 18 percent of all Americans aged twenty-five and older had completed four years or more of college; in 1970, the share was just 11 percent. In 1970, only about one in five had any college experience at all. By 1982, one person in three had had at least one year of college.

Formal education has become more valuable than learning from the school of hard knocks as the economy has become more complex. As the nation's wealth has risen, its young men and women have been freed from farms and production lines to spend more years in school, preparing for ever more challenging jobs. Machines built America, now computers are keeping it running. In the future, computers will accomplish ever more of the routine work that employed trained people before—accounting, inventory control, record keeping, and the like—enabling even more Americans to further their education.

America's educational profile is rising because younger Americans are replacing the older generation who grew up when it was less common to complete even high school. Every adult age group is better educated than the ones ahead of it. The children of the baby boom are far better educated than their parents. Age, in fact, is the best predictor of the amount of education a person has—more important than either sex or race.

It is as if the successive shocks of the Depression and World War II that created a family-oriented, child-centered era also created a consensus that education was America's best hope for the future. As more children were born, the concerns of the nation turned to caring for them. Schooling became the way to offer them a better world.

Less than half of Americans sixty-five or older in 1982 had completed high school. Only 9 percent were college graduates. A person aged sixty-five in 1982 was born in 1917. By the time he or she reached high school age, the Depression was in full swing. College was out of the question, and even completing high school was impossible for most.

People born a decade later—those aged fifty-five to sixty-four in 1982—were much more likely to be high school graduates. Almost two thirds of them finished high school. But World War II started just as this group came of college age. The war delayed college for some, but the GI bill made college attendance possible for many who would never otherwise have gone to college. The war ended college as a privilege of the wealthy elite and made it a right of the middle class.

The impact of the GI bill appears in the rapid change in college attendance rates among men. In 1982, 17 percent of men aged fifty-five to sixty-four had completed at least four years of college, almost twice as high a proportion (9 percent) as among women in this age group. A college education was America's way of rewarding the young men who fought in World War II. The women rewarded them by staying home to have large families.

Before it became common for men to attend college, the average woman was better educated than the average man. Women's median number of years of schooling was higher than men's because men were more likely than women to leave high school and take a job, whereas few Americans, men or women, went on to college. But by 1970, men's median number of years spent in school had begun to exceed women's because a higher share of men were continuing on to college, while fewer dropped out of high school. In the 1970s, the share of Americans who continued on to college increased dramatically for both men and women. By 1982, 27 percent of men aged twenty-five to thirty-four, and

21 percent of women in that age group, were college graduates. The increase was even greater for people who had had at least one year of college.

Differences in educational attainment may be the single greatest reason that young people today have a perspective on life that is different from their elders. The generation gap is an education gap. As well as vastly improving the odds of making money during one's working years, education also affects career expectations, social attitudes, and political behavior. Politicians used to get elected by waving American flags and kissing American babies. Educated voters have fewer babies to be kissed, but they are more likely to vote.

CLOSING THE EDUCATION GAP

Blacks have been closing the education gap with whites. As recently as 1970, only 10 percent of blacks aged twenty-five or older had had even one year of college, and only 4.5 percent had a college education. By 1982, the share who had completed at least one year of college had more than doubled—to 22 percent—and the share who were college graduates had risen to 9 percent.

Blacks still lag behind whites in educational attainment, but nowhere near as far behind as a decade or so ago. Among blacks, as among whites, the people in the youngest age groups have made the greatest gains in education. Blacks who were aged twenty-five to thirty-four in 1982 had double the college attainment of those who were in this age group in 1970. In 1982, 36 percent had had at least one year of college, and 13 percent were college graduates.

The proportion of young blacks who graduate from high school has risen by 26 percentage points in a dozen years. In 1970, 53 percent of blacks aged twenty-five to thirty-four had completed four years of high school. By 1982, the share had risen to 79 percent. In 1970, young blacks lagged 23 percentage points behind young whites in high school completion; in 1982 the gap had been cut by two-thirds, to 8 percentage points.

Despite this swift progress, nearly half of blacks do not possess a high school diploma, compared to less than one-third of whites. Americans forget how unequal the education system used to be. It has been only thirty years since the Supreme Court ruled that racially segregated education was unconstitutional, only twenty years since the civil rights movement, and only ten years since financial aid to low-income college students became widely available. Middle-aged and elderly blacks grew up before these events. Seven percent of blacks aged sixty-five or older are illiterate. Only 18 percent of elderly blacks have graduated from high school, only 7.5 percent have gone beyond high school, and just 3.8 percent hold a college degree. The older generation remains a world apart.

The gains of young blacks, however, have been so great that they have brought up blacks' overall educational averages astonishingly. In 1980, the median schooling blacks received was 12.2 years, less than one-half year behind whites. The average black person, counting the old as well as the young, had become a high school graduate. In contrast, as recently as 1970, the median was just under ten years for blacks; in 1960 it was eight years. In two decades, blacks have added four years to their median school attainment, more than twice the increase for whites.

The educational gains of the young have divided blacks not only according to generation, but also according to whether or not a young person has taken advantage of the new educational opportunities for blacks. Given the importance of education to occupational status, income and wealth, and mobility and opportunity, blacks whose education equals or exceeds that of whites are much more likely than in the past to join the American mainstream. But those blacks who are stuck in deteriorating central cities will not receive the same quality of education that blacks in affluent areas will receive or that most whites receive. They may improve the educational statistics, but they will not be able to change their lives.

The national legislation passed in the 1960s and 1970s gave low-income blacks a foothold on the educational ladder. By 1975, the share of black high school graduates who enrolled in college was the same as that for whites. Blacks made up 10 percent of all college undergraduates in 1982, only slightly less than the share of the total population that is black. In 1970, 350,000 black students were enrolled full time as undergraduates in college degree programs. Only six years later, the number had soared to 640,000 as government financial aid programs went into effect.

Since then, the number has grown more slowly because of recession and government belt-tightening and because there are fewer people in the traditional college-going age groups. In 1980, there were 660,000 black full-time undergraduate degree students, 3 percent more than in 1976. In addition, 450,000 black students were studying part time or in nondegree programs. In all, about 1.1 million blacks were enrolled in colleges and universities in 1982. Even the elite universities have opened their doors. Blacks made up 7 percent of Harvard's 1980 enrollment, 6 percent of Stanford's and Yale's, and over 7 percent of Princeton's. (Dartmouth, whose unofficial symbol used to be an Indian, leads the nation's prestige schools in the percentage of its student body that is American Indian, 1.5 percent; Harvard has just 0.3 percent.)

The percentage of blacks going to college has risen more rapidly than the percentage of whites. Private institutions accounted for all of the 20,000 increase in black full-time enrollment between 1976 and 1980. Blacks were 10.3 percent of all students at private colleges and universities in 1982, up from 5.8 percent in 1970. Two thirds of black students are now enrolled in colleges in which most of the students are white; only a little more than one quarter are in predominantly black institutions. And in 1981, for the first time, the three most popular fields of study at the undergraduate level were the same for blacks and whites alike—business, education, and the social sciences.

Black women have made even more impressive gains in education than black men. In 1981, 36,200 black women received bachelor's degrees, compared to 24,500 black men. At the master's level, 11,000 women received degrees, compared to 6,200 men. Only at the doctoral and first professional degree levels did black men outnumber black women. Nevertheless, black women received 29 percent more doctorates in 1981 than in 1976, and 8 percent more bachelor's degrees. Black men received 4 percent fewer bachelor's degrees in 1981 than in 1976 and 10 percent fewer doctorates.

Hispanics have not fared as well as blacks in education. Over 50 percent of Hispanics aged twenty-five and older do not have a high school diploma. Only 19 percent attended college for at least one year, and only 8 percent are college graduates. In 1982, Hispanics had a median of just eleven years of schooling. Hispanic women lag behind black women in education because they are more likely to live in traditional families in which women are wives and mothers first and independent learners and workers second. The fragmentation of the black nuclear family requires that black women fend for themselves, which means getting an education if possible. A majority of black women have completed high school, but only 44 percent of Hispanic women.

Blacks also may have an advantage over Hispanics in America's educational system because so many Hispanics are recent immigrants who come from countries with weak educational systems. For them language and culture can be barriers. As Hispanics become more inte-grated into the American culture, their educational attainment should rise.

DEMOGRAPHIC DEMAND AND THE SUPPLY OF SCHOOLING

Because primary and secondary education are compulsory under the law, public school enrollment trends closely follow population trends. The number of students peaked at 61 million in 1975, exactly eighteen years after the peak year for births, and the number has dropped since then as the number of births has dropped. As baby bust followed baby boom, education became a declining industry in the 1970s. In 1982, elementary enrollment was fully 19 percent below its peak year, 1970. High school enrollment was 10 percent below its peak in 1977. As the last members of the baby-boom generation—those Americans born in 1964—have moved through high school and into the work force or college, high school enrollments have declined further.

But elementary enrollments are beginning to rise again as the children born to the baby-boom generation start to attend school. The roller coaster of births gives educational planning a wild ride; and because public schools are a local concern the ups are accentuated in areas that are gaining population, whereas in areas that do not attract young adults with children, school enrollment may not rise at all, despite a national increase in the number of births.

As enrollments rise and fall across the country, so does the demand for teachers. Between 1982 and 1995, the demand for kindergarten and elementary school teachers will rise from 1.4 million to 1.9 million, but the demand for secondary school teachers will stabilize at about 1 million. College faculty members are on the government's list of endan-gered occupations—those expected to decline most rapidly between 1982 and 1995. However, elementary and kindergarten teachers rank eighth from the top in the number of new positions likely to be created over this period—with more than 500,000 new teaching jobs, a 37 percent increase.

From a glut of elementary school teachers in the early 1970s, the country is likely to face a shortage in the years ahead. Not only are there more such jobs, but also the proportion of full-time freshman students citing elementary or secondary education as their career choice fell to 4.7 percent in 1982, down from 22 percent in 1966. In 1983, however, the percentage of students interested in becoming elementary or secondary school teachers rose slightly, to 5.1 percent. The number of degrees awarded in education dropped 44 percent between 1972 and 1973 and 1980 and 1981, as prospective teachers realized that jobs no longer existed. Teaching jobs will start to open again just as college students' interest in becoming teachers is waning. The coming buyer's market in elementary school teachers should help boost women's employment further in the 1980s—women comprise only half of secondary school teachers, but 82 percent of elementary school teachers—and may even add a few more men to the roster of elementary teachers.

The reach of education has spread far beyond the traditional school-age years. Education in America now reaches almost from cradle to grave. Although total school enrollment has declined, enrollment both of small children in nursery school and of older adults in college has increased tremendously. There has been a surge of children into nursery schools. In 1982, over 1 million more young children were enrolled in nursery schools than in 1970, a rise of 96 percent. In 1965, only 11 percent of children aged three or four were enrolled in nursery school. In 1981, the share had more than tripled to 36 percent, or more than 2 million children.

In 1985, the last members of the baby-boom generation turn twenty-two, the traditional age of the college graduate. For the next two decades, colleges will face hard times. They will have to attract a higher share of high school graduates and broaden their reach into the nontraditional ages and groups that have not gone to college in the past if they wish to maintain enrollments. For some, it may be a matter of survival.

Enrollment in institutions of higher education increased over 47 percent during the 1970s, from 7.4 million people aged fourteen to thirty-four to 10.9 million. Although enrollment in four-year colleges grew only 33 percent, enrollment in two-year colleges soared 78 percent. In the future, a growing number of students will be attending college part time, rising to nearly 50 percent of all enrollments in 1992, versus just over 29 percent in 1982. The proportion of college students under thirty-five years old who go to school full time has been shrinking —from 78 percent in 1970 to 71 percent in 1982. Among students thirty-five and older, 80 percent go to school part time.

In 1972, 56 percent of college students were under age twenty-two; now 52 percent are aged twenty-two or older. So unusual was it for anyone who had reached age thirty-five to be in college that the government did not even publish such statistics in 1970. In 1982, however, about 1.4 million Americans aged thirty-five or older were attending college, and nearly twice as many of them were women as were men. Fully 183,000 women aged thirty-five or older were full-time students. Older women have been retooling, using education to compensate for a lack of work-force experience. Going back to school cannot take the place of work experience lost during the childbearing years, but it can help train women to fill the new jobs the economy has created or to expand their own horizons.

Adult education has gained in popularity, both because colleges are seeking new ways to keep classrooms full and teachers employed and because Americans have become more interested in learning and are able to afford to take courses as adults. Information about enrollment in adult education was first collected in 1978, a sign of how recent the trend is. Then, 18 million Americans were enrolled. By 1981, the number had risen to over 21 million; 54 percent of enrollees were between the ages of seventeen and thirty-four, and 56 percent were women.

Of the more than 37,000 adult education courses offered today, almost 25 percent are in business and 11 percent are in health care. Most people return to school for job-related reasons; 60 percent of enrollees cite job-related reasons for continuing their education. But more than one quarter of all people enrolled in adult education cite personal or social reasons. One third of all women enrollees give personal or social reasons. The people who take adult education courses are more likely to be professional or technical workers than the work force as a whole. Fifty-seven percent already have a college degree.

As colleges attract the older student, the number of students aged eighteen to twenty-one enrolled in colleges and universities should decline by about 21 percent between 1982 and 1992—down about 1.1 million, largely because the population aged eighteen to twenty-one will decline by over 3 million. The number of students aged twenty-five and older, however, will increase by about 19 percent, and the majority of them will be women.

America now has over 3,000 institutions of higher education, nearly 22 percent more than in 1970. Over 1,700 of these are private, and among the private schools, four-year colleges outnumber two-year colleges. The reverse is true of public institutions. America's higher education system is a mixture of public institutions, private schools, vocational colleges, institutes for continuing education, and so on. The country's educational institutions vary in size, mission, student characteristics, and almost everything else. But they share the problem of the declining college-age student population.

Even in an age of air travel as many college students stay close to home as go long distances to school. In 1980, only 8 percent of first-time college students traveled more than 500 miles to attend school, 27 percent traveled between 100 and 500 miles, and 15 percent traveled between 50 and 100 miles. Fifty percent traveled 50 miles or less. Of high school seniors heading for college in 1980, about three quarters planned to attend college in their state of residence. The proportion was lowest in New England, little more than half, and in the Middle Atlantic States, about two thirds. It was highest in the West South-Central States of Texas, Oklahoma, Louisiana, and Arkansas. The Northeast has more colleges per capita than any other region, but it lost more than 30,000 college students to other regions in 1981.

Sixteen states throughout the country send more students out of state to college than they receive from other states. This may not be a problem for Alaska, Nevada, and New Mexico, which are gaining population and have few private colleges, but it is a problem for such states as New York, Connecticut, and New Jersey, which are not gaining young people but have many colleges. New York, the nation's leading population loser of the 1970s, has more colleges and universities than any other state, and 210 of its 296 are private. In twenty-one other states, private colleges outnumber public ones, including some states that are not population growth centers—Illinois, Indiana, Iowa, Maine, Massachusetts, Michigan, Ohio, Pennsylvania, and Rhode Island.

Because the population is growing rapidly in the South and West, but much more slowly in the Northeast, the colleges of the Northeast will have to recruit a growing number of students from other parts of the country if they are to hold their own in enrollments. This job of recruitment may prove difficult, particularly as colleges in the West and South improve in quality and reputation. While colleges in Texas, California, and Florida expand, those in Massachusetts, New York, New Jersey, and Pennsylvania may have to contract.

Private liberal arts colleges are those most at risk. These colleges are centered in the Northeast, where the pool of college-age people will shrink the most. Some states are growing so rapidly that their college-age population will not decline at all—Florida, Louisiana, Texas, Oklahoma, and Utah, for example. But these states do not account for many of the small liberal arts colleges. The growing imbalance between the nation's educational centers and its centers of population growth will cause problems in America's huge educational system for the remainder of the century.

These trends are likely to speed the college enrollments of minority students. Minorities are increasing as a share of the young population, and they remain underrepresented as a share of college students. Although 81 percent of college students in 1980 were whites, 9 percent blacks, 4 percent Hispanics, and 0.7 percent American Indians, 2.4 percent were Asians or Pacific Islanders—a greater share than the young Asian and Pacific Islander population is in the United States.

Even in states with a high proportion of blacks and Hispanics, these groups have been underrepresented in college. The highest proportion of Hispanics in 1980, 25 percent, was enrolled in New Mexico. But 37 percent of all New Mexicans are Hispanic. The state with the highest share of blacks enrolled was Mississippi, with 30 percent. But 35 percent of Mississippi's total population is black.

In their scramble for students, America's colleges also are likely to become less American. More than 300,000 foreign students—many of them from the oil-producing countries—were attending American colleges and universities in 1980. Because America's birthrate is low, while most of the world's youth population is still growing rapidly, foreign student enrollments in the United States could continue to rise almost indefinitely.

EDUCATION AMONG THE STATES

The states vary widely in their commitment to provide schooling for their residents and in their residents' educational level. Nationally, 16 percent of Americans aged twenty-five and older were college graduates in 1980, but in six states 20 percent or more of residents held a college degree—Colorado, Alaska, Connecticut, Maryland, Hawaii, and Massachusetts. At the other extreme, only 10 percent of West Virginians were college graduates.

In Kentucky, 48 percent of all residents aged twenty-five and older in 1980 were high school dropouts. In South Carolina, the proportion was 46 percent, and in Mississippi, 45 percent. But only 17 percent of Alaskans aged twenty-five and older, and 20 percent of the residents of Utah, were high school dropouts.

Alaska spends more on education per elementary and secondary school student than any other state, over $6,000 in the 1980/81 school year. The national average was about $2,700. Only New York, New Jersey, and Wyoming, spent over $3,500 per student. Mississippi spent less than $1,800, and six other states spent less than $2,000, with Alabama, Tennessee, Georgia, Arkansas, and Kentucky just above Mississippi.

Whereas the median number of school years completed is fairly uniform across the country, ranging from a low of 12.1 years in Kentucky and South Carolina to a high of 12.8 years in Alaska, Colorado, and Utah, the median varies by race. Among whites, the median is 13 years or greater in two states, Alaska and Hawaii, and is lowest in Kentucky at 12.1 years. Among blacks, the median dips to 9.4 years in Mississippi.

Table 16 COLLEGE GRADUATES

U.S. Average, 16.2 Percent

States*		Cities*	
1 Colorado	23.0%	1 Bethesda, MD	51.5%
2 Alaska	21.1	2 Columbia, MD	48.2
3 Connecticut	20.7	3 Palo Alto, CA	46.7
4 Maryland	20.4	4 Brookline, MA	40.4
5 Hawaii	20.3	5 Lower Merion Township,	
6 Massachusetts	20.0	PA	39.6
7 Utah	19.9	6 Newton, MA	37.6
8 California	19.6	7 Berkeley, CA	37.5
9 Virginia	19.1	8 Irvine, CA	36.8
10 Vermont	19.0	9 Richardson, TX	36.1
11 Washington	19.0	10 Evanston, IL	35.6
12 New Jersey	18.3	11 Arlington, VA	35.5
13 New Hampshire	18.2	12 Newport Beach, CA	35.1
14 New York	17.9	13 Ann Arbor, MI	35.1
15 Oregon	17.9	14 Alexandria, VA	34.2
16 New Mexico	17.6	15 Silver Spring, MD	33.7
17 Delaware	17.5	16 Cleveland Heights, OH	33.5
18 Montana	17.5	17 Oak Park, IL	33.4
19 Arizona	17.4	18 Bellevue, WA	33.1
20 Minnesota	17.4	19 Walnut Creek, CA	32.9
21 Wyoming	17.2	20 Kendall, FL	32.4
22 Kansas	17.0	21 Plano, TX	32.1
23 Texas	16.9	22 Boulder, CO	32.0
24 Illinois	16.2	23 West Hartford, CT	31.4
25 Idaho	15.8	24 Cambridge, MA	31.1
26 Nebraska	15.5	25 Overland Park, KS	30.0
27 Rhode Island	15.4	26 Cherry Hill, NJ	29.7
28 Oklahoma	15.1	27 Troy, MI	29.5
29 Florida	14.9	28 Townson, MD	29.3
30 Wisconsin	14.8	29 Mission Viejo, CA	28.9
31 North Dakota	14.8	30 Santa Monica, CA	28.9
32 Georgia	14.6	31 Iowa City, IA	28.4
33 Nevada	14.4	32 Arlington Heights, IL	27.9
34 Maine	14.4	33 Farmington Hills, MI	26.6

States*		Cities*	
35 Michigan	14.3	34 Madison, WI	26.4
36 South Dakota	14.0	35 Southfield, MI	26.3
37 Iowa	13.9		
38 Louisiana	13.9	*The Bottom Ten*	
39 Missouri	13.9	454 Norwalk, CA	5.0
40 Ohio	13.7	455 Baldwin Park, CA	5.0
41 Pennsylvania	13.6	456 Roseville, MI	4.1
42 South Carolina	13.4	457 Compton, CA	4.1
43 North Carolina	13.2	458 South Gate, CA	4.0
44 Tennessee	12.6	459 Pico Rivera, CA	3.9
45 Indiana	12.5	460 Camden, NJ	3.8
46 Mississippi	12.3	461 El Monte, CA	3.6
47 Alabama	12.2	462 Dundalk, MD	3.4
48 Kentucky	11.1	463 East Los Angeles, CA	2.0
49 Arkansas	10.8		
50 West Virginia	10.4		
*Percent of population 25+		*Percent of population 18+	

Source: 1980 census

In nine other states, all in the South, the median number of school years completed by blacks is under 12. These states are Alabama, Arkansas, Florida, Georgia, Louisiana, North Carolina, South Carolina, Tennessee, and Virginia. Blacks have a median of over 13 years in two states—13.1 years in South Dakota and 13.7 years in Vermont. In these and five other states, blacks' median years of schooling is higher than that of the whites in those states: Idaho, Maine, Montana, New Hampshire, and North Dakota. These states are among those with the fewest black residents of any of the states. The five states combined had a 1980 black population of about 15,000.

Hispanic educational attainment exceeds white attainment in only three states: Maryland, Virginia, and Vermont. Vermont has twice as many Hispanics as blacks, but they total only 3,377. Maryland's Hispanics have the highest educational attainment, a median of 12.8 years. Texas has the lowest, 8.8 years. Educated people are more likely to move than those with less education. They have more opportunities, and the job market for professionals is nationwide, bringing blacks to North Dakota and Hispanics to Maryland.

In some states minorities dominate the public school system. More than 50 percent of all students in Mississippi are black, 43 percent of South Carolina's, and 42 percent of Louisiana's. New Mexico's public school enrollment is 47 percent Hispanic; followed by Texas, 30 percent; California, 25 percent; and Arizona, 24 percent. American Indians are 21 percent of Alaska's public school students, and Asians and Pacific Islanders are 71 percent of Hawaii's. In New Mexico, over 10 percent of all students have difficulty with the English language.

Education is the road to advancement. Almost all Americans start the journey, but the road soon becomes rocky, and some fall behind. The government has tried to pave the road (for example, over 50 percent of all public school students ride to school at public expense, up from only 38 percent in 1960), but some states do not spend enough money to keep the road in good repair. Some parents want their children to take a different path: Nearly 5 million youngsters attend private or parochial schools, primarily Catholic institutions. Although public school enrollments have dropped because of the decline in the number of youngsters, private school enrollments have remained fairly stable.

By one means or another, a larger share of young people are graduating from high school and enrolling in college, but rising enrollments have been accompanied by falling test scores. In 1980, SAT scores were at their all-time low, after falling steadily for over a decade. Today's college students are no longer solely the elite of America, as past generations of the college-educated were. College graduates still include the best and the brightest, but they include more of the mediocre as well. If the cost of broadening the reach of education is to pull down the averages, the benefit is to open wider the doors of opportunity to many who would otherwise be shut out.

People go to college not only to learn but also because they know it will help them to earn higher incomes and increase their chances of getting a good job. Education does not guarantee equality. Whites continue to earn more than blacks at every level of education, for example. In 1982, white men with a high school diploma had a median income greater than the median for black men who had college diplomas. But black incomes rise steadily with education, and the same is true for other minority groups and for women. Education pays off, and so a rising share of Americans—men and women, white and black, Asian and Hispanic—will seek an education in the future.

TRENDS TO WATCH

– The rising educational attainment of young Americans means that in the future society as a whole will become more educated, as young people age and replace the older generation. Today, young men and young women have equal rates of college attendance, and women out-number men in college. More than nine out of ten college students favor equal pay and job opportunities for both sexes.

– Education boosts annual income and lifetime earnings. Education has a profound effect on social attitudes. Education changes views about career, marriage, divorce, and childbearing. People with a college education have smaller families, they are much more concerned with health, nutrition, and fitness, and they are more active in politics and community affairs. Educated consumers are more sophisticated, demand higher quality products, and expect better service.

– As it becomes more common for people to attend college, the possession of a college degree will no longer define a small educational, social, and economic elite. Instead, it will become a dividing line between two broad groups of Americans.

13 | Divided We Earn

"There is still a middle of the road, but more Americans are somewhere off on the shoulders. More households are becoming affluent, because more wives have joined the labor force. But more households are poor, because a rise in divorce has made more women the sole earners in their families. Fewer are left in the middle."

Hard work, brains, and luck are not all it takes to get ahead in America. Increasingly, family status determines how much a person has. American incomes have become more polarized in recent years—a reversal of the pattern throughout most of this century when the middle class was growing rapidly, poverty was on the decline, and the great disparities in wealth were disappearing.

There is still a middle of the road, but more Americans are somewhere off on the shoulders. More households are becoming affluent, because more wives have joined the labor force. But more households are poor, because a rise in divorce has made more women the sole earners in their families. Fewer are left in the middle.

The middle class today consists primarily of traditional families, in which the husband works full time and the wife does not work, or works only part time to supplement the family's income. On either side of the middle are a greater share of households in which women play an important role as earners. When a woman's income represents a second income, family income increases dramatically. When a woman is divorced or separated, family income sinks.

The median income of married couples in which both husband and wife worked in 1982 was $30,342. For married-couple families in which the wife was not in the labor force, median income was $21,299, near the median income for all households. But for female-headed families, median income was only $11,484. Two-earner couples are the new rich, whereas women who must support families by themselves are the new poor.

The income gap widened during the past decade. The share of low-income households, those making under $15,000 in 1982 dollars, rose 3.9 percentage points between 1970 and 1982. During these same years, the share of high-income households, those making at least $35,-000, rose 3.5 percentage points. The share of middle-income households shrank. The proportion of those making between $15,000 and $25,000, fell 1 percentage point. And it dropped fully 6.5 percentage points for those with incomes between $25,000 and $35,000. The following table shows how middle-class ranks have thinned:

Table 17 THE SHRINKING MIDDLE

Distribution of Household Income, 1970 and 1982
(in percent, constant 1982 dollars)

| | Year | | Percentage |
	1970	1982	point change
Low income (under $15,000)	33.5%	37.4%	+3.9
Lower middle			
($15,000–$24,999)	24.6	23.6	−1.0
Upper middle			
($25,000–$34,999)	23.4	16.9	−6.5
High income ($35,000 plus)	18.5	22.0	+3.5

Source: Census Bureau

According to the Census Bureau's 1983 Current Population Survey, a nationwide sample of households, 7.4 million households, or nearly 9 percent of the nation's 84 million households in 1983, had an annual income of at least $50,000 for the year 1982. Another 11 million households, or over 13 percent of the total, earned between $35,000 and

$50,000. At the bottom end of the scale, 20 million households, or 24 percent of all households, earned less than $10,000,. Another 21.5 million households, or about 26 percent, earned between $10,000 and $20,000, while 23.8 million households, or 28 percent, earned between $20,000 and $35,000 in 1982.

Families headed by people in executive, administrative, or managerial jobs had the highest median income in 1982, $37,787, while service workers and farmers headed families with the lowest median incomes, $18,009 and $15,508, respectively. Families headed by people with a graduate degree were at the top of the income ladder in 1982, with a median income of $41,587. But those with an eighth grade education or less averaged only $13,443.

People living alone had the lowest median income of all in 1982, just $9,984. This type of household includes young people who have just entered the labor force, older people who have retired, and middle-aged people who have never gotten married or who are between marriages. Their income is less than half that of two-person households, who earned a median of $20,201 in 1982.

Men's median income is twice as high as women's, $13,950 for men versus just $5,887 for women in 1982. Not only do men tend to earn higher wages than women, but also a higher proportion of men are in the labor force. Of those in the labor force, a higher share of men than of women work full time, year-round. Women who worked full time, year-round, had a median income of only $13,663 in 1982, far below the $21,655 of men who worked full time throughout the year.

Income still varies markedly by region of the country. Median family income was highest in the Northeast in 1982, where it was $24,918, and lowest in the South, at $21,500. Median household income was highest in the West, at $21,192, and lowest in the South, at $18,591.

MOVING FORWARD, STANDING STILL

America takes pride in advancing the standard of living, offering each generation a better way of life. In the 1970s, however, if people advanced at all, their path was rocky and their route circuitous. Median family income rose from less than $10,000 in 1970 to more than $23,433 in 1980, but after adjusting for inflation, real median family income in 1980 was some $1,000 less than in 1970. In contrast, in the 1960s, real median family income rose over $6,000, and in the 1950s, it rose over $5,000.

And median family income still dropped by $1,000 despite the addition of over 8 million wives to the labor force in the 1970s. Real median income for families peaked in 1973, when the first oil embargo brought to an end two decades of economic growth.

Per capita income, or income per American, rose 13 percent in the 1970s, after adjusting for inflation, but primarily because the average number of children per family declined. Statistically, fewer mouths to feed means that each family member is better off, but to paint a picture of economic growth during the past decade is to make the doubtful assumption that the average parent became better off by having fewer children and that the average married couple became better off because the wife went to work.

For unrelated individuals, those people who were either living alone or with unrelated people, real income rose 25 percent. Most Americans living in these two types of household are elderly. Their incomes rose during the 1970s because the government increased Social Security benefits dramatically. Because the government indexed increases in retirement benefits to the unprecedented increases in the cost of living during the 1970s, families with no earners kept up with inflation better than families whose members had to work for a living. The improvement in the living conditions of the elderly came at the expense of the working population. Still, the incomes of the elderly remain low compared to those of working-age people. Social Security notwithstanding, many retired people live in poverty.

By some measures, the American standard of living did continue its upward momentum during the stagnant 1970s: In 1980, 98 percent of all households had at least one television set; the 99.9 percent of households that had electricity also had an electric coffee maker. The proportion of households with air conditioners rose from 37 percent in 1970 to over 57 percent in 1980. This statistic is witness not only to Americans' rising standard of living but also to population growth in the South and Southwest, parts of which would still be as deserted without air conditioning as Minneapolis would be without heat. The electric blanket now covers nearly two thirds of all households, up from only one half in 1970.

An economy in which virtually every household already has an electric coffee maker, a toaster, and a vacuum cleaner is a different place from the economy of the past. Mass markets have become saturated, so mass merchandising is less effective. The population trends of the 1950s and early 1960s supported the rapid growth of a mass market. Until the mid-1960s, couples paired off and had children in traditional

families, while rising levels of education and real income, not the infla-
tionary brand, increased the purchasing power of households.

Today, however, new households form not only when young people
pair off to begin families but also when young people postpone getting
married and when couples divorce and remarry. The trends that produced today's fragmented American households, although population
growth slowed radically, created the conditions that led the manufacturers and marketers of products to slice the marketplace into segments.

The middle-class consumer market of a generation ago was characterized by its similarities; the segmented market of this generation is
characterized by its differences. Businesses seek out markets by following population growth out beyond saturated suburbia and also by
studying which types of consumers are most likely to buy their product
and then trying to find where those consumers live and how to reach
them.

Such demographic characteristics as income, occupation, age, and
family status have always been important determinants of consumer
spending, but today they hold the key to success or failure. Because the
population is no longer growing rapidly, because some age groups are
increasing while others are decreasing in number, because families have
fractured, and because racial and ethnic flows have changed course,
new consumer markets are arising, while old ones are disappearing. The
rifle shot is replacing the shotgun's salvo in manufacturing and marketing.

Because today's households are not the same as those of the past
decade, it is misleading to compare American incomes in 1970 with
those of the 1980s. America did not stagnate in the 1970s after all, even
though the statistical averages give that impression. Instead, some people became much better off, while others ended the decade in worse
shape than they began it.

Because per capita income measures the income of individuals—
and so did not fluctuate with changes in living arrangements between
1970 and 1980—it is a better measure of the decade's changes in income
than are family or household income statistics, which changed not only
as people became better off or worse off but also as a large share of
people left certain types of living arrangements and entered others. The
real median income for all households was $1,500 less in 1982 than in
1970, in part because a smaller share of all households were families in
1980 than in 1970. Family income is generally higher than household

income because families are more likely to have more than one earner.

Real per capita income grew 18 percent nationally, after adjustment for inflation, in the 1970s. Areas of the country that gained population rapidly in the 1970s also gained rapidly in per capita income, a trend that reflects the link between economic opportunity and population shifts; a major reason people move is to better themselves. The states that grew the fastest in per capita income were those that began the 1970s with relatively low per capita incomes and in which the population grew rapidly. Mississippi, one of the country's poorest states, ranked first in per capita income growth, which rose 40 percent; and it gained 14 percent in population. New York, one of the richest states, grew slowest in per capita income, which rose only 4 percent; and its population dropped by 4 percent.

Real income in Mississippi rose by $1,500 per capita, but it was still only $5,327 in 1979. In New York State, income rose only $325 per capita, to nearly $7,500. Although the average New Yorker is still much richer than the average Mississippian, the gap has narrowed. The regional differences in per capita income shrank during the 1970s as jobs and people flowed South and West.

The South made particular progress; it grew 20 percent in population, nearly twice the national rate, and 28 percent in per capita income, far above the 18 percent U.S. average. Per capita income in the South was $6,813 in 1979; the U.S. average was $7,313. Still, six of the bottom-ten states in per capita income are in the South. Six western states rank among the top ten, and the West grew second fastest in per capita income during the decade, to surpass the Northeast as the nation's richest region, per capita.

Per capita income in the West in 1980 was $7,921; in the Northeast, $7,477. Although income in the Northeast rose 10 percent, far below the national average, in the West it rose at exactly the national average. Income in the North-Central States grew slightly below the average, maintaining third-place position among the four regions, $558 richer per person than the South.

Eleven states gained 30 percent or more in real per capita income in the 1970s, including the energy-rich states of Wyoming, Colorado, Texas, Louisiana, and Oklahoma. West Virginia and South Carolina gained over 35 percent in per capita income; Alabama, 30 percent. Only one state in the North grew over 30 percent—North Dakota. All but Missouri in the western half of the North-Central Region, the Farm Belt, grew faster than the national rate—averaging a 24 percent increase; whereas all except Wisconsin of the North-Central Region's eastern states, the Industrial Belt, grew below the national average. In the Northeast, only Maine, New Hampshire, and Pennsylvania came close to the 18 percent national average gain.

Among major metropolitan areas, as among the states, real per capita income grew fastest in those that began the decade with low incomes and gained rapidly in population. Big metropolitan areas that were losing population grew the slowest in per capita income. The New York metropolitan area gained only 2 percent; Newark, 6 percent; Chicago, 7 percent; and Los Angeles, 9 percent. But Houston gained 38 percent in per capita income; Denver-Boulder, 33 percent; and Atlanta, 32 percent.

Because a good education often accompanies a high income, places that rank high in education also rank high in income. Bethesda, Maryland, for example, ranks high in per capita income and is one of the few large cities the United States in which a majority of adults have graduated from college. Per capita income there is $17,600; and 58 percent of residents aged twenty-five or older are college graduates. But not all "educated" cities are wealthy. Such college towns as Madison, Wisconsin; Ann Arbor, Michigan; and Boulder, Colorado, rank high in education, but not in income, because neither their student nor their faculty residents are among America's top earners.

One of the poorest cities in America, among those of at least 50,000 residents, is East Saint Louis, Illinois. Per capita income there is just $3,700 and median household income, $7,700. Other cities that rank low in income in both these measures are Laredo, Texas; Camden, New Jersey; and Newark, New Jersey. Newport Beach, California, ranks at the top among large cities in per capita income with $18,100. Not only is it a long way geographically from Newport Beach to East Saint Louis, the distance in per capita income is just as far—the $14,400 gap is nearly twice the country's own per capita income.

When both population and income are growing, a metropolitan area's aggregate income can soar. *Aggregate income*—per capita income multiplied by the total population—is one measure of an area's attractiveness as a market. Although the huge metropolitan areas of the Northeast and Midwest had only sluggish gains in aggregate income in the 1970s, and New York and St. Louis actually ended the decade with a lower aggregate income than when they began, the large metropolitan areas of the West and the South were posting huge gains in aggregate income.

Houston's aggregate income doubled as people and dollars flocked to the oil city; Fort Lauderdale and Phoenix gained at least 90 percent. Thirteen large metropolitan areas gained over 50 percent in aggregate income; all were in the South or West, and ten of them were in the nation's big-three boom states: California, Texas, and Florida. The nation as a whole gained 32 percent in real aggregate income during the decade. In 1979, the national aggregate was $1.7 trillion.

Traditionally, the North has been the nation's richest region, but the regional balance is shifting. Aggregate income in the Midwest and the Northeast grew at a pace below the national average, while the South and the West, propelled by their booming metropolitan areas, narrowed the gap in wealth with the North. In 1970, the South ranked third in aggregate income, with $333.4 billion. The combination of a rapidly growing economy and a huge population increase pulled the nation's most populous region into first place as the region with the highest aggregate income by 1980—$513.5 billion. The South pushed the North-Central Region from first place to second, with $433.9 billion, and the Northeast from second place to third, with $367.4 billion in 1979. Although the South had a rise in aggregate income of 54 percent, the Midwest gained 22 percent and the Northeast 10 percent.

The South came of age during the 1970s—casting off its reputation as a humid backwater of racial prejudice and sleepy small towns and emerging as vigorous, growth oriented, and modern minded. Nowhere does this transformation show up so well as in aggregate income, which accounts for both population and income growth. The West grew impressively too, up 47 percent in aggregate income, but remained in fourth place because of its small population. The Rocky Mountain States as a group grew faster in aggregate income than any other of the nine census divisions, rising 73 percent. Nevada and Wyoming doubled their aggregate income. But California still dominates the western market, contributing $196 billion of the entire region's $342 billion in aggregate income. California's 38 percent gain was above the national average, but no match for Florida's 80 percent gain, Texas's 67 percent, or Georgia's 52 percent.

Even New Hampshire grew faster than California in aggregate income, up 46 percent, as it lured people and their incomes from heavily taxed Massachusetts. Behind only New York and Rhode Island, Massachusetts had the third-lowest growth rate of any state in real aggregate income in the 1970s. Although some areas of the North did not fare badly, their growth has been but a shadow of the tremendous expansion in much of the rest of the country as income is becoming more evenly distributed across the face of America.

PEOPLE IN POVERTY

In the 1950s, estimates were that nearly 25 percent of Americans were poor. One of the goals of government for the past generation has been to eliminate poverty, largely through the Great Society programs of the 1960s. The poverty level fell rapidly through the 1960s, before leveling off in the 1970s at around 12 percent.

The antipoverty programs have not worked if the test is to eliminate poverty. The poor are still with us. In the 1980 census, nearly 28 million people, or 12.5 percent of the population, fell below the poverty level. In 1982, following two recession years, over 34 million people were living in poverty, or 15 percent of the population. The official poverty level in 1982 was an income of $5,019 for a single person and $9,862 for a family of four. The government arrives at the definition by multiplying the Agriculture Department's estimate of the cost of a minimum adequate diet by three, on the grounds that families spend about one third of their income on food.

Blacks are three times as likely as whites to be poor. Whereas only 12 percent of whites lived in poverty in 1982, 36 percent of blacks were poor. And 30 percent of Hispanics were living in poverty. Because whites are a majority of the population, despite their lower poverty rate poor whites outnumber poor blacks by more than two to one and poor Hispanics by more than five to one. In 1982, over 23 million whites lived in poverty compared to fewer than 10 million blacks and just over 4 million Hispanics.

Women who are heads of families, regardless of race, are particularly prone to poverty. The poverty rate for families headed by women with no husband present was over 40 percent in 1982, compared to a rate of 8 percent for married-couple families.

Rural poverty still exists in America. Because of its rural poverty, the South is still the only region to exceed the 15 percent national poverty rate in 1982. Among states, the poverty rate for persons ranged from a high of 24.5 percent in Mississippi, according to the 1980 census, to a low of 8 percent in Wyoming. Mississippi also had the highest poverty rate for families, 19.5 percent, while Wyoming and Nevada tied for the lowest, 5.9 percent.

Rural areas are on the upswing, and cities now face growing poverty. Nearly one third of the residents of Newark, New Jersey, fell below the poverty line, according to the 1980 census, which measured income received in 1979. Newark had the highest poverty rate of any large city in the nation. It was the only large northeastern city to be among the top ten in rate of poverty for persons in 1970. In 1980, it was joined by Hartford and New Haven, Connecticut, and Paterson, New Jersey.

Atlanta, Georgia, ranked second in poverty rate according to the 1980 census. Twenty-eight percent of its residents were poor. Among the nation's 169 cities of 100,000 population or more in 1980, fully 106 exceeded the national poverty rate in 1979. The city with the lowest poverty rate was Livonia, Michigan, with only 2.2 percent. Only 5 other cities of 100,000 population or more, had poverty rates below 5 percent: Warren and Sterling Heights, Michigan; Fremont, Sunnyvale, and Torrance, California.

Poverty is not what it used to be, now that almost all homes have television sets and other appliances that used to be luxuries. Moreover, poverty statistics do not reflect the value of such government benefits as food stamps that raise a poor family's standard of living. Including the market value of government noncash subsidies for the poor would reduce the number of people counted as living in poverty. Among the elderly, for example, counting noncash government benefits, primarily the value of subsidized medical care, as household income would reduce the share of elderly poor from nearly 15 percent of all people aged sixty-five and older to less than 4 percent.

Nor, for that matter, do income statistics for middle and upper incomes reflect tax breaks, subsidized pensions, and other benefits. Noncash benefits provided by government and private employers alike have become widespread. In 1982, an incredible 89 percent of all American households, or 75 million households, received at least one noncash benefit—Medicare, school lunches, pensions, or employer-provided health care. Almost 15 million households, or 17 percent of the total, received benefits available only to those whose income fell below a certain level. The median income of these latter households was about $8,000, versus over $21,000 for all households receiving noncash benefits. Money may not go as far as it once did, but nonmoney is going further.

Defining poverty is a political act and, therefore, hotly contested. How should one count the poor? What does it mean to be poor? But even including the full market value of all government noncash benefits, some 22 million people, or 10 percent of the total population, lived below the poverty level in 1982. Some were young people just setting out on their own, whose incomes will rise as they grow older. Others were victims of the recession, the people economic recovery has pulled back above the poverty line. But many were households headed by elderly women unable to earn enough money to escape poverty.

Between 1979 and 1982, more than 8 million additional Americans fell below the poverty line, and this is a conservative measure. In one sense, these poor are even worse off than those of the early 1960s because today's average American family no longer spends as much as the one third of its income on food as the government assumes in its poverty calculations. But by another measure, the number of poor is no greater than two decades ago, since about the same proportion of the population today as in 1960 has an income below one half of the U.S. median income. Measurement aside, poverty has become more democratic than ever, for millions less a chronic condition than a phase. Young people become poor when they leave the family home to seek their first job, women become poor when divorce splits their home, and elderly women become poor when they become widows.

But the image of poverty that most Americans hold has not kept pace with the changing portrait of the poor. A generation ago some families were poor because the breadwinner husband lost his job or lacked marketable skills. Women who lived in poverty then were likely to be the wives of poor men. Today, poor women are likely to head their own household. In 1959, two thirds of the poor lived in families headed by men. By 1982, this proportion had dropped to less than half. Today, 59 percent of poor blacks live in families headed by a woman, as do 24 percent of poor whites. The new faces of poverty are female and black.

The proportion of children who live in poverty has dropped since 1960 as families have become smaller. Still, nearly 40 percent of the poverty population today are children under age eighteen. Of these, more than half live in single-parent families headed by women. In 1960, less than one quarter of children in poverty lived in this type of family.

Because black families have fragmented more than white families, black poverty has grown more than white poverty. A much higher share of black households are single-parent families headed by women. Had family composition been the same in 1980 as it was in 1970, according to the Census Bureau, the poverty rate for blacks would have been under 20 percent in 1980, instead of nearly 29 percent. But dramatic family changes did occur, and today the best predictor of female poverty is marital status. The decisions a woman makes, or has made for her, about marriage, childbearing, and divorce directly affect her odds of falling into or staying out of poverty. These shifts in family status are far more important determinants of whether a woman lives in poverty than any other factor.

Conservatives argue that if women would only remain married, they would not be poor. Liberals argue that family disintegration reflects social changes beyond the control of the poor. The one side dreams of reducing poverty by restoring the traditional family. The other side wants more government support for the unfortunate. But neither side recognizes that women have become earners in their own right instead of secondary earners behind their husbands. The task is neither to return them to their husbands nor to cushion their fall from grace, but rather to recognize that society has changed.

Women face new responsibilities equal to, and sometimes greater than, those of men. A woman with two children, working full time throughout the year at the minimum wage, would still be below the poverty line. Add the costs of child care and other work-related expenses, and the woman worker becomes even poorer. Poverty today affects not only a hard core of unemployables or hard-luck cases but, increasingly, women who are raising children without husbands, whose jobs pay too little to allow them to succeed.

EARNING AND SPENDING

Like poverty, affluence is a matter not only of money but also of definition, A couple in their forties earning $25,000 a year and trying to send two children to college cannot be considered affluent, but a couple approaching retirement, whose children are grown and who have substantial equity in their home, could be living comfortably on $25,000 a year. As a group, the elderly possess more spending power than their low incomes suggest because they have fewer financial obligations, and the same is true of young people who live alone.

The same forces that are changing the face of the poverty population are creating a new kind of affluence. Many wives have propelled their families into affluence when their incomes are added to their husbands' incomes. In 1982, married couples in which both husband and wife worked full time had a median income of over $36,000.

Between 1970 and 1981, the number of married couples in which both husband and wife were employed rose 28 percent, whereas the number in which only the husband worked declined 28 percent. Households in which both husband and wife work have outnumbered those in which only the husband works since the late 1960s, but the gap is widening. In 1970, the husband, but not the wife, worked in 19.6 million households; by 1981, the number had dropped to 14 million. In

1970, 20.5 million households contained two-income couples; by 1982, their number had risen to 25.9 million.

Six million wives earned more than their husbands in 1981, 12 percent of all couples. In 2 million couples, the wife was the sole provider; in many such families, the husband had retired while a younger wife continued to work. Nearly four out of ten wives who earned more than their husbands in 1981 had completed more years of schooling than had their husbands. More than one third were in professional and managerial jobs, compared to only one quarter of wives who earned less than their husbands. Women who were secondary earners were concentrated in clerical, service, and sales jobs. American incomes have long reflected educational and occupational differences. Men who graduate from college and fill executive or professional jobs have always had much higher lifetime earnings than men who do not. But now this is becoming true of women.

Women earners play an important role in lifting some cities upward in income rankings, because some areas that have high percentages of women in the labor force also have high incomes. Among cities of 50,000 population or more, women's labor-force participation rates range from a high of 69 percent in Columbia, Maryland, a planned community between Baltimore and Washington, D.C., to a low of 26 percent in Miami Beach, where not too many men work either. Columbia ranks high in median household income ($29,900); Miami Beach ranks low ($8,500).

Surprisingly wide gaps in women's labor-force participation appear among the states—from Nevada's top ranking 60 percent to West Virginia's low of 37 percent. States at the bottom of the rankings include Kentucky, Louisiana, Arkansas, Alabama, Florida, Pennsylvania, Mississippi, New Mexico, and North Dakota. States near the top include Alaska, Hawaii, Colorado, New Hampshire, Maryland, Minnesota, North Carolina, Connecticut, and Massachussetts.

According to the 1980 census, Alaska led the nation in the share of families with incomes of $50,000 or more, at 18 percent, twice as high as second-place Hawaii's 9 percent. Connecticut, Maryland, New Jersey, and California came next, all 8 percent or more. In eight other states the proportion was over 6 percent—Illinois, Virginia, Michigan, Nevada, Delaware, New York, and Colorado. The national average was 5.6 percent. In Maine, only 2.2 percent of its families had incomes of at least $50,000, according to the census, the smallest share of any state. The only other states below 3 percent in the share of affluent households were South Dakota, Arkansas, and Mississippi.

Table 18 WOMEN IN THE LABOR FORCE

U.S. Average, 50.0 Percent

States		Cities	
1 Nevada	59.8%	1 Columbia, MO	68.9%
2 Alaska	57.9	2 Bloomington, MN	67.4
3 Hawaii	56.5	3 Alexandria, VA	66.5
4 Colorado	54.8	4 Westminster, CO	66.5
5 New Hampshire	54.4	5 Mountain View, CA	65.9
6 Maryland	54.3	6 Redondo Beach, CA	65.9
7 Minnesota	54.0	7 Paradise, NV	65.8
8 North Carolina	53.7	8 Aurora, CO	65.7
9 Connecticut	53.6	9 Garland, TX	65.5
10 Massachusetts	52.8	10 Irving, TX	65.1
11 Wisconsin	52.7	11 Reno, NV	65.0
12 South Carolina	52.4	12 Schaumburg, IL	64.7
13 California	52.4	13 Anchorage, AK	64.5
14 Rhode Island	52.2	14 Mesquite, TX	64.5
15 Georgia	51.9	15 Arlington, VA	64.2
16 Virginia	51.9	16 Sunnyvale, CA	63.8
17 Vermont	51.7	17 Irvine, CA	63.6
18 Illinois	51.5	18 Iowa City, IA	63.2
19 Delaware	51.4	19 Cerritos, CA	63.1
20 Wyoming	51.4	20 Rochester, MN	63.1
21 Nebraska	51.1	21 Daly City, CA	62.9
22 Kansas	50.8	22 Arlington, TX	62.8
23 Texas	50.7	23 Santa Clara, CA	62.6
24 New Jersey	50.5	24 Madison, WI	62.1
25 Washington	50.4	25 West Covina, CA	62.0
26 Indiana	50.3	26 Lincoln, NE	61.9
27 Oregon	50.2	27 Richardson, TX	61.7
28 Iowa	50.0	28 Tempe, AZ	61.6
29 Utah	49.4	29 Arvada, CO	61.5
30 Missouri	49.2	30 Inglewood, CA	61.3
31 South Dakota	49.1	31 Fremont, CA	60.8
32 Montana	48.9	32 Costa Mesa, CA	60.6
33 Idaho	48.8	33 Mount Prospect, IL	60.6
34 Tennessee	48.8	34 Charlotte, NC	60.6
35 Michigan	48.7	35 Palo Alto, CA	60.4
36 New York	48.2		
37 Ohio	48.0	*The Bottom Ten*	
38 Maine	47.8	454 Port Arthur, TX	41.5
39 Arizona	47.6	455 Altoona, PA	41.5
40 Oklahoma	47.1	456 Youngstown, OH	41.1
41 North Dakota	46.9	457 Camden, NJ	41.1
42 New Mexico	46.2	458 East St. Louis, IL	40.7
43 Mississippi	45.8	459 Largo, FL	40.5
44 Pennsylvania	45.6	460 Laredo, TX	39.6
45 Florida	45.5	461 Huntington, WV	39.5

States		Cities	
46 Alabama	45.1	462 Pompano Beach, FL	39.4
47 Arkansas	44.5	463 Miami Beach, FL	25.9
48 Louisiana	44.1		
49 Kentucky	43.6		
50 West Virginia	36.5		

Source: 1980 Census

Increasingly, climbing the ladder to financial success will require a team effort. The saying "behind every successful man stands a woman" will take on new meaning, although the ladders will probably have to be widened to allow couples to stand side by side. Wives' incomes make it easier for men to lighten their heavy burden of being the principal wage earner in most families. The earnings of husbands in two-income families are less, on average, than those of husbands in traditional families.

Two-income couples are of two types: those in which both husband and wife work as professionals, managers, or administrators, and those in which only one partner (or neither partner) works as a professional or manager. Surveys taken by the National Opinion Research Center during the past five years show that just 10 percent of married couples with earnings were the dual-career couples so often depicted in the media—those with two professions. But 45 percent received two paychecks, and another 45 percent supported themselves on the earnings of only one spouse. Two-income couples may now be in the majority, but two-career professional couples are a small fraction of the American marketplace.

One-paycheck couples are older, on average, than two-paycheck couples, dual-career householders better educated—nearly one third have graduate-level education and over half have a college degree—than either one-paycheck householders or those with two sources of earnings, but in which neither partner is a professional. The incomes of dual-career couples reflect their superior education—two thirds have incomes of $25,000 or more. As companies have noticed, Yuppies, Yumpies, and other forms of these young, affluent households carry more economic clout than their small numbers might suggest.

Although women's wages are rising, workers in the upper-income brackets are still largely men. Fewer than 5 percent of working wives had incomes of $25,000 or more in 1982. Only about 114,000 women (including both married and unmarried) had incomes of at least $75,-

000, versus over 1 million men. In 1981, the Internal Revenue Service calculated that there were 4.5 million Americans with assets of $300,-000 or more. These 2 percent of Americans control nearly one quarter of the country's total wealth. Only one third of these Americans were women, but the women's average net worth was higher than the men's —$637,000 versus $471,000. Some women fall into poverty when their husband dies; others become wealthy through inheritance. Fewer than one third of the wealthy women were younger than fifty, compared to nearly one half of the men.

THE MEANING OF AFFLUENCE

Inflation erodes the meaning of affluence. In inflation-adjusted dollars, the share of households earning at least $50,000 peaked in 1979 and has since declined. Taxation, as everybody will tell you, also erodes spendable income, and the progressive income tax erodes the spendable income of the rich more than that of the poor—on the theory that the rich will miss their money less because they have more. Allowing for the tax bite, median household income in 1980 was not the $17,710 measured before taxes, but just $14,550, 18 percent less. Before taxes, more than 4.4 million households had incomes of $50,000 or more. After taxes, their number had dropped to 1 million. Across the board, paying taxes depresses income (as well as depressing taxpayers).

Perhaps to fight this taxing depression, Americans have been going underground. Almost one quarter of all households say they earn money they do not normally report on their income tax returns. In 1980, more than 80 percent of households purchased goods or services in the cash-only market, undocumented transactions amounting to $42 billion. The government estimates it collects taxes on less than one quarter of this total. Most people do not live it up with their underground gains, but rather spend it on food and home repairs.

American spending patterns shifted in the 1970s not only because of taxes but also because of rising oil prices and shrinking households. Oil consumed 11 percent of American incomes in 1980–81, compared to 7 percent in 1972–73, according to the government's consumer expenditure surveys. Hardest hit by oil price increases were the poor, who spend a higher proportion of their income on basics. The 20 percent of households with the lowest incomes devote nearly 80 percent of their income to food, energy, and household basics. The top 20 percent devote only 20 percent of their income to these items—

leaving more for luxuries, automobiles, travel, and investments.

Americans are spending a smaller share of their budgets on food than a decade ago, in part because their family size is smaller. They have been shifting their food spending from the home to restaurants. Fast-food establishments now dot, and sometimes blight, the landscape. In the early 1960s, consumers spent almost five times as much on food at home as on food away from home. Twenty years later, they spent only twice as much. Two-earner couples spend more of their food budgets on food away from home than do other households, and they spend more on energy, convenience goods, and transportation.

After taxes have been paid, and daily necessities paid for, some households manage to have money left for luxuries. The Census Bureau and the Conference Board, a business research organization, studied this discretionary spending, defining households with discretionary income as those with an income at least 30 percent higher than necessary to maintain a comfortable standard of living for households of a certain size, age, and geographic location. In all, over 25 million households had discretionary income in 1980, or 31 percent of all households.

The average after-tax income of these well-off households was $26,-962, and an average $7,644 of this amount was available for spending on goods and services beyond the necessities—a national total of $193 billion. The federal government could virtually eliminate its deficit without causing deprivation if it simply were to tax away all this discretionary money each year—perhaps as part of a national "back to basics" campaign. But it would be unlikely to rally much discretionary support for such a proposal.

Households with the most money to spare are headed by people in their prime earning years of the forties and early fifties, when earnings peak. Average after-tax income peaks in the forty-five to forty-nine age group at $32,665. Discretionary income peaks in the same age group, at an average $9,177. But between ages fifty-five and fifty-nine, when for most people the children have grown up and necesssities command a smaller share of a family's budget, the share of households with discretionary income peaks. Life may begin at forty, but "discretionary" life hits full stride at fifty-five.

A close relationship exists between discretionary dollars and years of education. The more education the head of a household possesses, the higher that household's discretionary income. Although fewer than one third of households have any discretionary income, one half of households headed by a college graduate have money to spare. The proportion is even larger for those households whose head has gone to graduate school. Average discretionary income for households headed by people with a graduate school education was over $11,000 in 1980 —an impressive amount of extra cash.

THE AFFLUENT FUTURE

As the baby-boom generation becomes a larger share of all workers and as the country's educational level continues to rise, national income should rise too. The 1970s were a time of rising divorce rates and rapid growth among young households, trends that depressed income. The number of households will be growing more slowly in the years ahead, but because a growing share of people will be middle-aged and more couples will have two earners, real incomes should rise. In another ten years, the affluent, middle-aged, husband-wife, baby-boom household will be a dominant feature of the economy.

So many factors affect income—economic growth, divorce rates, women's labor-force participation rates, and education and occupation —that income projections are only guesses. The Census Bureau shies away from them. Private forecasters, however, point to rising affluence. Data Resources Inc. (DRI), the Lexington, Massachussetts, forecasting firm, projects that median household income in real terms will rise from about $20,000 in 1980 to $25,000 in 1995, measured in constant 1982 dollars. A smaller share of all households will be in the low-income brackets and a higher share will be at the top levels.

The number of households earning at least $50,000, according to DRI, will triple between 1980 and 1995. As a share of all households, they will rise from just 8 percent to 18 percent. Household earnings of less than $20,000 will decline from 49 percent of all households in 1980 to just 41 percent in 1995. Overall, the share of households with an annual income below $40,000 should fall from 84 percent in 1980 to 72 percent in 1995. Those with $40,000 or more will rise from 16 percent of all households in 1980 to 28 percent in 1995, nearly doubling.

These income projections are not guaranteed (or your money back), but the direction of the trends seems certain: The aging of the baby-boom generation and the rise of the two-income couple, both powerful forces, should boost markets that cater to the affluent for the rest of this century. More products will emphasize quality, convenience, and culture.

This is not to say that poverty will be eliminated. To the contrary, a society with rising affluence must also cope with a new kind of poverty. Americans of the next decade will have moved far from the society of the 1950s, when men toiled to achieve a middle-class life for their wives and families. Now, women, too, help determine the fortunes of their families—for richer or for poorer.

TRENDS TO WATCH

– Rising affluence is in store for America, because a growing share of households will contain two earners and the baby-boom generation will be reaching its peak earning years.

– *Discretionary income*—the amount of income remaining after paying taxes and buying necessities—should rise as well, in part because the average household will contain fewer children.

– Even as affluence is growing, however, the proportion of Americans who are poor will also grow, because relatively more households will consist of single people or families headed by women without husbands.

– The relative size of the middle class will shrink, because the number of traditional husband-wife families in which the husband works but the wife does not will become a smaller share of all households.

The Canadian People

"Canadians, like their southern neighbors, favor the Sunbelt. The Canadian Sunbelt, however, stops just north of Detroit."

To know Canada demographically, simply know the United States and divide by ten. Canadians share many trends with their southern neighbors, but there is only one Canadian for about every ten residents of the United States. The Canadian population numbered 24 million at the time of that country's 1981 census, compared to 230 million in the United States in 1981.

Canadians do not like to think of themselves as one tenth of Americans. Nor do they like the habit U.S. residents have of reserving the term *Americans* for themselves. Canadians are Americans too. In some ways, Canada is different from the United States. In other ways, including its baby-boom generation, migration westward, and changes in how its people live, Canada's trends parallel those of the United States.

The Canadian climate helps to explain why a country second in land area only to the Soviet Union has so few residents. Canada, as a whole, is so sparsely populated that it is as if the residents of New York, Los Angeles, and Chicago were to have the entire United States, and then some, all to themselves. Canada's population grew 13 percent during the decade between the 1971 and 1981 censuses, slightly more than the growth of the U.S. population. But in the latter half of the 1970s, growth slowed to about 1 percent per year, only one third the rate of a generation earlier. Canadians are having fewer children, on average, than in the past.

At the peak of the Canadian baby boom, in the late 1950s, Canadian women were averaging 3.9 children apiece. More recently, however, fertility has dropped sharply, and Canadian women now average well below 2 children apiece. In consequence, like the United States, the Canadian population is becoming middle-aged. The median age of Canadians recorded by the 1981 census was almost thirty, up from twenty-eight in the 1976 Canadian census. (Canada takes a census every five years.) The rise in the Canadian median age is even more rapid than the trend in the United States, but its causes are the same: There are proportionately fewer children in the Canadian population, Canadians are living longer, and the Canadian baby-boomers are growing older. The number of Canadians aged sixty-five or older rose three times as fast as the general population.

Fluctuations in Canadian fertility over the past three decades have created a roller coaster effect in the age distribution of Canada that closely resembles that of the United States. Even though the average woman has been having fewer children than past generations, the number of preschool children in Canada increased 3 percent between the 1976 and 1981 censuses because the large baby-boom generation reached the childbearing years. However, the number of children between the ages of five and nineteen declined, reflecting the Canadian baby bust of the 1960s and early 1970s. As in the United States, the fastest-growing age groups in Canada are now in their thirties, the leading edge of the baby boom.

The number of people in the average Canadian household has dropped steadily. In the 1981 census, average household size was just 2.9 persons per household, only slightly higher than the U.S. figure. To look inside the shrinking Canadian household is to find changing living arrangements—the postponement of marriage, an increase in divorce, a decline in childbearing, a lengthening life span, and an increasing probability that widowed Canadians will live alone rather than move in with relatives—all trends that are reshaping households in the United States as well.

Young Canadians are marrying later than in the past. As recently as 1976, 46 percent of Canadian women were married by the age of twenty-one. By 1981, the share had dropped to 40 percent. One Canadian household in five in 1981 contained a person living alone, up from 17 percent five years earlier. Households containing six persons or more dropped from being 10 percent of all households in 1976 to become just 6 percent in 1981.

The number of single-parent families increased 28 percent between 1976 and 1981, married couples by only 9 percent. Women headed 80 percent of single-parent families. Still, 5.6 million Canadian households contain a husband and wife—two thirds of the country's 8.3 million households—whereas there were only 714,000 single-parent families in 1981. Divorce has become commonplace in Canada, just as it has in the United States. The divorced population rose by almost 66 percent between 1976 and 1981. But divorced Canadians accounted for only 2.5 percent of the total adult population in 1981, some 500,000 people. Remarriage rates are high and a rising share of all marriages are remarriages.

THE CANADIAN SUNBELT

Canadians, like their southern neighbors, favor the Sunbelt. The Canadian Sunbelt, however, stops just north of Detroit. Only a few hardy Canadians—fewer than 1 percent—live in the Yukon and in the Northwest Territories. Most of the population is concentrated in the southern border of the country—as far south as a Canadian can go without emigrating.

More than 60 percent of Canadians live in the provinces of Ontario and Quebec, and Ontario is the most populous of Canada's twelve provinces. The 1981 census counted 8.6 million people there, more than one third of the total population. Quebec has 6.4 million residents, more than one quarter of all Canadians. Next in size is British Columbia, with 2.7 million residents, and Alberta, with 2.2 million. Manitoba has slighty more than 1 million residents, and all the other provinces have fewer than 1 million. The Yukon, an enormous expanse of territory, has only 23,000 inhabitants, and the Northwest Territories, an even vaster province stretching into the Arctic, has only 46,000 residents.

The western provinces are growing rapidly, whereas population growth has slowed in Canada's east. Alberta grew 38 percent and British Columbia 26 percent between 1971 and 1981, as Canadians moved west. These were the only two populous provinces to grow faster than the national rate of 13 percent for the decade. The Yukon gained 26 percent in population and the Northwest Territories 31 percent, not because of migration to those provinces so much as because of the high fertility of their Indian and Inuit residents.

Ontario grew 12 percent. Quebec grew only 7 percent because fertility dropped in the province, despite its largely Catholic population. The lowest growth rates were in Saskatchewan and Manitoba, Canada's Midwest, both of which gained less than 5 percent in population.

Canada's population is redistributing itself in a westward direction. The western provinces gained migrants during the 1970s, while most of the eastern and central provinces lost migrants. For the first time in thirty years, Ontario's share of the total population declined. Quebec's dropped as well, but the western provinces all gained. Regional shifts reflect the experience of Canada's metropolitan areas. Much more than the U.S. population, Canadians are concentrated in major metropolitan areas. More than one out of four Canadians lives in Montreal, Toronto, or Vancouver.

With a population of about 3 million, Toronto is Canada's largest metropolitan area, home to 12 percent of all Canadians. In contrast, only 4 percent of U.S. residents live in New York, the largest U.S. metropolis. Montreal has almost 3 million residents, and Vancouver has 1.3 million. Of Canada's twenty-four metropolitan areas, only these three had populations over 750,000 in 1981.

The fastest-growing Canadian metropolitan areas between 1976 and 1981 were Calgary and Edmonton, both in Alberta—Canada's Mountain State. Calgary grew by 26 percent and Edmonton by 19 percent. In contrast, Toronto grew by just 7 percent, Montreal by less than 1 percent. The Ottawa-Hull metropolitan area, in which the Canadian capital is located, grew by just 4 percent in this five-year period. Two metropolitan areas lost population—Windsor and Sudbury, the former being the center of the Canadian automobile industry and the latter a nickel-producing area. Both suffered economic setbacks.

Mirroring the rural renaissance in the United States, Canadians are beginning to move to the less populous parts of the country and from crowded cities to less densely settled suburbs. Canada's two largest cities lost population between the two most recent censuses. Despite a population decline within the cities of Toronto and Montreal, their suburbs grew in population, especially the outer suburbs.

As in the United States, it is the rural Canadian population that is growing fastest. Between 1976 and 1981, the number of Canadians who lived in rural areas grew 9 percent, compared to just 5 percent in urban areas, which in Canada are those areas with a population of at least

1,000 and a population density of at least 400 people per square kilometer. As a result, the share of rural Canadians has risen in recent years, while the urban population has dropped. Still, some three quarters of all Canadians are urban. Even in the Yukon and the Northwest Territories, at least half of the population lives in urban areas.

As a result of Canada's population shifts, the four western provinces and the two territories now contain 28.9 percent of all Canadians, up from 26.8 percent a decade earlier. In the preceding twenty years, the West's share hardly increased at all. The share in the Atlantic Provinces dropped from 9.5 percent of Canadians to 9.2 percent between 1971 and 1981. Quebec lost 1.5 percentage points, falling to 26.4 percent of the total population during the decade. Ontario's share of the total population decined for the first time since 1951. It peaked at 35.9 percent in 1976, but dropped to 35.4 percent in 1981.

As many as 85 percent of Canadians were living in their province of birth at the time of the 1981 census, compared with only 64 percent of U.S. residents who were living in their state of birth at the time of the 1980 census. In Quebec, 92 percent of residents were born in the province. In Alberta and British Columbia, the most popular destinations for Canadian migrants during the 1970s, about 50 percent of the residents were born outside the province they now live in. And nearly 20 percent came from other countries. Quebec and Ontario are old Canada, still split between French and English, whereas Alberta and British Columbia may be the Canada of the future.

THE CULTURE GAP

If you telephone a government office in Canada, you will be greeted in two languages, English and French. Canada is officially a bilingual country. However, Canadians who can speak both official languages are highly concentrated in eastern Canada. More than 50 percent of bilingual Canadians live in Quebec; another 25 percent live in Ontario. According to the census, only 15 percent of Canadians are able to speak both English and French—up hardly at all from the 13.5 percent in 1971—or from the 13 percent fifty years ago. Thirty percent of bilingual Canadians have English as a mother tongue, and 61 percent have French.

French-speaking Canadians are more likely to learn English than English-speaking Canadians are to learn French. However, this pattern may be changing. In Quebec Province, the proportion of residents who are able to speak both English and French rose from less than 28 percent in 1971 to more than 32 percent a decade later. In the 1981 census, more than half of Quebec's people whose mother tongue was English reported being able to speak French, up from little more than one third a decade earlier

Language is such an important political issue in Canada that the census contains three separate measures of language ability: *mother tongue*, which is the language first learned in childhood and still understood; *home language*, which is the language a person usually speaks at home; and *official language*, which is a person's ability to speak either French or English.

According to the 1981 census, 61 percent of Canadians say English is their mother tongue; and 68 percent speak English at home. For 26 percent of Canadians, French is their mother tongue and 25 percent speak French at home. French Canadians are less likely than English-speaking Canadians to retain their mother tongue as the language used at home. Canada's immigrants are more likely to adopt English than French.

Seven percent of Canadians speak a language other than French or English at home. Although the number of Canadians speaking Italian, German, and Ukrainian fell during the 1970s, those speaking Indo-Pakistani languages increased over 300 percent. Spanish was up almost 200 percent, and Chinese 140 percent. The 1981 census recorded over seventy-five different mother tongues, most spoken by only small groups of people.

Even more than the United States, Canada is a land of immigrants. Sixteen percent of the Canadian people were born outside of Canada, whereas only 6 percent of U.S. residents were born outside the United States. Canada now has almost 4 million immigrants.

Before the 1970s, two of every three Canadian immigrants came from Europe. Between 1978 and 1981, however, fewer than one of every three arriving immigrants came from Europe; 44 percent came from Asia. Thus, Europeans are becoming a smaller share of the Canadian foreign-born population. In 1971, Europeans were 80 percent of all Canadians who had been born in another country; by 1981, their share had dropped to 67 percent, while the share of Asians and Latin Americans was growing. The total number of Canadians born in Europe actually declined during the past decade, reflecting their older age. The number of Canadians whose birthplace is Asia, however, rose 228 percent.

Whereas the United States forbids its census takers to ask about religion, Canada's census includes a question about religion. Canada is a nation of Catholics and Protestants. Some 47 percent of Canadians are Catholic, up 13 percent since 1971. Protestants are next, at 41 percent of the population. However, Catholics are a majority in only two provinces, Quebec, where they are 88 percent of all residents, and New Brunswick, where they are 54 percent. Elsewhere Protestants outnumber Catholics.

The third most popular answer to the religion question, however, was "no religion," a response given by 7 percent of the people—88 percent more than a decade earlier. The fastest-growing religious group are the Buddhists, up 223 percent during the 1970s, a consequence of immigration from Asia, but the Buddhists are not about to overtake the atheists: The country had 52,000 Buddhists in 1981, a scant 0.2 percent of all Canadians.

English and French still dominate Canada's ethnic landscape. In Newfoundland, more than 90 percent of residents are of British origin; in Quebec, 80 percent are of French origin. Among Canadians reporting a single ancestry in the 1981 census, 40 percent listed British and 27 percent French. Far behind was German, with 5 percent. Only 3 percent of Canadians reported Italian ancestry; and 2 percent reported Ukrainian, the fifth largest group. Native Peoples was the sixth largest ethnic group counted in the census, at some half-million. The 1981 census was the first in which Canadians could report more than a single ancestry, but only 8 percent of them did so—compared to about 33 percent of United States residents.

Because Canada is so influenced by immigration, Canadian census statistics dwell on immigrant status, language, and ethnicity, whereas the U.S. census is obsessed by race. But one searches Canadian census data in vain for tabulations by race. Canada has few blacks, and the census does not ask about race. Only 45,000 Canadians reported that their ethnic origin was African.

These differences in statistics reflect the two countries' different histories. The United States has faced difficulties integrating its large black minority into the mainstream, so the census charts racial progress in detail. But whites of different ethnic backgrounds have merged into the mainstream with comparatively little problem, so officials have less interest in examining their progress. In Canada, however, the large unassimilated minority is French, not black.

CANADIAN CHARACTERISTICS

The labor force in Canada has grown almost three times as fast as the rate of population growth during the past two decades, as the baby-boom generation swelled the ranks of workers and more women joined the labor force. Overall, almost 12 million Canadians were in the labor force at the time of the 1981 census. Over 7 million workers were in Quebec and Ontario provinces, but fewer than 13,000 in the Yukon.

Between 1971 and 1981, the number of women in Canada's labor force jumped 61 percent, versus a rise of only 24 percent for men. A majority of Canadian women now work outside the home, and 52 percent of Canadian wives, up from 37 percent in 1971. By 1981, women workers had become 41 percent of Canada's total work force, just 1 percentage point lower than that in the United States.

Women have been gaining in male-dominated professions. In 1981, there were over five times more women engineers, six times more women lawyers, three times more women accountants, and four times more women bus drivers than in 1971. Still, almost half of all women workers are in the teaching, clerical, and health occupations. Almost 9 percent of the members of the male labor force in Canada are self-employed, but only 3 percent of Canadian women.

Although the total labor force grew about 38 percent, finance, insurance, and real estate occupations grew almost 74 percent. A long-term decline in the agricultural labor force that began in the 1930s halted during the decade, except in the three prairie provinces that make up Canada's Midwest. In British Columbia, the number of workers in agriculture rose 37 percent. In all, the agricultural work force remained stable at slightly fewer than one-half million.

As in the United States, manufacturing is on a down trend. Thirty years ago, about one quarter of all Canadian workers were in manufacturing. Now, according to the 1981 census, only 18.5 percent are. Employment in manufacturing grew more slowly than employment in any other sector except agriculture in the 1970s. These labor-force trends reflect the changing pattern of Canadian economic and technological development.

The occupational group that includes law, social work, and library and museum work grew 138 percent in the 1970s in Canada, the fastest growing of any occupational group. Managerial and administrative occupations grew 118 percent; natural sciences, engineering, and math grew 72 percent; and artistic, literary, and recreational occupations were up 105 percent. The economy is now almost evenly divided between white-collar and blue-collar occupations. As in 1971, clerical workers are the largest single occupational group, accounting for 18 percent of all workers in 1981. Next comes services with 12 percent, and sales with 9 percent.

Employment growth was strongest in the extreme west and in Newfoundland. In Newfoundland, Alberta, British Columbia, the Yukon, and the Northwest Territories, labor-force growth exceeded the national average. The new jobs are not in the manufacturing industries of Canada's great cities, or on the farms of Manitoba and Saskatchewan, but rather in the offices, shops, and service industries out west.

Canadians are spending more years in school. The percentage of the population aged fifteen or older with a college degree virtually doubled in the past decade, rising from just 4.8 percent in 1971 to 8 percent in 1981. In the five years between the 1976 and 1981 censuses, while the population grew only 6 percent, the number of Canadians with a university degree rose by more than one third. In Alberta, 9.6 percent of residents aged fifteen or older held a college degree in 1981. Although 9 percent of Ontario residents had a college degree, only 7.1 percent of Quebec residents had a degree in 1981. Newfoundland had the lowest level of university-educated residents of any province, just 4.7 percent.

Over 70 percent of Canadians aged fifteen or older have at least completed secondary school. Meanwhile, the number who do not have at least a ninth grade education has dropped steadily, and now stands at about one in five.

Women are going to school in increasing numbers. Between 1971 and 1981, the number of women aged twenty-five or older in school full time rose 70 percent, twice the rate for men. Part-time attendance for women rose 146 percent, nearly three times the men's rate. As in the United States, women are playing a quick game of catch-up in education.

A better educated population and an economy with a higher share of white-collar jobs among its work force have meant that income is growing for Canadians. While inflation-adjusted median household income in the United States stagnated in the 1970s, it rose fully 20 percent in Canada. Median household income was $21,300 (Canadian) in 1980, up sharply from an inflation-adjusted $17,800 in 1970. Much of the income growth took place during the first half of the 1970s, however; recession marred the progress subsequently.

Nationally, one Canadian household in five had an income over $35,000 in 1980, compared to just one in eight a decade earlier. Families fared better than other types of households. Median family income was $26,700 in 1980, up 28 percent during the decade. The rise in family income reflects the trend to families in which there are two earners. Three quarters of all Canadian families had at least two earners in 1980, up from less than two thirds in 1970. In 1980, nearly eight out of ten women had an income either from a job or from a pension.

Women have narrowed the income gap with men in Canada, compared to a decade ago, but men still earn twice the amount that women do. For women, median income in 1980 was $8,400, a 34 percent increase in real dollars from 1970. Men's income was $16,900, up 19 percent. Women's incomes have helped push family income upward, but for women who do not live in families, life is more difficult. Over one half of the 3 million Canadians who live alone or with someone other than relatives are women, and more than one third of them are over age sixty-five. Men who live alone or with unrelated people are younger and have higher incomes than women. For men living outside of a family, median income in 1980 was $10,700; for women, it was only $6,600.

Incomes are highest in the Canadian West. In the Yukon, the median household income was $27,700 in 1980. In British Columbia and Alberta, both migrant magnets, household incomes were also greater than the average—over $24,500 in Alberta and $23,000 in British Columbia. In the provinces of Ontario and Quebec, however, median income was only $22,600 and $20,000, respectively. The province with the lowest median household income in 1980 was Prince Edward Island, just $16,400, followed by New Brunswick, less than $18,000. Among metropolitan areas, Calgary had the highest average household income—$30,600 in 1980, followed by Edmonton, $28,900, and Toronto, $28,800.

Almost two thirds of Canadian households are occupied by their owners, whereas one third of the nation's 8.3 million occupied private dwellings are rented. More than one in five homeowners spent at least one quarter of their income on housing in 1981, and the proportion has probably risen since then, as housing costs have risen in Canada, as in the United States.

Reflecting the popularity of small households in the 1980s, condominiums are sprouting in Canada, and a question about condominiums appeared on the census form in 1981 for the first time. The census counted 171,000 condominiums, 2 percent of all households. But the proportion of condo owners is higher in Ontario, British Columbia, and Alberta. Almost half of Canada's housing stock is more than twenty years old. But in such recently settled areas as the Yukon and North-west Territories, over half has been built in the past ten years.

The similarities between Canada and the United States are striking. Both have had a baby boom and a baby bust. Families are fragmenting, women are joining the labor force in record numbers. People are shifting out of the central cities and into the suburbs and the countryside beyond. The population of the remote areas is growing rapidly. Agriculture is stagnant, manufacturing is declining, and the service sector is booming.

But the two countries' different minorities shape their culture and their concerns. Race relations—black versus white, and consequently, rich versus poor, city versus suburb, educated versus uneducated, and professional versus the less skilled—are critical to discussions of what kind of a country the United States is likely to become. But in Canada, it is ethnic relations—the French versus the English, and consequently, the French language versus the English language, Catholic versus Protestant, and Quebec versus other provinces—that will shape the future. Each country monitors changes in the status of its dominant minority, but without being able to change the status of the minority so that monitoring is no longer necessary.

The appearance of Spanish-speaking enclaves in the United States are heightening United States concerns about language, while the rapid increase in the number of Asian immigrants to Canada may heighten the racial concerns of that country. The two countries will remain different, but their demographic trends may become even more alike.

15 | Ten Trends Shaping America

"There is no blueprint for the future, and no certainty that the future will be better than the past. But out of the turmoil of demographic change may come a new strength.

"Americans are not as divided as their demographics."

Where do demographic trends lead? What kind of future do the numbers foretell? Ten powerful demographic trends are altering America.

TREND 1: SOCIETY IS BECOMING MIDDLE-AGED.

America is becoming middle-aged, less concerned with the fantasies of youth and more concerned with the facts of making a living.

In the years ahead, the baby boom will become the dominant influence on America's tastes, spending and savings patterns, use of leisure time, and government and industry. By the turn of the century, the baby-boom generation will be aged thirty-six to fifty-three, a majority of the labor force, a majority of legislators, journalists, and opinion leaders. By then, the youth culture of the 1960s and 1970s will have faded, and middle age will be in full bloom.

Except for the Internal Revenue Service, nobody pays much attention to middle-aged people. They are too old for the educators, too young for Social Security, and too dull for the media. But middle-aged folks are at their productive peak. They are more likely than any other age group to live in a family, stay in one place, and vote. Employment is high, and median income peaks between the ages of forty-five and fifty-four.

Between 1985 and 1995, the number of Americans aged thirty to fifty-five will grow by more than 20 million, as the baby-boom generation occupies this age group. At the same time, there will be nearly 9 million fewer people aged fifteen to thirty in 1995 than there are today, as the smaller baby-bust generation succeeds the baby-boomers among America's young adults.

This transition should be a powerful and positive force for the economy. As the baby-boom generation takes command of the middle age groups, America should enjoy a renaissance of productivity after more than a decade of stagnation. For the rest of this century and into the next, the markets that cater to adults—travel, entertainment, and personal service—will be growing.

Markets for youngsters and jobs for teachers also will get a boost because baby-boom parents will be having children. In 1995, when the baby-boom generation has made its impact on the childbearing years, there will be 5 million more children in the preteen years than there are today. A higher share of children than in the past will be firstborn, a consequence of the smaller families in favor with today's parents. People spend more on their first child. And because so many baby-boom families contain two earners, parents have more money to spend per child.

Because people are living longer, the grandparents of the future will have more years in which to dote on their grandchildren. But America will not soon become a nation of elders. Although the median age will be rising sharply, and the number of people sixty-five and older has already surpassed the number of teen-agers, the number of Americans aged sixty-five and older will increase more slowly during this decade than in the 1970s. Between 1990 and 2000, the sixty-five-plus age group will grow at its slowest rate ever, because the small group of people born during the Depression enters its retirement years.

The number of people aged eighty-five and over will increase over 50 percent between 1980 and 1990, as the health of the elderly improves, but the number of elderly is small. Currently, fewer than 3 million people are aged eighty-five and older; by 1995 there will be just

3.8 million. In contrast, 36 million Americans are now in their thirties, and by 1995 the number will be 44 million. A middle-aged America will not become an elderly nation until the baby-boom generation reaches old age a generation from now.

TREND 2: WOMEN ARE GROWING IN IMPORTANCE.

Women will become an increasingly important force in society. As they continue to gain in the labor force and in education, their status will continue to become more equal to that of men. The proportion of women in the labor force has been steadily increasing.

The older generation is giving way to the newer, which expects women to work—and so more women are working. Young women are more likely than older women to work. Over 70 percent of women in their twenties are in the labor force, compared with under 45 percent of those aged fifty-five to sixty-four. In 1970, less than one third of women with preschool children were in the labor force; today half are working, and the majority full time. Their children, too, will expect to work.

As women are better accepted in the labor force, they will fill increasingly senior positions and carry more weight in business and government. The 1970s brought a revolution in attitudes about women's place and a surge of women into the workplace. The 1980s are bringing rising expectations about women's wages and career opportunities.

Although it is commonly heard that over half of all women are now in the labor force, the statistics are even more dramatic when they include only working-age women, not also those of retirement age. Among women of working age, almost two thirds are in the labor force.

Neither is it true that all women who do not work are homemakers. Women are still much more likely to be found around the home than are men, but nearly 5 million women aged sixteen and older are not in the labor force because they are going to school. Women attending school are over 6 percent of all working-age women. In fact, less than one in five women aged twenty to twenty-four today is keeping house —neither working nor going to school. In the twenty-five to forty-four age group, just over one in four is keeping house.

Young women have twice the college experience of older women.

More than one woman in five aged twenty-five to twenty-nine has completed college, compared to less than one in ten among women age fifty and older. As the younger generation replaces the older, women's educational attainment is approaching that of men and may soon exceed it.

The changing role of women has enormous implications for women and men alike, as well for businesses and government programs. It is not that today's young women are busier—women have always been busy. Instead, they see the world differently from their mothers. Their new attitudes and changing roles have changed men's attitudes and roles. Demographically, it is getting harder to tell young men and women apart.

Businesses are beginning to reflect these changes in their advertising and marketing. Women are no longer appendages of men. In a world in which more than 70 percent of American women in their twenties are in the labor force and 20 percent are college graduates, women want to think of themselves as attractive, successful, and independent—able to enjoy life, not just work their way through stacks of dishes.

TREND 3: THE EDUCATIONAL LEVEL IS RISING.

Americans will continue to gain in education. The trend to rising educational attainment for men and women alike reflects the superior education experience of members of the baby-boom generation who are replacing those who grew up when it was uncommon to spend so many years in school.

Baby-boomers are fundamentally different from previous generations, not only because of the size of their age group but also because of their education. Education alters attitudes and behavior. Educational differences between the generations imply long-lasting changes in occupational preferences, income levels, and political behavior. The rise in education is nothing short of a revolution in American life.

By the turn of the century, over 20 percent of American adults will be college graduates, and virtually everybody will complete high school. Because educated people expect education for their children, the educational revolution is likely to bring lasting changes. As the general educational level rises, those who fail to participate in the educational opportunities will find themselves further removed from the mainstream of society.

TREND 4: NEW LIVING ARRANGEMENTS ARE EMERGING.

The American family is not dead, but no longer is it the stereotypical family of the 1950s. Instead, family members as individuals have arisen from the ashes of the traditional family. Living arrangements will continue to change. People once moved through life's stages in chorus, now they engage in a more modern dance, freed from rigid rules about what is proper for young men and young women.

As long ago as 1967, traditional families in which only the husband was employed became the minority of all married couples with earnings. Today's Americans marry later, have fewer children, and divorce more readily—leaving mothers, or sometimes fathers, to raise their children, or their only child, alone.

As the baby-boom generation reaches the family years during the remainder of this decade and the next, however, families will become more numerous. Over 90 percent of all Americans marry, and among families with children, two is still the most popular number. But the image of the typical American family consisting of four people—mom, dad, and two kids—is gone probably forever. Average family size—dividing the total number of people who live in families by the number of families—is now closer to three than four. But is there a typical family at all?

It is still too early to tell whether the children of fragmented families will be different from past generations of children as they grew into adulthood. Families have never been as stable as traditionalists have proclaimed. Except for the 1950s, fragmentation has been a fact of family life. In earlier years, death, not divorce, disrupted young families. Few parents lived many years together after their children had grown and left home. Now, they face many years together because life expectancy has risen, but half of them choose to split apart.

TREND 5: THE LABOR FORCE IS FRACTURING ALONG NEW LINES.

The labor force is being split into segments that are different from the traditional blue-collar, white-collar split. In the service sector, jobs are growing rapidly both in the high-education, high-skill areas and in the low-education, low-skill areas. Computer-related occupations are among the fastest-growing; but so are janitorial occupations. The single occupation adding the most workers in the 1970s was secretaries.

As the two-earner couple becomes the norm, a variety of services is growing to meet their time-scarce schedules—convenience restaurants, mail-order shopping, home delivery services, twenty-four-hour banking, for example. These industries pay low wages to the many waitresses, messengers, and clerks, but high wages to the marketers, planners, and executives. The growing array of specialized services will further divide the country into highly educated professionals, managers, and administrators, on one end, and poorly paid clerks, on the other.

America in 2000 will have a labor force even less dependent on manufacturing than it is today. The nation has come far from the blue-collar, white-collar society of midcentury. But it has much further to go. Instead of selling more cars every year, for example, Detroit will have to sell better cars, and cars for different types of customers who have different needs. For each car sold, more energy will need to be devoted to selling the potential buyers and to customer service.

TREND 6: THE EARNINGS GAP IS WIDENING.

Changes in family structure, education, and the labor force will change the earnings patterns of Americans. A country that has aspired to eliminate poverty and to build a middle-class society now finds both poverty and affluence on the rise, at the expense of the middle.

However, instead of a wealthy elite consisting of robber barons and industrial magnates, a group that could be taxed for the benefit of the middle class and whose philanthropy could support the less fortunate, a portion of the middle class is becoming wealthy. The new rich are not capitalists; their affluent life-style depends not on the labor of others but rather on their own labor—and increasingly on the labor of both husband and wife. Such families do not look kindly on efforts to tax away their money.

Millions of families, particularly those headed by the highly educated baby-boom generation, have two incomes because that is what it takes to live comfortably today. In 1982, two-earner families had a median income nearly 50 percent higher than single-earner families. By 1990, the average American family should be better off than in 1980, but being substantially better off requires two incomes. At the other end, the new poor are women, and particularly black women, who must support their families on a single income, earned in the low-paying service occupations.

The number of upper-income households has been growing faster than the total number of households largely because so many wives have joined the labor force. But low-income households have been growing as well, as more families split and women support themselves. The middle-income group is becoming a smaller share of all households because it consists primarily of traditional families. America in the twenty-first century will have to cope with both a new form of affluence and a new form of poverty.

TREND 7: THE ORIGINS OF IMMIGRANTS ARE CHANGING.

American society will change ethnically because immigrants are now coming from different places. Immigration from Europe has dropped to less than one fifth of all immigration, whereas immigration from Asia has increased to more than one third. Mexico has replaced Germany as the number-one country of origin for America's foreign born.

Immigration has increased rapidly in the past decade, and the drop in the U.S. birthrate has made immigration a greater percentage of total population growth. These trends have heightened ethnic awareness and raised voices calling for new curbs on immigration as well as demands to control illegal immigration. America may still be a melting pot, but the differences in the backgrounds of new immigrants and American citizens are much greater than they used to be when almost all immigrants came from Europe.

Such rapid change creates social stresses. Blacks, for example, express concern that the rapid increase in the number of Hispanic immigrants diverts public attention from the problems of America's largest racial minority. The 1980 census counted about 15 million Hispanics, versus 27 million blacks, but the number of Hispanics rose 61 percent in the 1970s, the number of blacks rose only 17 percent.

Immigrants to America traditionally have held low-paying jobs that other Americans do not want. Once they get started, however, they rapidly improve their status. Immigrants from East Asia, still a small number, are particularly achievement oriented and well educated. Their median income already exceeds that of whites, in part because so many family members work. In time, the society may absorb them as it has other new groups, and our culture will add an Asian dimension.

When the economy is moving upward, the assimilation process works more smoothly than it did in the 1970s, a time of economic stagnation and high immigration. If the mid- to late-1980s and the 1990s are a time of economic growth for the world economy, and political tensions do not create new streams of refugees, the pressures to migrate should lighten, and the United States will be better able to absorb immigrants.

TREND 8: PEOPLE AND JOBS ARE SPREADING OUTWARD.

Americans will become more dispersed geographically. The nation's population density increases every year because the population is growing while the national borders remain fixed, but the average American lives in a less densely settled place than a decade ago.

The nation had a historic reversal in metropolitan and nonmetropolitan growth rates between 1970 and 1980. As a group, the biggest cities lost people during a decade when the total population grew 11 percent. The top thirty cities lost more than 1 million people. People say they prefer a less densely settled living environment, and they have been voting with their feet. Areas that offer attractive life-styles have been growing, whether in the South or the North, whereas crowded cities have been losing those who can afford to leave.

The spread of people reflects the spread of the new kinds of jobs. It is easier to find employment in suburban and nonmetropolitan areas, and businesses have found it profitable to leave the big cities. Better communications and the service economy no longer force businesses to cluster together. The big cities of America became big because they were port or rail distribution centers—New York, Boston, Cleveland, Chicago, New Orleans, Denver, Los Angeles. The hubs of the future are in computer terminals, communications satellites, telephones, and airplanes and in Express Mail. Population concentration is less important than it used to be for enterprise. The decline of manufacturing and the rise of services mean fewer large plants but more offices, shops, and stores.

Americans are not returning to the cities, as stories about young people revitalizing city neighborhoods have suggested. Selective neighborhood renovation has not offset the loss of residents from other parts of cities. Also, those returning to cities have smaller families than those they replace. Families with children continue the exodus to suburbia and beyond. The apparent renewal of interest in city living was largely an effect of the baby-boom generation's reaching the age when Americans first set up their own households. As the small baby-bust generation reaches young adulthood, and baby-boomers have families, it may appear that young adults are fleeing the cities. But this trend, too, will reflect the country's changing age structure.

America may not become less metropolitan in the future than it is today, but the meaning of the word *metropolitan* will change. About three quarters of all Americans live in metropolitan areas. As areas around the metropolis grow, they join the metropolitan area, and as smaller cities grow in population, the government reclassifies them as metropolitan. The metropolitan population may not decline, but by the turn of the century, the once broad differences between the cities and the countryside will be even smaller than they are today. The cities were once the only places to find cultural amenities, and they attracted people from the countryside. Now, city problems often outweigh their attractions, while the countryside offers urban amenities—and there are still places to park.

TREND 9: REGIONAL DIFFERENCES ARE DIMINISHING.

The flows of Americans across the country are creating a nationwide economy and culture to an extent that was unknown two decades ago. Because of these flows, America's regions will become more alike. As the South and West continue growing, their growth will increase their similarity to the country's former growth areas, the Northeast and Midwest, which are retooling to reverse their decay.

Regional growth results from the same trends that cause metropolitan and nonmetropolitan shifts. In the past, growth in the South and West lagged behind the Northeast and Midwest. But in the 1970s, the southern states grew rapidly, while some northern states lost population. The relationship was not simple cause and effect. Northern cities have been losing migrants for many decades. In the 1970s, however, the migration out of the North appeared more dramatic because falling birthrates meant fewer births to compensate for the migration losses.

For the rest of this century, the South and West will continue above-average growth in population; the Northeast and Midwest will face below-average growth. This trend contains the seeds of continued growth in the South and West, because movers tend to be young adults.

As they settle down and raise families, their children will further increase the population of today's growth states. Meanwhile, northern cities that cannot attract migrants will face continued pressures on their tax base that could deny them the ability to rebuild their cities to attract business and new residents.

Growth begets more growth; decline invites further decline. The shift of population from one region to another is a powerful trend that is not easily turned around. The imbalance in regional growth will bring a growing share of seats in the House of Representatives to states in the South and West. These shifts should strengthen the political power of America's growth regions and weaken that of its old seats of power.

Migration is a dynamic process; there are flows and counterflows, a continual sorting out of people. Employment opportunities encourage migration, but migration out of one state reduces the potential number of future migrants from that state, whereas heavy migration to another state eventually reduces its appeal for new migrants. In the fast-growing Rocky Mountain States, for example, the availability of water is a check on unlimited population growth.

Eventually, growth slows, an area matures, and the problems of size limit further growth. The boom states of the South have actively sought businesses, but corporations may look increasingly to the population-rich countries in Asia and elsewhere abroad for the cheap labor they once sought in the South. The older cities of the Northeast and Midwest have already faced the facts of economic change; for other states, such change is still in the future.

TREND 10: INTERNATIONAL TRENDS ARE BECOMING MORE IMPORTANT.

The world beyond the United States' borders is becoming far more important to Americans. Sometime during 1988, the world's population will pass 5 billion, double the total in 1950. By the year 2000, 6 billion people will live on earth. Most Americans still look to Europe for their heritage, but America's future may lie in less familiar territory.

Each year, over 90 percent of the increase in the world's population occurs in developing nations—all the countries of the world except the United States, Canada, the Soviet Union, the European countries, Japan, Australia, and New Zealand, which are considered to be developed. For every ten people added to the world's population, only one lives in a modern industrialized country.

In 1950, about two thirds of all people lived in Asia, Latin America, and Africa; today, three quarters live there. In the next century, the share will rise to over 80 percent. Although 1.2 billion people live in countries with modern economies, 3.5 billion live in those still on the road to modernization—although there are wide variations in where they stand along the road. The developed countries will gain only 115 million people before the turn of the century; excluding China, the rest of the world will gain 1.1 billion. China alone will gain more people between now and the turn of the century than will the entire developed world.

An income gap and a generation gap separate the world's nations. Of the 126 countries that contained at least 1 million people in 1980, only 14 had a per capita gross national product (GNP) of over $10,000. Per capita GNP is the value of the country's goods and services divided by its total population. Over half of the world's people live in countries where per capita GNP is below $360. In poor countries, many people do not even participate in the cash economy, but live at subsistence levels on small farms. In the poorest countries, per capita income is below $100 per year—an amount many Americans earn in less than one day.

Except for the oil-rich Arab countries, wealthy countries all have aging populations. Relatively few children are born each year, and people live into their seventies. The poor countries all have young populations. Many children are born, but few people live to retire. Birthrates are falling nearly everywhere in the world, but they are much lower in developed nations than elsewhere. The world's median age is rising from its low point of 21.7 years in 1970; today, it is 23, and it should reach 26 years by 2000. But a twenty-year gap in median age will continue to separate the oldest countries from the youngest.

Even if birthrates were to fall rapidly throughout the developing world, it would be many years before populations stabilized. Population growth has a momentum that does not stop immediately after the brakes are put on. When the large generations produced by today's high birthrates enter the childbearing years, they will produce large numbers of children, even if the average woman in the future has fewer children. These population dynamics command America's attention, as the American people become an ever-smaller share of the world's people.

The world's past may have been rural, but its future is becoming urban. By the year 2000, more people will live in urban areas than in rural areas—the first time in history this has occurred. In 1950, just eight urban areas contained at least 5 million residents. Today, there are nearly thirty such areas. By the turn of the century, about sixty "super cities" will have passed the 5 million mark.

Americans have grown up with the notion that New York is the world's Big Apple, and from 1950 to 1975, New York was the largest metropolitan area in the world. But in 1975, Tokyo surged ahead. Today, the Tokyo-Yokohama area contains over 27 million people, versus 17 million for the New York area. In 1950, London was the world's second largest metropolitan area with about 10 million residents. Now, London has dropped to tenth place, just behind Buenos Aires.

Huge urban areas are arising as the people of developing nations flock to the cities to seek a better life. In 1950, the Mexico City area had just 3 million people, and it ranked sixteenth among world metropolitan areas. Today, the Mexico City area ranks third, with about 17 million people. By 1990, it will have passed New York in population, and soon thereafter it will become the world's largest metropolis, home to some 28 million residents.

The once mighty cities of Chicago, Paris, and Los Angeles are moving down in the world rankings as the rate of population growth in the United States and Europe declines and people spread from large cities to the countryside. But in the developing nations, people are still moving in the opposite direction. The world's big cities are becoming bigger than anyone imagined they could. Forty years from now, the only North American or European metropolis among the world's twenty-five largest will be New York, which will rank fourteenth—the spot held by Calcutta in 1980. Calcutta was synonymous with urban poverty and overcrowding when that city was home to only 4.7 million people in 1950. Today, Calcutta has over 10 million residents. By 2025, even the smallest of the world's twenty-five largest urban areas will have more than 15 million residents.

A host of other urban areas are reaching the size that once gave a city world-class status. In the next century, such areas as Shanghai and Peking in China; Bombay, Calcutta, Delhi, and Madras in India; Manila in the Philippines; and Dacca in Bangladesh, will supplant the major North American and European capitals as the world's greatest metropolitan centers.

As more people are drawn to cities, housing, transportation, and sanitation facilities all become overburdened. The world will have to construct as many new schools in just the next generation as it has constructed in the past century if it hopes to educate its children. A population that doubles in a generation continually requires twice as much food, twice as many jobs, twice as many housing units just to maintain a constant standard of living.

When a country cannot provide opportunities for its people, but opportunities exist elsewhere, people migrate—whether to the oil fields of Saudi Arabia or the lettuce fields of California. For some developing countries, the money that migrants send home is a key source of foreign exchange. Almost 5 million foreigners help the Arab Gulf States enjoy a high standard of living. West Germany and France have imported workers by the millions to maintain their economic growth. In good times, the receiving countries welcome such labor because their economies are growing. But when recession strikes, foreign workers are unwelcome.

Developed countries, the United States among them, will continue to attract migrants from developing countries because of the differences in the standards of living between the rich countries and the poor countries. The waiting lines are long. As the cities of Asia, Latin America, and Africa fill to overflowing, while countries on wealthier continents face the eventual prospect of population decline if their low birthrates continue, pressure for further international migration will rise.

At current population growth rates, it will take the United States seventy-two years to double its population. But India and Indonesia will double their populations in about thirty-two years, and Mexico in twenty-nine years. Americans are becoming an ever-smaller share of the world's population. The world's countries are separated by an income gap, an age gap, and a huge imbalance in population. Some Asian economies are growing far more dynamically than those of the United States or Europe. The world of the future will not look like the world of the past; and America should be looking to the future.

Demographics have divided America. The challenge for the future is to build a new foundation from the fragments. Can the country find a common purpose, achieve goals, even speak a single language? The American people must decide.

Politicians have long divided the electorate into voting blocks—the ethnic vote, the black vote, the elderly vote, and so forth. In seeking favor with one group, politicians alienate other groups. In the past, it was possible to find pools of support among key demographic groups without losing the mainstream, but today the currents of difference can flow stronger than the mainstream. The role of leadership is to unite, not to conquer by dividing the people into ever-finer fragments.

Businesses increasingly rely on their ability to identify promising market segments among the mass of consumers in order to make a profit. As politicians slice the electorate, so marketers slice consumers because purchasing behavior differs by demographics. But what of the trends that have reshaped the marketplace and that reflect so many differences among Americans?

Today's trends have a pattern to them. Millions of Americans are breaking the social bonds that tied them to the past. People are choosing to live alone instead of crowding in with relatives; divorce is not a rejection of the institution of marriage, but rather an expression of hope for a better relationship; people are moving out of cities to seek a better life in less crowded surroundings; women are no longer isolated in the home; immigrants escape oppression and stagnation at home to find opportunity in America.

Traditional roles are being swept aside. New roles are not fixed. Family relationships are being reshaped; cities are being altered; cultural patterns are changing; men's and women's roles are being redefined. There is no blueprint for the future, and no certainty that the future will be better than the past. But out of the turmoil of demographic change may come a new strength.

Americans are not as divided as their demographics.

America's 100 Largest Cities: A Statistical Profile

This Appendix presents a unique list of the nation's one hundred most populous cities, alphabetically, ranked by ten important indicators.

The nation's one hundred largest cities contain some 50 million Americans. These cities vary not only in size—from top ranking New York City, with over 7 million people, to Greensboro, North Carolina, 100th on the list with just over 150,000 people—but also in such characteristics as the share of households that contain married couples (Warren, Michigan, leads), the percentage of immigrants among all residents (Miami, Florida, is tops), and the proportion of residents who are college graduates (Madison, Wisconsin, wins this one).

   The list is arranged alphabetically. Readers can pick a city (their city) and learn how it ranks, compared with the nation's other large cities. Akron, Ohio, for example, first alphabetically, ranks last in the percentage of Hispanics, with less than one half of 1 percent at the time of the 1980 census. Akron is low in average housing value, the percentage of women in the work force, and the percentage of residents who are college graduates. Yonkers, New York, which is last alphabetically, is one of the nation's oldest cities—ranking third in median age, with 34.4 years; St. Petersburg, Florida, is the oldest city ranked, with a median age of 42.2 years.

There are fascinating differences among American cities that appear in the rankings, which this section invites readers to discover for themselves. And the flavor of the cities is revealed in the rankings: San Francisco is a city of singles with a foreign flavor; Buffalo, a traditional working-class city. See for yourself.

CITY: AKRON, OH

Characteristic	Rank	Value
Population size	59	237,177
Percent black	46	22.19
Percent Hispanic	100	.49
Percent foreign born	63	3.66
Median age (years)	28	30.1
Percent college graduates	83	10.05
Percent women in labor force	93	46.01
Percent married-couple households	51	50.6
Median household income ($)	59	14,703
Average housing value ($)	76	38,234

CITY: ALBUQUERQUE, NM

Characteristic	Rank	Value
Population size	44	331,767
Percent black	93	2.31
Percent Hispanic	6	33.76
Percent foreign born	57	4.53
Median age (years)	68	28.6
Percent college graduates	12	19.78
Percent women in labor force	43	53.48
Percent married-couple households	18	56.41
Median household income ($)	24	16,514
Average housing value ($)	31	60,142

CITY: ANAHEIM, CA

Characteristic	Rank	Value
Population size	63	219,311
Percent black	97	1.23
Percent Hispanic	18	17.14
Percent foreign born	16	14.10
Median age (years)	54	28.8
Percent college graduates	65	11.99
Percent women in labor force	14	59.15
Percent married-couple households	16	57.79
Median household income ($)	8	20,026
Average housing value ($)	7	104,858

CITY: ANCHORAGE, AK

Characteristic	Rank	Value
Population size	78	174,431
Percent black	82	5.38
Percent Hispanic	52	2.89
Percent foreign born	47	4.99
Median age (years)	95	26.3
Percent college graduates	18	18.37
Percent women in labor force	2	64.50
Percent married-couple households	8	60.67
Median household income ($)	1	27,375
Average housing value ($)	8	95,439

CITY: ARLINGTON, TX

Characteristic	Rank	Value
Population size	94	160,113
Percent black	91	2.82
Percent Hispanic	42	4.07
Percent foreign born	61	3.92
Median age (years)	89	27
Percent college graduates	6	20.98
Percent Women in labor force	3	62.75
Percent married-couple households	5	63.63
Median household income ($)	6	21,136
Average housing value ($)	20	66,103

CITY: ATLANTA, GA

Characteristic	Rank	Value
Population size	29	425,022
Percent black	2	66.62
Percent Hispanic	76	1.35
Percent foreign born	84	2.30
Median age (years)	55	28.8
Percent college graduates	32	16.29
Percent women in labor force	56	51.44
Percent married-couple households	97	35.32
Median household income ($)	98	11,296
Average housing value ($)	49	48,018

CITY: AURORA, CO

Characteristic	Rank	Value
Population size	96	158,588
Percent black	80	6.82
Percent Hispanic	39	5.15
Percent foreign born	45	5.26
Median age (years)	79	27.9
Percent college graduates	8	20.29
Percent women in labor force	1	65.69
Percent married-couple households	7	60.74
Median household income ($)	5	21,698
Average housing value ($)	16	72,325

CITY: AUSTIN, TX

Characteristic	Rank	Value
Population size	42	345,544
Percent black	61	12.18
Percent Hispanic	12	18.79
Percent foreign born	53	4.83
Median age (years)	97	26.2
Percent college graduates	5	21.60
Percent women in labor force	7	60.40
Percent married-couple households	64	47.52
Median household income ($)	58	14,709
Average housing value ($)	39	54,647

CITY: BALTIMORE, MD

Characteristic	Rank	Value
Population size	10	786,775
Percent black	7	54.77
Percent Hispanic	80	.99
Percent foreign born	68	3.13
Median age (years)	26	30.2
Percent college graduates	89	9.15
Percent women in labor force	79	48.23
Percent married-couple households	86	41.34
Median household income ($)	81	12,811
Average housing value ($)	91	32,414

CITY: BATON ROUGE, LA

Characteristic	Rank	Value
Population size	62	219,419
Percent black	20	36.39
Percent Hispanic	67	1.93
Percent foreign born	73	2.90
Median age (years)	94	26.5
Percent college graduates	19	18.22
Percent women in labor force	59	51.11
Percent married-couple households	47	51.01
Median household income ($)	51	15,158
Average housing value ($)	32	59,194

CITY: BIRMINGHAM, AL

Characteristic	Rank	Value
Population size	50	284,413
Percent black	5	55.62
Percent Hispanic	96	.72
Percent foreign born	100	1.13
Median age (years)	35	29.7
Percent college graduates	81	10.45
Percent women in labor force	78	48.29
Percent married-couple households	61	48.00
Median household income ($)	92	11,951
Average housing value ($)	85	35,438

CITY: BOSTON, MA

Characteristic	Rank	Value
Population size	20	562,994
Percent black	45	22.45
Percent Hispanic	35	6.47
Percent foreign born	10	15.46
Median age (years)	56	28.8
Percent college graduates	39	15.19
Percent women in labor force	49	52.68
Percent married-couple households	98	34.66
Median household income ($)	84	12,530
Average housing value ($)	72	40,295

CITY: BUFFALO, NY

Characteristic	Rank	Value
Population size	39	357,870
Percent black	34	26.71
Percent Hispanic	57	2.49
Percent foreign born	40	6.15
Median age (years)	19	30.9
Percent college graduates	91	8.88
Percent women in labor force	99	44.18
Percent married-couple households	85	41.72
Median household income ($)	95	11,593
Average housing value ($)	99	26,000

CITY: CHARLOTTE, NC

Characteristic	Rank	Value
Population size	47	314,447
Percent black	28	31.13
Percent Hispanic	81	.98
Percent foreign born	77	2.78
Median age (years)	45	29.3
Percent college graduates	20	18.21
Percent women in labor force	6	60.59
Percent married-couple households	36	53.55
Median household income ($)	20	16,917
Average housing value ($)	40	54,150

CITY: CHATTANOOGA, TN

Characteristic	Rank	Value
Population size	87	169,550
Percent black	27	31.72
Percent Hispanic	92	.75
Percent foreign born	97	1.28
Median age (years)	22	30.3
Percent college graduates	70	11.47
Percent women in labor force	68	49.82
Percent married-couple households	34	54.00
Median household income ($)	76	13,564
Average housing value ($)	75	38,617

CITY: CHICAGO, IL

Characteristic	Rank	Value
Population size	2	3,005,078
Percent black	16	39.83
Percent Hispanic	23	14.08
Percent foreign born	13	14.48
Median age (years)	42	29.4
Percent college graduates	72	11.25
Percent women in labor force	62	50.85
Percent married-couple households	81	43.64
Median household income ($)	46	15,452
Average housing value ($)	83	36,254

CITY: CINCINNATI, OH

Characteristic	Rank	Value
Population size	32	385,457
Percent black	24	33.85
Percent Hispanic	89	.84
Percent foreign born	78	2.75
Median age (years)	47	29.1
Percent college graduates	53	13.73
Percent women in labor force	73	48.80
Percent married-couple households	91	40.09
Median household income ($)	83	12,675
Average housing value ($)	50	47,555

CITY: CLEVELAND, OH

Characteristic	Rank	Value
Population size	18	573,822
Percent black	13	43.75
Percent Hispanic	49	3.11
Percent foreign born	42	5.81
Median age (years)	33	29.8
Percent college graduates	99	5.15
Percent women in labor force	95	45.09
Percent married-couple households	79	43.75
Median household income ($)	88	12,277
Average housing value ($)	92	31,735

CITY: COLORADO SPRINGS, CO

Characteristic	Rank	Value
Population size	66	215,150
Percent black	81	5.54
Percent Hispanic	31	8.54
Percent foreign born	48	4.99
Median age (years)	74	28.2
Percent college graduates	26	17.61
Percent women in labor force	39	53.95
Percent married-couple households	11	59.54
Median household income ($)	37	15,948
Average housing value ($)	24	62,599

CITY: COLUMBUS, GA

Characteristic	Rank	Value
Population size	88	169,434
Percent black	23	34.22
Percent Hispanic	61	2.20
Percent foreign born	64	3.65
Median age (years)	81	27.7
Percent college graduates	82	10.12
Percent women in labor force	70	49.39
Percent married-couple households	15	58.33
Median household income ($)	78	13,353
Average housing value ($)	79	37,230

CITY: COLUMBUS, OH

Characteristic	Rank	Value
Population size	19	564,866
Percent black	47	22.07
Percent Hispanic	85	.93
Percent foreign born	72	2.91
Median age (years)	86	27.2
Percent college graduates	52	13.81
Percent women in labor force	32	55.44
Percent married-couple households	66	47.13
Median household income ($)	55	14,834
Average housing value ($)	61	44,988

CITY: CORPUS CHRISTI, TX

Characteristic	Rank	Value
Population size	60	231,999
Percent black	83	5.09
Percent Hispanic	4	46.65
Percent foreign born	49	4.99
Median age (years)	88	27.1
Percent college graduates	64	12.29
Percent women in labor force	52	51.78
Percent married-couple households	4	64.35
Median household income ($)	22	16,799
Average housing value ($)	61	44,554

CITY: DALLAS, TX

Characteristic	Rank	Value
Population size	7	904,074
Percent black	29	29.32
Percent Hispanic	28	12.22
Percent foreign born	4	6.07
Median age (years)	63	28.7
Percent college graduates	27	17.52
Percent women in labor force	11	59.61
Percent married-couple households	60	48.39
Median household income ($)	29	16,227
Average housing value ($)	28	60,489

CITY: DAYTON, OH

Characteristic	Rank	Value
Population size	70	203,371
Percent black	19	36.94
Percent Hispanic	88	.86
Percent foreign born	86	2.03
Median age (years)	70	28.5
Percent college graduates	94	8.15
Percent women in labor force	81	48.13
Percent married-couple households	73	45.15
Median household income ($)	90	12,146
Average housing value ($)	95	30,816

CITY: DENVER, CO

Characteristic	Rank	Value
Population size	24	492,365
Percent black	63	12.00
Percent Hispanic	14	18.73
Percent foreign born	39	6.23
Median age (years)	27	30.2
Percent college graduates	10	20.12
Percent women in labor force	21	56.79
Percent married-couple households	82	43.35
Median household income ($)	45	15,506
Average housing value ($)	18	68,818

CITY: DES MOINES, IA

Characteristic	Rank	Value
Population size	74	191,003
Percent black	79	6.89
Percent Hispanic	70	1.74
Percent foreign born	71	2.95
Median age (years)	38	29.6
Percent college graduates	58	13.26
Percent women in labor force	17	57.84
Percent married-couple households	40	53.26
Median household income ($)	23	16,717
Average housing value ($)	63	44,719

CITY: DETROIT, MI

Characteristic	Rank	Value
Population size	6	1,203,339
Percent black	3	63.03
Percent Hispanic	59	2.36
Percent foreign born	43	5.67
Median age (years)	64	28.7
Percent college graduates	98	6.78
Percent women in labor force	94	45.83
Percent married-couple households	88	40.97
Median household income ($)	69	13,981
Average housing value ($)	100	23,265

CITY: EL PASO, TX

Characteristic	Rank	Value
Population size	28	425,259
Percent black	89	3.2
Percent Hispanic	1	62.54
Percent foreign born	6	21.37
Median age (years)	98	25.6
Percent college graduates	71	11.39
Percent women in labor force	92	46.33
Percent married-couple households	3	64.93
Median household income ($)	65	14,232
Average housing value ($)	56	45,906

CITY: FLINT, MI

Characteristic	Rank	Value
Population size	95	159,611
Percent black	14	41.38
Percent Hispanic	58	2.44
Percent foreign born	80	2.67
Median age (years)	93	26.7
Percent college graduates	95	7.17
Percent women in labor force	91	46.42
Percent married-couple households	67	47.04
Median household income ($)	18	17,181
Average housing value ($)	96	29,472

CITY: FORT WAYNE, IN

Characteristic	Rank	Value
Population size	80	172,196
Percent black	56	14.31
Percent Hispanic	64	2.03
Percent foreign born	83	2.43
Median age (years)	69	28.6
Percent college graduates	79	10.58
Percent women in labor force	34	55.13
Percent married-couple households	43	52.10
Median household income ($)	33	16,038
Average housing value ($)	84	35,579

CITY: FORT WORTH, TX

Characteristic	Rank	Value
Population size	33	385,166
Percent black	44	22.75
Percent Hispanic	26	12.60
Percent foreign born	55	4.75
Median age (years)	46	29.3
Percent college graduates	51	13.84
Percent women in labor force	44	53.27
Percent married-couple households	25	55.27
Median household income ($)	49	15,304
Average housing value ($)	67	41,881

CITY: FRESNO, CA

Characteristic	Rank	Value
Population size	65	218,202
Percent black	70	9.77
Percent Hispanic	9	23.49
Percent foreign born	26	8.27
Median age (years)	76	28.1
Percent college graduates	61	12.89
Percent women in labor force	57	51.28
Percent married-couple households	44	51.95
Median household income ($)	63	14,426
Average housing value ($)	22	62,963

CITY: GRAND RAPIDS, MI

Characteristic	Rank	Value
Population size	75	181,843
Percent black	52	15.84
Percent Hispanic	48	3.17
Percent foreign born	54	4.8
Median age (years)	70	28
Percent college graduates	63	12.66
Percent women in labor force	55	51.53
Percent married-couple households	45	51.94
Median household income ($)	47	15,452
Average housing value ($)	80	36,963

CITY: GREENSBORO, NC

Characteristic	Rank	Value
Population size	100	155,684
Percent black	25	32.89
Percent Hispanic	93	.75
Percent foreign born	91	1.74
Median age (years)	57	28.8
Percent college graduates	15	18.98
Percent women in labor force	20	56.86
Percent married-couple households	38	53.29
Median household income ($)	36	15,971
Average housing value ($)	42	51,800

CITY: HONOLULU, HI

Characteristic	Rank	Value
Population size	36	365,048
Percent black	98	1.17
Percent Hispanic	38	5.25
Percent foreign born	7	18.63
Median age (years)	12	31.4
Percent college graduates	13	19.72
Percent women in labor force	10	60.11
Percent married-couple households	27	54.92
Median household income ($)	9	19,897
Average housing value ($)	1	156,379

CITY: HOUSTON, TX

Characteristic	Rank	Value
Population size	5	1,595,167
Percent black	32	27.55
Percent Hispanic	17	17.59
Percent foreign born	22	9.75
Median age (years)	82	27.6
Percent college graduates	24	18.11
Percent women in labor force	13	59.21
Percent married-couple households	46	51.27
Median household income ($)	11	18,474
Average housing value ($)	29	60,431

CITY: HUNTINGTON BEACH, CA

Characteristic	Rank	Value
Population size	85	170,505
Percent black	99	.57
Percent Hispanic	32	7.87
Percent foreign born	20	10.36
Median age (years)	58	28.8
Percent college graduates	9	20.15
Percent women in labor force	8	60.3
Percent married-couple households	10	59.94
Median household income ($)	2	24,015
Average housing value ($)	2	130,048

CITY: INDIANAPOLIS, IN

Characteristic	Rank	Value
Population size	12	700,719
Percent black	48	21.77
Percent Hispanic	86	.91
Percent foreign born	87	1.91
Median age (years)	48	29
Percent college graduates	59	13.25
Percent women in labor force	30	55.82
Percent married-couple households	29	54.64
Median household income ($)	16	17,279
Average housing value ($)	70	41,303

CITY: JACKSON, MS

Characteristic	Rank	Value
Population size	71	202,893
Percent black	11	46.93
Percent Hispanic	95	.73
Percent foreign born	99	1.2
Median age (years)	83	27.5
Percent college graduates	16	18.94
Percent women in labor force	18	57.24
Percent married-couple households	35	53.72
Median household income ($)	56	14,926
Average housing value ($)	47	48,213

CITY: JACKSONVILLE, FL

Characteristic	Rank	Value
Population size	22	540,920
Percent black	36	25.35
Percent Hispanic	68	1.82
Percent foreign born	74	2.86
Median age (years)	49	29
Percent college graduates	75	10.98
Percent women in labor force	58	51.18
Percent married-couple households	20	56
Median household income ($)	53	14,926
Average housing value ($)	77	38,176

CITY: JERSEY CITY, NJ

Characteristic	Rank	Value
Population size	61	223,532
Percent black ·	31	27.71
Percent Hispanic	15	18.68
Percent foreign born	9	16.26
Median age (years)	30	29.9
Percent college graduates	86	9.59
Percent women in labor force	77	48.4
Percent married-couple households	78	43.95
Median household income ($)	82	12,787
Average housing value ($)	90	32,488

CITY: KANSAS CITY, KS

Characteristic	Rank	Value
Population size	93	161,093
Percent black	37	25.30
Percent Hispanic	40	4.76
Percent foreign born	79	2.7
Median age (years)	65	28.7
Percent college graduates	96	7.17
Percent women in labor force	61	50.94
Percent married-couple households	28	54.86
Median household income ($)	50	15,210
Average housing value ($)	93	31,666

CITY: KANSAS CITY, MO

Characteristic	Rank	Value
Population size	27	448,154
Percent black	33	27.29
Percent Hispanic	47	3.26
Percent foreign born	75	2.84
Median age (years)	23	30.3
Percent college graduates	55	13.55
Percent women in labor force	25	56.14
Percent married-couple households	59	49.33
Median household income ($)	41	15,859
Average housing value ($)	71	40,321

CITY: KNOXVILLE, TN

Characteristic	Rank	Value
Population size	77	175,030
Percent black	54	14.53
Percent Hispanic	94	.75
Percent foreign born	93	1.64
Median age (years)	40	29.5
Percent college graduates	60	13.13
Percent women in labor force	80	48.14
Percent married-couple households	57	49.73
Median household income ($)	91	11,971
Average housing value ($)	78	37,884

CITY: LAS VEGAS, NV

Characteristic	Rank	Value
Population size	89	164,674
Percent black	59	12.81
Percent Hispanic	33	7.73
Percent foreign born	29	7.96
Median age (years)	34	29.8
Percent college graduates	87	9.42
Percent women in labor force	12	59.4
Percent married-couple households	39	53.27
Median household income ($)	14	17,468
Average housing value ($)	17	69,868

CITY: LEXINGTON-FAYETTE, KY

Characteristic	Rank	Value
Population size	68	204,165
Percent black	58	13.21
Percent Hispanic	99	.62
Percent foreign born	85	2.08
Median age (years)	78	28
Percent college graduates	14	19.28
Percent women in labor force	24	56.5
Percent married-couple households	32	54.18
Median household income ($)	38	15,915
Average housing value ($)	33	58,592

CITY: LINCOLN, NE

Characteristic	Rank	Value
Population size	81	171,932
Percent black	94	1.83
Percent Hispanic	74	1.44
Percent foreign born	67	3.19
Median age (years)	85	27.3
Percent college graduates	25	17.84
Percent women in labor force	5	61.91
Percent married-couple households	26	55.13
Median household income ($)	19	17,094
Average housing value ($)	44	51,121

CITY: LITTLE ROCK, AR

Characteristic	Rank	Value
Population size	98	158,461
Percent black	26	32.24
Percent Hispanic	90	.83
Percent foreign born	89	1.85
Median age (years)	50	29
Percent college graduates	7	20.44
Percent women in labor force	19	57.23
Percent married-couple households	48	50.85
Median household income ($)	42	15,796
Average housing value ($)	43	51,703

CITY: LONG BEACH, CA

Characteristic	Rank	Value
Population size	37	361,334
Percent black	66	11.19
Percent Hispanic	24	13.96
Percent foreign born	15	14.22
Median age (years)	24	30.3
Percent college graduates	46	14.63
Percent women in labor force	69	49.58
Percent married-couple households	80	43.65
Median household income ($)	48	15,394
Average housing value ($)	9	93,098

CITY: LOS ANGELES, CA

Characteristic	Rank	Value
Population size	3	2,966,850
Percent black	51	16.99
Percent Hispanic	7	27.48
Percent foreign born	4	27.12
Median age (years)	24	30.3
Percent college graduates	33	16.08
Percent women in labor force	37	54.17
Percent married-couple households	74	45.09
Median household income ($)	43	15,735
Average housing value ($)	4	115,244

CITY: LOUISVILLE, KY

Characteristic	Rank	Value
Population size	49	298,455
Percent black	30	28.23
Percent Hispanic	98	.68
Percent foreign born	95	1.39
Median age (years)	9	31.8
Percent college graduates	77	10.88
Percent women in labor force	82	48.06
Percent married-couple households	71	46.05
Median household income ($)	89	12,274
Average housing value ($)	88	32,903

CITY: LUBBOCK, TX

Characteristic	Rank	Value
Population size	79	173,979
Percent black	74	7.94
Percent Hispanic	13	18.77
Percent foreign born	70	2.96
Median age (years)	100	25.2
Percent college graduates	35	15.65
Percent women in labor force	27	55.89
Percent married-couple households	9	60.39
Median household income ($)	44	15,732
Average housing value ($)	65	43,773

CITY: MADISON, WI

Characteristic	Rank	Value
Population size	84	170,616
Percent black	92	2.67
Percent Hispanic	75	1.43
Percent foreign born	56	4.71
Median age (years)	90	27
Percent college graduates	1	26.39
Percent women in labor force	4	62.07
Percent married-couple households	70	46.12
Median household income ($)	25	16,510
Average housing value ($)	25	62,376

CITY: MEMPHIS, TN

Characteristic	Rank	Value
Population size	14	646,356
Percent black	9	47.58
Percent Hispanic	87	.88
Percent foreign born	96	1.29
Median age (years)	71	28.4
Percent college graduates	67	11.68
Percent women in labor force	53	51.73
Percent married-couple households	50	50.7
Median household income ($)	68	14,039
Average housing value ($)	68	41,706

CITY: MIAMI, FL

Characteristic	Rank	Value
Population size	41	346,865
Percent black	39	25.08
Percent Hispanic	2	55.98
Percent foreign born	1	53.70
Median age (years)	2	38.0
Percent college graduates	73	11.10
Percent women in labor force	63	50.73
Percent married-couple households	69	46.18
Median household income ($)	99	11,075
Average housing value ($)	36	55,401

CITY: MILWAUKEE, WI

Characteristic	Rank	Value
Population size	16	636,212
Percent black	43	23.11
Percent Hispanic	41	4.16
Percent foreign born	50	4.98
Median age (years)	59	28.8
Percent college graduates	85	9.74
Percent women in labor force	38	54.03
Percent married-couple households	65	47.14
Median household income ($)	35	16,028
Average housing value ($)	59	45,533

CITY: MINNEAPOLIS, MN

Characteristic	Rank	Value
Population size	34	370,915
Percent black	75	7.67
Percent Hispanic	77	1.28
Percent foreign born	51	4.92
Median age (years)	36	29.7
Percent college graduates	17	18.56
Percent women in labor force	38	54.03
Percent married-couple households	95	38.36
Median household income ($)	64	14,351
Average housing value ($)	35	56,532

CITY: MOBILE, AL

Characteristic	Rank	Value
Population size	72	200,396
Percent black	21	36.27
Percent Hispanic	78	1.2
Percent foreign born	88	1.88
Median age (years)	60	28.8
Percent college graduates	54	13.62
Percent women in labor force	87	47.13
Percent married-couple households	30	54.48
Median household income ($)	61	14,587
Average housing value ($)	51	47,092

CITY: MONTGOMERY, AL

Characteristic	Rank	Value
Population size	76	177,857
Percent black	17	39.25
Percent Hispanic	84	.95
Percent foreign born	98	1.24
Median age (years)	75	28.2
Percent college graduates	31	16.42
Percent women in labor force	51	52.17
Percent married-couple households	24	55.4
Median household income ($)	54	14,900
Average housing value ($)	58	45,539

CITY: NASHVILLE-DAVIDSON, TN

Characteristic	Rank	Value
Population size	25	455,663
Percent black	42	23.23
Percent Hispanic	97	.71
Percent foreign born	92	1.68
Median age (years)	37	29.7
Percent college graduates	42	14.83
Percent women in labor force	31	55.81
Percent married-couple households	31	54.38
Median household income ($)	32	16,109
Average housing value ($)	46	48,656

CITY: NEWARK, NJ

Characteristic	Rank	Value
Population size	46	329,248
Percent black	4	58.3
Percent Hispanic	16	18.62
Percent foreign born	12	14.49
Median age (years)	91	27
Percent college graduates	100	5.11
Percent women in labor force	90	46.44
Percent married-couple households	94	38.54
Median household income ($)	100	10,118
Average housing value ($)	89	32,719

CITY: NEW ORLEANS, LA

Characteristic	Rank	Value
Population size	21	557,515
Percent black	6	55.25
Percent Hispanic	45	3.44
Percent foreign born	62	3.89
Median age (years)	66	28.7
Percent college graduates	49	14.20
Percent women in labor force	88	46.90
Percent married-couple households	84	42.19
Median household income ($)	93	11,814
Average housing value ($)	23	62,752

CITY: NEW YORK, NY

Characteristic	Rank	Value
Population size	1	7,071,639
Percent black	38	25.28
Percent Hispanic	11	19.88
Percent foreign born	5	23.61
Median age (years)	5	32.7
Percent college graduates	47	14.63
Percent women in labor force	86	47.14
Percent married-couple households	77	43.98
Median household income ($)	70	13,854
Average housing value ($)	34	57,296

CITY: NORFOLK, VA

Characteristic	Rank	Value
Population size	55	366,979
Percent black	22	35.2
Percent Hispanic	62	2.16
Percent foreign born	60	3.98
Median age (years)	99	25.5
Percent college graduates	92	8.46
Percent women in labor force	90	46.81
Percent married-couple households	52	50.38
Median household income ($)	85	12,509
Average housing value ($)	62	44,832

CITY: OAKLAND, CA

Characteristic	Rank	Value
Population size	43	339,337
Percent black	10	46.95
Percent Hispanic	29	9.46
Percent foreign born	18	12.54
Median age (years)	15	31.3
Percent college graduates	22	18.18
Percent women in labor force	54	51.58
Percent married-couple households	96	37.01
Median household income ($)	72	13,780
Average housing value ($)	12	80,958

CITY: OKLAHOMA CITY, OK

Characteristic	Rank	Value
Population size	31	403,243
Percent black	15	14.51
Percent Hispanic	51	2.91
Percent foreign born	76	2.83
Median age (years)	31	29.9
Percent college graduates	37	15.43
Percent women in labor force	40	53.87
Percent married-couple households	22	55.87
Median household income ($)	39	15,907
Average housing value ($)	48	48,055

CITY: OMAHA, NE

Characteristic	Rank	Value
Population size	48	314,267
Percent black	62	12.05
Percent Hispanic	60	2.34
Percent foreign born	65	3.23
Median age (years)	43	29.4
Percent college graduates	45	14.69
Percent women in labor force	41	53.80
Percent married-couple households	41	53.09
Median household income ($)	27	16,374
Average housing value ($)	73	39,612

CITY: PHILADELPHIA, PA

Characteristic	Rank	Value
Population size	9	1,688,210
Percent black	18	37.83
Percent Hispanic	44	3.81
Percent foreign born	37	6.39
Median age (years)	10	31.7
Percent college graduates	90	9.09
Percent women in labor force	98	44.36
Percent married-couple households	72	45.21
Median household income ($)	80	13,169
Average housing value ($)	98	27,789

CITY: PHOENIX, AZ

Characteristic	Rank	Value
Population size	9	789,704
Percent black	85	4.77
Percent Hispanic	21	14.79
Percent foreign born	44	5.65
Median age (years)	52	28.9
Percent college graduates	57	13.32
Percent women in labor force	36	54.35
Percent married-couple households	14	58.61
Median household income ($)	15	17,419
Average housing value ($)	26	61,823

CITY: PITTSBURGH, PA

Characteristic	Rank	Value
Population size	30	423,938
Percent black	40	23.95
Percent Hispanic	91	.79
Percent foreign born	46	5.23
Median age (years)	6	32.7
Percent college graduates	68	11.66
Percent women in labor force	96	44.70
Percent married-couple households	75	44.37
Median household income ($)	77	13,408
Average housing value ($)	81	36,947

CITY: PORTLAND, OR

Characteristic	Rank	Value
Population size	35	366,423
Percent black	76	7.65
Percent Hispanic	63	2.05
Percent foreign born	34	7.09
Median age (years)	13	31.4
Percent college graduates	21	18.21
Percent women in labor force	45	53.15
Percent married-couple households	76	44.22
Median household income ($)	57	14,782
Average housing value ($)	30	60,349

CITY: PROVIDENCE, RI

Characteristic	Rank	Value
Population size	99	156,804
Percent black	64	11.91
Percent Hispanic	36	5.51
Percent foreign born	17	13.49
Median age (years)	32	29.9
Percent college graduates	66	11.98
Percent women in labor force	71	49.09
Percent married-couple households	83	43.25
Median household income ($)	97	11,437
Average housing value ($)	54	46,191

CITY: RICHMOND, VA

Characteristic	Rank	Value
Population size	64	219,214
Percent black	8	51.28
Percent Hispanic	82	.97
Percent foreign born	90	1.84
Median age (years)	20	30.5
Percent college graduates	34	15.72
Percent women in labor force	42	53.55
Percent married-couple households	90	40.43
Median household income ($)	75	13,606
Average housing value ($)	60	45,134

CITY: RIVERSIDE, CA

Characteristic	Rank	Value
Population size	83	170,876
Percent black	78	6.91
Percent Hispanic	19	16.09
Percent foreign born	28	8.02
Median age (years)	80	27.8
Percent college graduates	43	14.8
Percent women in labor force	47	52.81
Percent married-couple households	13	58.92
Median household income ($)	13	17,849
Average housing value ($)	15	73,283

CITY: ROCHESTER, NY

Characteristic	Rank	Value
Population size	57	241,741
Percent black	35	25.75
Percent Hispanic	37	5.36
Percent foreign born	25	8.38
Median age (years)	53	28.9
Percent college graduates	74	11.07
Percent women in labor force	60	51.08
Percent married-couple households	92	40.02
Median household income ($)	74	13,641
Average housing value ($)	97	27,902

CITY: SACRAMENTO, CA

Characteristic	Rank	Value
Population size	52	275,741
Percent black	57	13.36
Percent Hispanic	22	14.10
Percent foreign born	21	10.04
Median age (years)	14	31.4
Percent college graduates	38	15.37
Percent women in labor force	67	49.84
Percent married-couple households	68	46.78
Median household income ($)	60	14,604
Average housing value ($)	27	61,708

CITY: ST. LOUIS, MO

Characteristic	Rank	Value
Population size	26	453,085
Percent black	12	45.5
Percent Hispanic	79	1.18
Percent foreign born	81	2.62
Median age (years)	11	31.6
Percent college graduates	93	8.18
Percent women in labor force	84	47.62
Percent married-couple households	93	39.02
Median household income ($)	96	11,511
Average housing value ($)	94	31,010

CITY: ST. PAUL, MN

Characteristic	Rank	Value
Population size	54	270,230
Percent black	84	4.81
Percent Hispanic	53	2.79
Percent foreign born	52	4.86
Median age (years)	41	29.5
Percent college graduates	36	15.62
Percent women in labor force	35	54.96
Percent married-couple households	62	47.98
Median household income ($)	34	16,029
Average housing value ($)	37	55,015

CITY: ST. PETERSBURG, FL

Characteristic	Rank	Value
Population size	58	238,647
Percent black	50	17.13
Percent Hispanic	69	1.79
Percent foreign born	31	7.74
Median age (years)	1	42.2
Percent college graduates	62	12.71
Percent women in labor force	100	42.69
Percent married-couple households	58	49.41
Median household income ($)	94	11,798
Average housing value ($)	66	42,748

CITY: SALT LAKE CITY, UT

Characteristic	Rank	Value
Population size	90	163,033
Percent black	96	1.56
Percent Hispanic	34	7.67
Percent foreign born	32	7.65
Median age (years)	61	28.8
Percent college graduates	11	19.88
Percent women in labor force	50	52.30
Percent married-couple households	63	47.85
Median household income ($)	79	13,211
Average housing value ($)	21	64,444

CITY: SAN ANTONIO, TX

Characteristic	Rank	Value
Population size	11	785,809
Percent black	77	7.32
Percent Hispanic	3	53.67
Percent foreign born	27	8.25
Median age (years)	87	27.2
Percent college graduates	78	10.8
Percent women in labor force	83	47.74
Percent married-couple households	12	59.05
Median household income ($)	73	13,775
Average housing value ($)	86	35,263

CITY: SAN DIEGO, CA

Characteristic	Rank	Value
Population size	8	875,538
Percent black	73	8.85
Percent Hispanic	20	14.84
Percent foreign born	11	14.95
Median age (years)	72	28.4
Percent college graduates	23	18.15
Percent women in labor force	48	52.81
Percent married-couple households	56	49.91
Median household income ($)	26	16,408
Average housing value ($)	6	105,465

CITY: SAN FRANCISCO, CA

Characteristic	Rank	Value
Population size	13	678,974
Percent black	60	12.69
Percent Hispanic	27	12.4
Percent foreign born	3	28.3
Median age (years)	4	34.1
Percent college graduates	2	24.02
Percent women in labor force	23	56.51
Percent married-couple households	99	34.37
Median household income ($)	40	15,866
Average housing value ($)	3	117,947

CITY: SAN JOSE, CA

Characteristic	Rank	Value
Population size	17	629,442
Percent black	86	4.57
Percent Hispanic	10	22.29
Percent foreign born	14	14.44
Median age (years)	84	27.5
Percent college graduates	30	16.8
Percent women in labor force	9	60.13
Percent married-couple households	6	60.89
Median household income ($)	4	22,886
Average housing value ($)	5	106,160

CITY: SANTA ANA, CA

Characteristic	Rank	Value
Population size	69	203,713
Percent black	87	3.94
Percent Hispanic	5	44.49
Percent foreign born	2	30.51
Median age (years)	96	26.3
Percent college graduates	88	9.18
Percent women in labor force	26	56.09
Percent married-couple households	17	57.60
Median household income ($)	12	18,362
Average housing value ($)	11	85,539

CITY: SEATTLE, WA

Characteristic	Rank	Value
Population size	23	493,846
Percent black	71	9.42
Percent Hispanic	56	2.58
Percent foreign born	19	11.26
Median age (years)	7	32.4
Percent college graduates	3	22.79
Percent women in labor force	28	55.88
Percent married-couple households	87	41.02
Median household income ($)	28	16,254
Average housing value ($)	14	74,031

CITY: SHREVEPORT, LA

Characteristic	Rank	Value
Population size	67	205,776
Percent black	15	41.15
Percent Hispanic	73	1.47
Percent foreign born	94	1.46
Median age (years)	62	28.8
Percent college graduates	50	14.15
Percent women in labor force	46	52.92
Percent married-couple households	33	54.17
Median household income ($)	52	15,043
Average housing value ($)	57	45,887

CITY: SPOKANE, WA

Characteristic	Rank	Value
Population size	82	171,300
Percent black	95	1.62
Percent Hispanic	72	1.59
Percent foreign born	58	4.44
Median age (years)	21	30.5
Percent college graduates	48	14.34
Percent women in labor force	85	47.33
Percent married-couple households	55	49.98
Median household income ($)	71	13,853
Average housing value ($)	55	46,140

CITY: SYRACUSE, NY

Characteristic	Rank	Value
Population size	86	170,105
Percent black	53	15.7
Percent Hispanic	66	1.94
Percent foreign born	33	7.65
Median age (years)	67	28.7
Percent college graduates	56	13.36
Percent women in labor force	72	48.91
Percent married-couple households	89	40.65
Median household income ($)	86	12,321
Average housing value ($)	87	33,270

CITY: TACOMA, WA

Characteristic	Rank	Value
Population size	97	158,501
Percent black	72	9.10
Percent Hispanic	55	2.62
Percent foreign born	35	7.09
Median age (years)	39	29.6
Percent college graduates	76	10.97
Percent women in labor force	97	44.62
Percent married-couple households	49	50.71
Median household income ($)	62	14,546
Average housing value ($)	45	49,010

CITY: TAMPA, FL

Characteristic	Rank	Value
Population size	53	271,523
Percent black	41	23.41
Percent Hispanic	25	13.17
Percent foreign born	36	6.87
Median age (years)	8	32
Percent college graduates	80	10.49
Percent women in labor force	74	48.74
Percent married-couple households	53	50.09
Median household income ($)	87	12,318
Average housing value ($)	82	36,759

CITY: TOLEDO, OH

Characteristic	Rank	Value
Population size	40	354,635
Percent black	49	17.44
Percent Hispanic	50	3.09
Percent foreign born	69	3.1
Median age (years)	44	29.4
Percent college graduates	84	9.87
Percent women in labor force	75	48.74
Percent married-couple households	37	53.3
Median household income ($)	31	16,200
Average housing value ($)	69	41,691

CITY: TUCSON, AZ

Characteristic	Rank	Value
Population size	45	330,537
Percent black	88	3.5
Percent Hispanic	8	24.84
Percent foreign born	30	7.92
Median age (years)	73	28.4
Percent college graduates	44	14.72
Percent women in labor force	66	49.96
Percent married-couple households	42	52.64
Median household income ($)	67	14,086
Average housing value ($)	41	53,296

CITY: TULSA, OK

Characteristic	Rank	Value
Population size	38	360,919
Percent black	65	11.87
Percent Hispanic	71	1.74
Percent foreign born	82	2.59
Median age (years)	29	30
Percent college graduates	28	17.48
Percent women in labor force	33	55.14
Percent married-couple households	23	55.69
Median household income ($)	21	16,872
Average housing value ($)	38	54,956

CITY: VIRGINIA BEACH, VA

Characteristic	Rank	Value
Population size	56	262,199
Percent black	69	10.01
Percent Hispanic	65	2
Percent foreign born	59	4.18
Median age (years)	92	26.9
Percent college graduates	29	17.39
Percent women in labor force	29	55.84
Percent married-couple households	2	66.70
Median household income ($)	7	20,203
Average housing value ($)	19	67,711

CITY: WARREN, MI

Characteristic	Rank	Value
Population size	92	161,134
Percent black	100	.23
Percent Hispanic	83	.97
Percent foreign born	23	8.93
Median age (years)	25	30.3
Percent college graduates	97	7.06
Percent women in labor force	64	50.35
Percent married-couple households	1	68
Median household income ($)	3	23,857
Average housing value ($)	52	46,904

CITY: WASHINGTON, DC

Characteristic	Rank	Value
Population size	15	638,333
Percent black	1	70.24
Percent Hispanic	54	2.78
Percent foreign born	38	6.35
Median age (years)	17	31.2
Percent college graduates	4	22.11
Percent women in labor force	15	58.19
Percent married-couple households	100	30.47
Median household income ($)	30	16,211
Average housing value ($)	10	90,728

CITY: WICHITA, KS

Characteristic	Rank	Value
Population size	51	279,272
Percent black	67	10.83
Percent Hispanic	46	3.38
Percent foreign born	66	3.22
Median age (years)	51	29
Percent college graduates	40	15.11
Percent women in labor force	22	56.64
Percent married-couple households	21	55.99
Median household income ($)	17	17,214
Average housing value ($)	53	46,723

CITY: WORCESTER, MA

Characteristic	Rank	Value
Population size	91	161,799
Percent black	90	2.83
Percent Hispanic	43	3.99
Percent foreign born	24	8.5
Median age (years)	18	31.1
Percent college graduates	69	11.5
Percent women in labor force	76	48.55
Percent married-couple households	54	49.99
Median household income ($)	66	14,116
Average housing value ($)	74	39,064

CITY: YONKERS, NY

Characteristic	Rank	Value
Population size	73	195,351
Percent black	68	10.58
Percent Hispanic	30	8.67
Percent foreign born	8	16.67
Median age (years)	3	34.4
Percent college graduates	41	14.89
Percent women in labor force	65	50
Percent married-couple households	19	56.21
Median household income ($)	10	18,719
Average housing value ($)	13	74,721

Notes on Sources

In more than six years of following demographic trends, I have read virtually every article that has appeared discussing Census Bureau data and their significance. In many ways, this book is a digest of my experience. The ideas of many of the nation's demographers—in the Census Bureau, at universities, and at demographic institutes—are reflected here.

Many of the numbers in this book come from the U.S. Census Bureau, either directly from Census Bureau reports or indirectly from articles that use census data. These numbers are current as of June 1984, when they were checked and updated.

These notes, organized by chapter, are intended not only to credit these many sources but also to draw the readers' attention to those places where they can find further information. This is not an inclusive list, but rather a list of those sources I found most helpful in writing this book. Analyses and reports of data continue to be published from the 1980 census and later surveys, and I urge the interested reader to look for them.

These notes reflect three types of sources: Census Bureau publications; articles from *American Demographics* magazine; and sources such as journal articles or statistical publications from government agencies other than the Census Bureau. For each chapter I list my principal sources, divided into these three categories. Because the Census Bureau is the Mother Ship of demographics, some more words about the 1980 census are in order:

The 1980 census was primarily a census of households. Every occupied housing unit in the nation received—or should have received—a questionnaire on Census Day, April 1, 1980, asking questions about the people living in the household and about their housing conditions.

A longer form of the census questionnaire went to a sample of about 17 percent of households everywhere except localities with fewer than 5,000 residents, where such a sample would be statistically too small to produce reliable results. In such small areas, the sample size was larger.

On its sample questionnaire, the Census Bureau asked for a broad range of information, from the age of each person living in the household (question 5), to whether the household has air conditioning (question H. 27). The answers people gave to such questions determine much of what we know about ourselves as Americans today.

Most people told the census takers the truth. The demographers at the Census Bureau know that not everybody told the truth, but because there are so many answers from the millions of households surveyed, the faulty responses tend to cancel one another out. Some census items are more prone to error than others—more people lie about their income than their age, for example—but overall the census is probably among the most reliable information anywhere in the world, even if it is not perfect.

The Census Bureau, having collected millions of pieces of information, tabulated the data and made the findings available in a variety of different forms, from printed reports to computer tapes. The Census Bureau is responsible not only for taking a census every decade but also for conducting surveys throughout the decade to update its information.

In fact, we do not need the census to tell us the trends at the national, regional, or state level. The Census Bureau's Current Population Survey tells us much of what we need to know. This is a monthly survey of some 60,000 households. Every March, the Census Bureau asks detailed demographic questions of these households. Many of the statistics in this book rely on Current Population Survey data for information that is more current than the material from the 1980 census.

No survey is as comprehensive as the census, however, neither does any survey provide information for areas as small as towns or neighborhoods, as the census is able to do. The value of a census is not only the broad range of questions that are answered, but also the geographic detail. The census provides a head count for about 2.5 million city blocks, but not much data about these blocks. As the size of the geographic area increases, so does the amount of information tabulated for the area.

We know more about the nation's population as a whole than we do about each one of its more than 3,000 counties. And we know more about the demographic characteristics of counties than we do about those of neighborhoods. It would be too expensive and complicated to tabulate detailed information for very small areas, and such detail might reveal information about individuals living there that would violate the census provisions for confidentiality—and besides, who would be interested in such detail?

Most statistics found in this book are for the nation as a whole, for regions, states, cities, and counties. Only local planners, people studying commuting or researchers looking into the dynamics of neighborhood change, want census details for small areas. The rest of us are more interested in the broad trends.

THE ESSENTIAL CENSUS

I am a fan of the Census Bureau. It is a government agency with integrity. In some countries, census data are political footballs. Some statistical offices play the numbers close to their chest. In the United States, the Census Bureau has kept out of partisan politics and it has never been racked by scandal. The bureau literally offers an open book of numbers. Some people even complain that the bureau's book is too open—so inclusive that it resembles the Manhattan telephone directory more closely than a statistical guidebook.

In arguments over the extent of poverty in America and the effectiveness or failure of government programs, in discussions of unemployment or housing policy, in debates over immigration's impact, in analyses of consumer markets or changing mores, competing sides use the same census data to marshal and refute arguments. This is as it should be, but we should not take the fact for granted.

If some of the numbers in this book, say those pertaining to the status of blacks, were systematically wrong, a false portrait would emerge. If the Census Bureau falsified its numbers to prove a political point, policies would be made, money spent, and books written based on faulty information; and society would suffer. America's political leaders, despite temptations, for the most part have been wise enough to recognize the value of objective statistics, collected and analyzed by professionals, for all to use. At the Census Bureau, only the census director and a few assistants are political appointments.

The pursuit of statistical wisdom has not stopped politicians from trying to influence the Census Bureau or even to impugn its numbers. After the 1980 census, cities filed more than fifty lawsuits to get the numbers changed to adjust for an assumed undercount of blacks. But decade after decade, the Census Bureau's reputation remains high, even at a time when the accepted wisdom in this country is that government is wasteful and dishonest.

In virtually every aspect of information about our society, the Census Bureau provides valuable numbers and helps us to understand our demographic characteristics and to chart social trends. The bureau is not glamorous or exciting, but it is absolutely necessary.

SOURCES

A few census publications have been invaluable to virtually every chapter of this book. I refer to these below and do not mention them again chapter by chapter, with one or two exceptions. These key publications provide basic information about Americans according to such characteristics as age, race, sex, and place of birth. These publications are available in a national summary and for each of the fifty states.

All Census Bureau publications, and those of other government agencies, are available from the following address: Superintendent of Documents, U.S. Government Printing Office, Washington, DC 20402. There is a charge for most publications.

1980 Census of Population: Characteristics of the Population
    PC80-1-A Number of Inhabitants
        A1 National Summary
        A13 Hawaii . . . etc. (one number per state)
    PC80-1-B General Population Characteristics
        B1 National Summary
        B13 Hawaii . . . etc.
    PC80-1-C General Social and Economic Characteristics
        C1 National Summary
        C13 Hawaii . . . etc.
    PC80-1-D Detailed Social and Economic Characteristics
        D1 National Summary
        D13 Hawaii . . . etc.

The Census Bureau releases similar series for housing characteristics and also provides other publications for both housing and population characteristics. These are numbered as follows:

HC80-1 1980 Census of Housing
PCH80-1 1980 Census of Population and Housing

Those who need advice on which publications contain specific types of statistics can obtain help from the Census Bureau's Data User Services Division, Bureau of the Census, Washington, DC 20230. The bureau publishes user guides, catalogues, and so forth.

Other publications from the Census Bureau that proved useful for many chapters of this book, and that anyone who wants to know the facts about Americans would find valuable as references, include:

Statistical Abstract of the United States, 1984. (The government publishes a new edition every year.)
Historical Statistics of the United States, Colonial Times to 1970 Bicentennial, U.S. Bureau of the Census, 2 parts.
U.S. Bureau of the Census State and Metropolitan Area Data Book, 1982.

1: THE POWER OF POSITIVE DEMOGRAPHICS

Like the introduction, this chapter relies on a broad range of sources, including many newspaper and magazine articles that have reported on demographics. These include *The Wall Street Journal, The New York Times, Business Week, Fortune,* and *Newsweek,* which have been among the general circulation publications that have paid the most attention to demographics.

American Demographics magazine is the principal source of reliable demographic information and this chapter relies heavily on items contained in that magazine's "Openers" section, which contains news of note about demographics compiled by the editors. *American Demographics* is part of Dow Jones & Co. and has offices at P.O. Box 68, Ithaca, NY 14850.

The "demographic surprises" attributed to demographer Calvin Beale that are mentioned in this chapter come from "U.S. Population: Where We Are: Where We're Going," *Population Bulletin* 37, no. 2, Population Reference Bureau, Washington, DC, June 1982. The Population Reference Bureau is a reliable source of information about demographic trends, and its population bulletin series is widely read for current information on new developments in the field. The bureau is a private nonprofit corporation.

2: GENERATION GAPS

Census Bureau publications:
Household and Family Characteristics, March 1983, *Current Population Reports,* P-20, no. 388, 1984.
Money Income of Households, Families, and Persons in the U.S., 1982, *Current Population Reports,* P-60, no. 142, 1984.
Projections of the Population of the U.S. by Age, Sex, and Race: 1983–2080, *Current Population Reports,* P-25, no. 982, 1984.
Voting and Registration in the Election of November, 1982, *Current Population Reports,* P-20, no. 383, 1983.
American Demographics magazine:
Barbara A. Price, "What the Baby Boom Believes" (May 1984).
Bryant Robey, "Age in America" (July/August 1981).
Bryant Robey, "Entering Middle Age" (February 1984).
Bryant Robey and Cheryl Russell, "The Year of the Baby Boom" (May 1984).
Other sources:
Eileen Crimmins, "Changing Patterns of American Mortality Decline," *Population and Development Review* 7 (1981).
Jacob S. Siegel and Jeffrey S. Passel, "New Estimates of the Number of Centenarians in the United States," *Journal of the American Statistical Association* 71 (1976).

3: SPLITTING THE NUCLEAR FAMILY

Census Bureau publications:
Household and Family Characteristics, March 1983, *Current Population Reports,* P-20, no. 388, 1984.
Marital Status and Living Arrangements, March 1982, *Current Population Reports,* P-20, no. 349, 1983.
American Demographics magazine:
Paul C. Glick, "How American Families are Changing" (January 1984).
Arthur J. Norton, "Keeping Up with Households" (February 1983).
Cheryl Russell, "The Condo Craze" (March 1981).

Graham B. Spanier, "Living Together in the Eighties" (November 1982).

James A. Weed, "Divorce: Americans' Style" (March 1982).

Arthur F. Young and F. John Devaney, "What the 1980 Census Shows about Housing" (January 1983).

Other sources:

Atlas of Demographics, U.S. by County, Infomap, Inc., Boulder, CO, 1982.

4: NEW WOMEN, NEW MEN

Census Bureau publications:

Child Care Arrangements of Working Mothers, 1982, *Current Population Reports,* P-23, no. 129, 1983.

Fertility of American Women, June 1983, *Current Population Reports,* P-20, no. 386, 1984.

Household and Family Characteristics, March 1983, *Current Population Reports,* P-20, no. 388, 1984.

Marital Status and Living Arrangements, March 1982, *Current Population Reports,* P-20, no. 349, 1983.

Projections of the Population of the U.S. by Age, Sex, and Race: 1983–2080, *Current Population Reports,* P-25, no. 982, 1984.

American Demographics magazine:

Bryant Robey, "For Women Only" (November 1983).

Daphne Spain and Suzanne M. Bianchi, "How Women Have Changed" (May 1983).

Other sources:

Advance Report of Final Natality Statistics, National Center for Health Statistics, 1981.

5: BALANCING THE REGIONS

Census Bureau publications:

Estimates of the Population of States, July 1, 1983, *Current Population Reports,* P-25, no. 944, 1983.

Geographical Mobility: March 1975–March 1980, *Current Population Reports,* P-20, no. 368, 1981.

Illustrative Projections of State Populations, 1975–2000, *Current Population Reports,* P-25, no. 796, 1979.

John Long, "Population Deconcentration in the United States," *Special Demographic Analyses,* CDS 81-5, 1981.

State of Residence in 1975 by State of Residence in 1980, 1980 Census PC80-S1-9.

American Demographics magazine:

Bryant Robey and Cheryl Russell, "Altered States" (September 1983).

Bryant Robey and Cheryl Russell, "The States in 1990" (December 1983).

Cheryl Russell, "Inside the Shrinking Household" (October 1981).

Other sources:

Larry Long, "Population Redistribution in the United States: Issues for the 1980s," *Population Trends and Public Policy* 5, no. 3, Population Reference Bureau, 1983.

6: CITIES, SUBURBS, AND BEYOND

Census Bureau publications:

Farm Population of the United States, 1982, *Current Population Reports,* P-27, no. 56, 1983.

John Long, "Population Deconcentration in the United States," Special Demographic Analyses, CDS 81-5, 1981.

American Demographics magazine:

Richard L. Forstall, "Is America Becoming More Metropolitan?" (December 1981).

Philip N. Fulton, "Are We Solving the Commuting Problem?" (November 1983).

Jane Newitt, "Behind the Big City Blues" (June 1983).

Cheryl Russell, "Life on the Fringes" (May 1982).

Other sources:

Larry Long and Diana DeAre, "The Slowing of Urbanization in the U.S." *Scientific American* (July 1983).

Kevin P. McCarthy, Metropolitan Suburbs: Profile and Prospects, unpublished paper presented to the Population Association of America, 1983.

7: THE ETHNIC MOSAIC

Census Bureau publications:

Ancestry of the Population by State: 1980, 1980 Census *Detailed Population Characteristics* PC80-S1-10, 1983.

Characteristics of the Foreign-Born, special tabulations, 1984.

Race of the Population by State, 1980, 1980 Census *Detailed Population Characteristics* PC80-S1-3, 1981.

Twenty Censuses: Population and Housing Questions, 1790–1980. U.S. Bureau of the Census, 1979.

American Demographics magazine:

Edith McArthur, "How Wide Is the Language Gap?" (May 1981).

Bryant Robey and Cheryl Russell, "All Americans" (February 1984).

Bryant Robey, "America, Out of Focus" (April 1981).

Bryant Robey, "Ethnics on Parade" (August 1981).

Other sources:

Frank D. Bean, Allan G. King, and Jeffrey S. Passel, "The Number of Illegal Migrants of Mexican Origin in the United States: Sex Ratio-based Estimates for 1980," *Demography* 20, no. 1 (February 1983).

Reynolds Farley and Michael J. Levin, "Ancestry of the U.S. Population," unpublished paper presented to the Population Association of America, May 1984.

8: FROM SOUTH OF THE BORDER

Census Bureau publications:

"The Condition of Hispanics in America Today," paper presented at hearings of Subcommittee on Census and Population, House of Representatives, 1984.

1980 Census of Population, Characteristics of the Population, General Social and Economic Characteristics, PC80-1-C1, 1983.

American Demographics magazine:

Cheryl Russell, "The News about Hispanics" (March 1983).

Other sources:

Cary Davis, Carl Haub, and JoAnne Willette, "U.S. Hispanics: Changing the Face of America," *Population Bulletin* 38, no. 3, Population Reference Bureau, 1983.

Projections of Hispanic Population for the United States, 1990 and 2000, Center for Continuing Study of the California Economy, Palo Alto, CA, 1984.

9: THE ASIANS

As of the end of 1984, the Census Bureau had yet to issue a report profiling Asians. Census Bureau statistics in this chapter come from the author's analysis of 1980 census data contained in the census reports outlined at the beginning of these notes.

In September 1984, the Population Institute of the East-West Center, with which I am currently affiliated, held an important conference on Asian immigration to the United States at which new statistics and analyses were presented. This chapter draws heavily on papers presented at that conference. The conference papers have since been published under the title *Asia-Pacific Immigration to the United States,* which is available from the East-West Center, 1777 East-West Road, Honolulu, Hawaii 96848.

In particular the following conference papers proved helpful:

James T. Fawcett, Fred Arnold, and Urmil Minocha, "Asian Immigration to the United States: Flows and Processes," unpublished paper, September 1984.

Linda W. Gordon, "Southeast Asian Refugee Migration to the United States," unpublished paper, September 1984.

Michael J. Levin, "Pacific Islanders in the United States," unpublished paper, September 1984.

Peter C. Smith and Robert W. Gardner, "Asian Americans: Growth and Change in the 1970s," unpublished paper, September 1984.

Other sources:

Robert Pear, "Immigration and the Randomness of Ethnic Mix," *The New York Times,* October 2, 1984.

10: BLACK AND WHITE GAPS

Census Bureau publications:

Money Income of Households, Families, and Persons in the U. S., 1982, *Current Population Reports,* P-60, no. 142, 1984.

Jeffrey S. Passel, Jacob S. Siegel, and Gregory Robinson, Coverage of the National Population, *Current Population Reports,* P-23, no. 115, 1981.

The Social and Economic Status of the Black Population, *Current Population Reports,* P-23, no. 80, 1979.

Daphne Spain and Larry Long, "Black Movers to the Suburbs," Center for Demographic Studies, CDS-80-4, 1981.

American Demographics magazine:

Reynolds Farley and Suzanne M. Bianchi, "The Growing Gap between Blacks" (July 1983).

Reynolds Farley, "The Long Road: Blacks and Whites in America" (February 1980).

Gordon Green and Edward Welniak, "Changing Families, Shifting Incomes" (February 1983).

Larry Long and Diana DeAre, "The Suburbanization of Blacks" (September 1981).

Other sources:

Milton D. Norris, "A National Profile of Black Elected Officials," *Focus,* Joint Center for Political Studies 12, no. 2 (February 1984).

"Unemployment Rates by Sex and Age, Seasonally Adjusted, Table 6," *Monthly Labor Review* 107, no. 5 (May 1984).

11: WHAT COLOR IS YOUR COLLAR?

Census Bureau publications:

Detailed Occupations and Years of School Completed by Age, for the Civilian Labor Force by Sex, Race, and Spanish Origin, 1980, PC80-S1-8.

American Demographics magazine:

Carol Boyd Leon, "Occupational Winners and Losers" (March 1983).

Martha Farnsworth Riche, "The Blue Collar Blues" (November 1983).

Bryant Robey and Cheryl Russell, "A Portrait of the American Worker" (March 1984).

State Demographics: Population Profiles of the Fifty States, compiled by the *American Demographics* magazine editors, Dow Jones/Irwin, Homewood, IL, 1984.

Bureau of Labor Statistics publications:

Employment and Earnings, various editions.

Occupational Outlook Handbook, 1982–83.

Occupational Outlook Quarterly, Fall 1983.

Occupational Projections and Training Data, 1982 edition, Bulletin 2202.

12: DEGREES OF DIFFERENCE

Census Bureau publications:

Money Income of Households, Families, and Persons in the U.S., 1982, *Current Population Reports,* P-60, no. 142, 1984.

National Center for Education Statistics publications:

W. Vance Grant and Leo J. Eiden, Digest of Education Statistics, 1982.

W. Vance Grant and Thomas D. Snyder, Digest of Education Statistics, 1983–84.

High School Graduates: Projections for the 50 States: 1982–2000, American Freshmen, 1983.

Valena White Plisko, ed., The Conditions of Education, 1983 edition, Statistical Report.

13: DIVIDED WE EARN

Census Bureau publications:

Characteristics of the Population Below the Poverty Level, 1982, P-60, no. 144, 1984.

Estimates of Poverty Including the Value of Noncash Benefits: 1979 to 1982, Technical Paper no. 51, 1983.

A Marketer's Guide to Discretionary Income, a Joint Study of the Conference Board and the Census Bureau, 1983.

Money Income of Households, Families, and Persons in the U.S., 1982, *Current Population Reports,* P-60, no. 142, 1984.

American Demographics magazine:

Suzanne Bianchi, "Wives Who Earn More than Their Husbands" (July 1984).

Demographic Forecasts, "Households and Income in 1995" (April 1984).

Gordon Green and John Coder, "Counting What You Keep" (February 1984).

Beth B. Hess, "New Faces of Poverty" (May 1983).

Dave M. O'Neill, "Living Standard Standards" (August 1983).

"Opener," "The Rich Are Different" (November 1983).

Bryant Robey and Cheryl Russell, "How Consumers Spend" (October 1983).

Cheryl Russell, "Underground Economy" (October 1983).

Daphne Spain and Steven Nock, "Two Career Couples, a Portrait" (August 1984).

Special Research Section, "How They Rank" (December 1983).

Other sources:

Labor Force Statistics Derived from the Current Population Survey: *A Databook* vol. 1, Bulletin 2096, Bureau of Labor Statistics, 1982.

14: THE CANADIAN PEOPLE

The statistics in this chapter come from statistical reports obtained from Statistics Canada, that nation's census bureau. In addition, three articles from *American Demographics* were of value:

Edward Pryor and Douglas Norris, "Canada in the Eighties" (December 1983).

Edward Pryor and Malcolm Britton, "What Canada's 1981 Census Found" (July 1983).

Cheryl Russell, "Demographics of the Dominion" (July–August 1980).

15: TEN TRENDS SHAPING AMERICA

This chapter draws on the sources used in earlier chapters of this book. The information about international trends comes from the following sources:

American Demographics magazine:

David B. Lewis, "International Demographics: The Meaning Behind the Numbers" (February 1982).

"Opener," "The Five Million Club" (February 1984).

Cheryl Russell, "Haves and Have Nots" (September 1981).

Other sources:

Estimates and Projections of Urban, Rural, and City Populations, 1950–2025; the 1980 Assessment, United Nations, New York, 1982.

World Bank Atlas, 1983, World Bank, Washington, DC, 1984.

World Population Data Sheet, Population Reference Bureau, 1983.

Readers interested in a regular source of reporting on international statistics and demographic trends should consult *International Demographics,* published monthly by American Demographics, Inc., Ithaca, New York.

APPENDIX: AMERICA'S 100 LARGEST CITIES: A STATISTICAL PROFILE

The original data from which these rankings were made come from computer tapes of the 1980 census. Market Statistics, a data firm in New York City, provided the base rankings from which the tables in this book were constructed.

Acknowledgments

This book could not have been written without the assistance of Cheryl Russell, who helped in every step of the research and writing. Her knowledge of demography and her sense of what is important improved this book immeasurably. During our work together, Ms. Russell was research director of American Demographics, Inc., and last year she succeeded me as editor of *American Demographics* magazine.

All the editors of *American Demographics* were helpful. Research assistant Diane Haggblom did the computer calculations to produce the city rankings found in the Appendix. Demographic Institute Director Bickley Townsend read an early version of several chapters and offered suggestions. Editors Doris Walsh, Martha Riche, and Caroline Eckstrom were valuable as sources of ideas and encouragement.

To *American Demographics'* publisher Peter Francese I owe my gratitude, not only for providing an atmosphere in which writing such a book was possible but also for allowing me a brief, but vital, leave of absence to complete its writing and editing, freed from the rigors of putting out a monthly magazine. He also made several key suggestions about chapter organization.

Susan Robey read the entire manuscript, part of it twice, to make suggestions that resulted in greater clarity. Her editing skills have made this a better book. Demographer Charles Hirschman, a professor at Cornell University, also read the manuscript and helped improve it.

With Cheryl Russell's help, I have checked the numbers in this book and believe them to be accurate and the most current numbers available as of June 1984. However, I alone am responsible for any errors of fact or interpretation that undoubtedly appear among the hundreds of statistics contained in these pages. I have tried to be careful, avoiding the bold but unsubstantiated claims for which futurists and trend spotters are famous, and notorious—because they so often turn out to be wrong.

The inspiration for this book, and much of the material in it, springs from articles that have appeared in *American Demographics,* for which I was the editor from the magazine's inception in 1979 until the summer of 1984, before leaving to join the East-West Center in Honolulu. Most of the ideas about trends are not original to me, but have been suggested by people far more expert than I. There is not room in this section to express my gratitude to all of them individually. However, in my Notes on Sources, I report, chapter by chapter, on the major material I used for this book. Readers who want more information on any of the subjects found here will find these articles and research reports a rich source.

The experts at the Census Bureau deserve special thanks. The statistics and analysis that the Census Bureau's demographers publish are the foundation for every investigation of America's changing population. The Census Bureau contains a knowledgeable, professional, interesting, open, and helpful group of people. Without them, neither I nor anyone else would be able to have confidence in our observations about demographic trends.

Truman Talley, my editor and publisher, urged me to write *The American People,* and I have appreciated his guidance and support during the past two years of writing. Finally, the East-West Population Institute in Honolulu provided me with office space, living quarters, and breathing room in order to edit these chapters, and I am grateful to the Institute's director, Lee-Jay Cho, and to Morley Gren for making these arrangements. My thanks to Ruth Sahara for her help in typing portions of the manuscript in its final stages.

Honolulu   BRYANT ROBEY
February 1985

Index

Bryant Robey was born in 1940 in Cambridge, Massachusetts, and grew up in Cleveland, Ohio. He graduated from Amherst College in 1962 with a degree in English and received a master's degree from Harvard University the following year. In 1978, he became the founding editor of *American Demographics* magazine in Ithaca, New York, where he worked until 1984. The magazine became part of Dow Jones & Company in 1981. Mr. Robey now lives in Honolulu, Hawaii, where he is director of public affairs for the East-West Center and a specialist at the center's Population Institute.